PENGUIN

SABRE

ACCLAIM FOR SABRE SQUADRON

'A remarkable story that has made regimental history …
sends your heart racing from the prologue' *Darlington
Northern Echo*

'Cameron Spence pulls no punches relaying this gripping
non-fictional account … if you liked *Bravo Two Zero*
and *Immediate Action* … you'll enjoy this book. It's by
far the best one yet' *Dorset Evening News*

'Spence's willingness to make such revelations elevates
Sabre Squadron above its precursors, as does his ability
to capture with graphic intensity the almost palpable
tension wrought during six weeks behind enemy lines'
Yorkshire Evening Post

'Written with the pace and style of a novel, this is the true
story of an SAS patrol's six weeks behind enemy lines …
exciting and highly readable' *South Wales Argus*

'*Sabre Squadron* is the story of how he [Spence] and 29 fellow SAS members spent six weeks deep behind enemy lines in the midst of Saddam's forces ... adding to the legendary reputation of the world's most famous special forces' *Yorkshire Post*

'A magnetic, authentic account of war with a patrol' *Edinburgh Evening News*

'Breathtaking daring and ingenuity ... it is a story so incredible that the reader would be forgiven for thinking its plot could have been dreamed up by a Hollywood scriptwriter. It may read like a thriller but Cameron Spence was there' *Bolton Evening News*

'Earthily authentic language and an arsenal of exotic weapons go into an authentic description of battle. This is a book that also fascinates because of its unglamorous details' *Sunday Mercury*

SABRE
SQUADRON

CAMERON SPENCE

PENGUIN BOOKS

PENGUIN BOOKS

UK | USA | Canada | Ireland | Australia
India | New Zealand | South Africa

Penguin Books is part of the Penguin Random House group of companies
whose addresses can be found at global.penguinrandomhouse.com

Penguin
Random House
UK

First published by Michael Joseph 1997
Published in Penguin Books 1998
This edition published 2020
-001

Printed and bound in Great Britain by Clays Ltd, Elcograf S.p.A.

ISBN: 978–1–405–94388–8

www.greenpenguin.co.uk

ABOUT THE AUTHOR

Cameron Spence was a senior NCO in A Squadron, 22 SAS, deployed behind Iraqi lines for six weeks during the Gulf War. *Sabre Squadron* is his account of that operation

For Vince Phillips and Shug Denbury,
the two members of A Squadron
who didn't come home.

CONTENTS

ACKNOWLEDGEMENTS

There are a number of people who I'd like to thank for their part in making *Sabre Squadron* happen: Mark Lucas who has been instrumental in helping get this project off the ground; Nick Cook, who has not only done a fantastic job, but has also become a very good friend since Mark first brought us together; Nish Bruce, a colleague and good friend, whose good advice and support have been invaluable; the team from Michael Joseph and Penguin and last, but by no means least, Jade, for her confidence, support and understanding throughout.

PROLOGUE

I was crashed out when I heard the word. Buzz's voice was low and hoarse, but it still went off in my sleep-starved brain like a klaxon.

Stand-to, stand-to. Enemy.

Before I'd even opened my eyes, Tom shook me. Three times, hard. He needn't have bothered. I'd gone from unconscious to full adrenalin rush in a second. I kicked off the sleeping bag – my maggot – and grabbed my webbing, which I'd been using for a pillow. This contained all the things I needed most – extra magazines, grenades, spare water bottles, food and my baccy-tin survival kit.

Bright sunlight broke through the cam-net, hitting me full in the eyes. It took a second to locate my M16, another to slip the webbing over my upper body. As I did so, I was aware of frantic movement to my left as Jeff stirred himself into action. I'd been asleep next to the front wheel; Jeff had taken the rear slot. Both had offered protection from the relentless wind and sand.

Sleep. A lifetime away.

Laughter. Chat. A brew and a fag before I settled down to rest. These had been my last memories. Now, we were in the grip of a drama – one that I had no bloody comprehension of. I felt helpless, filled with a need to know what was happening. But discipline took over. First things first.

I chucked my maggot into my Bergen and hurled the whole damned lot into the back of the vehicle. There was a whirl of motion on the edge of my vision as Jeff, Tom and Nick did the same.

From his position, I guessed Nick must have been at the back of the vehicle making a brew when the balloon went up. Tom had been round the other side, probably cleaning his M16. He must have leaped the bonnet like a human flea to get to me. Now he was taking up a firing position on this side of the engine. His angle of aim at least gave me an indication of the direction of threat.

With my 16 in my right hand, I joined him. Four bodies battling to get organized in a camouflaged tent, nine-tenths of which was filled with a fighting vehicle.

Above me, Nick jumped up behind the Mk19 grenade launcher and disengaged the locking lever, pulling it down and to the right with a vicious *kerklunk*. Fighting the netting above him, he then swivelled the heavy support weapon through 270 degrees, kicking Bergens aside to give him freedom of movement.

Behind me, Jeff hurled the stove, brew-kit, a couple of mugs, a Jerry-can and the remnants of lunch into the back of the vehicle. He then locked the tail-gate upright.

Silence. We were ready.

It had taken us around twenty seconds. And in that time, no one had said a word.

Now, I felt my heart. It was pounding in my chest like it was about to burst.

Slow it down, Cameron, mate. If you have to start shooting, your aim had better be steady or we might as well all throw in the towel and be done with it.

Slow, steady breaths brought my pulse down to something workable.

Without taking my eyes off the horizon, I reached for the binoculars I always kept under the commander's seat. To my right, I heard Tom engage the buckle of his belt-kit, the light scrape of his M16 as the magazine touched the bonnet.

I expected to hear the rumble of an engine, the clank of a tank-track; something that would give threat-density and distance. But all I heard was the wind and the flap of the cam-net. It was as close to silence as I'd ever come since crossing over the border into Saddam's backyard.

Shit.

That could mean a company of Republican Guards coming for us on foot.

The nerves in my stomach tightened.

'What have we got?' I asked, raising the binos to my face. It took me a second to adjust the focus past the cam-net and onto the endless, table-top flat expanse of desert beyond.

Before Tom could answer, I replayed the things in my mind I already knew.

Buzz had been acting as forward sentry for Tony's vehicle. Tony's wagon, Taff's and mine had been grouped in a 20 metre cluster 200 metres from the rest of the convoy. There, spread over a 150 metre arc, three other Land Rovers had been positioned to protect the Unimog Mother Support Craft. The weather was clear. Visibility was good – out to nine or ten kilometres in this piss-poor terrain. They'd have had to be comatose not to have seen whatever it was that had grabbed Buzz's attention.

'Enemy vehicle,' Tom replied. 'That's all Buzz said.'

The permutations were endless. What kind of vehicle? Was it the only one or were there others? Was this an isolated move or the final play in a carefully crafted set of manoeuvres that had succeeded in surrounding us?

It was then that the CO's words came back to me. *Prepare yourselves mentally for the worst. If the shit hits the fan you won't be coming home.*

I tapped the sidearm on my belt to make sure it was still there. If the worst had happened, there was no bloody way I was going to let them take me.

I nudged Tom in the ribs. 'Death or glory, eh?'

'Shut the fuck up, Cammy, and listen.'

'Can you hear anything?'

'Jack-shit, mate, but –'

And then, we saw it, traversing across our front about 700 metres away. Given the range and the haze it was difficult to make out, but it looked like one of their Russian-made liaison vehicles, a large jeep-type thing called a GAZ. This one had the canvas pulled up so there was no knowing how many people might be inside. Could be just a driver; could be a half a dozen fully armed troops.

The jeep began to slow. They'd been haring across the desert, nothing to see for miles, until seven tumuli had loomed into view on the otherwise blemishless horizon. Of course, they were bloody going to slow down. Two big questions remained: what did they think we were? And would they stop?

I felt Tom willing the GAZ to go on. But at the same time, I knew he was thinking the same as me: if they didn't come to some pretty obvious conclusions, they deserved to have their bloody heads knocked in.

Five hundred metres after we first spotted it, the jeep stopped.

Nick and Tom swore. Three metres away, I heard a rasp of oaths – a faint echo – from Taff's vehicle. This thing was rapidly achieving critical mass.

The GAZ sat there, engine idling, its occupants watching us from a safe distance. The thought crossed my mind. Perhaps they were calling in reinforcements. An air strike. The seconds ticked by. The tension was unbearable.

'Maybe they'll just fuck off,' Tom said.

I knew he didn't believe it any more than I did.

The stand-off continued. I don't know how long the GAZ stayed there. It could have been two minutes; it could have been ten.

Tom edged along the bonnet until he reached the wheel where I'd been sleeping. Out of the corner of my eye, I saw him take up a firing position just behind the grenade launchers on the front bumper.

Suddenly, the jeep began to move. For a moment, it looked like they'd decided to keep going, but the driver was simply pulling a slow turn. Five seconds later, the GAZ was headed directly for us.

There was a chorus of 'shits' from under the cam-net. I hunkered down behind the front of our vehicle, elbows propped on the bonnet, my 16 trained on the advancing column of dust. There was a flurry of activity behind me as Nick primed the Mk19, pumping a grenade into the chamber with the cocking handle. The 19 is a big weapon, but with those huge hands of his, Nick always managed to make it look easy.

'I'm going round the back,' Jeff rasped. 'If the bloody thing goes noisy, I'll make a break for it.'

'Make sure they don't get away,' Tom said out the corner of his mouth.

I half-turned to where Jeff had taken up station. He was crouched by the rear bumper. 'You got a white-phos, yeah?'

He nodded, grimly. A white-phosphor grenade burns everything instantaneously within a 25 metre area. It beat HE as the weapon of choice in a situation like this. Chuck a white-phos in the back of that thing and it wouldn't stand a chance. But first Jeff had to get to it. And then, he had to make sure the damn thing was on target. If he missed, then we'd really be in the shit.

The jeep was moving towards us at a steady pace, a trail of dust in its wake. It was no longer a case of if this thing was going to go down, but when. At around 200 metres from us, the driver had a choice: make for our cluster of nets or the group with the Unimog. In a growing feeling that this whole thing was somehow preordained, I watched the driver turn the wheel towards us. He was clearly visible behind the shit-spattered windscreen.

Each bloke took his own bead on the GAZ as it approached. There was one last thing I had to know before we were in shit-or-bust silent-running. Without looking up, I called softly to Nick. 'Can you see anything else out there, or is this it?'

'Nothing, mate,' he shot back. 'But that doesn't mean it's not there.'

Now, I looked at him, but my eyes did the talking. Too bloody right.

The GAZ pulled up ten metres from our nets in a flurry of dust and grit.

None of us moved a muscle. My last memory of Nick was a fleeting glimpse of his huge head, as he trained the Mk19 on the main body of the vehicle. The veins in his neck were sticking out and throbbing. He looked as ugly as sin.

I could make out a couple of faces now behind the dust and the flies that covered the windscreen – and something else, a lighter hue in the shadows, which could have been a third. It was impossible to tell if there were people in the back. I had to presume there were.

Ten metres wasn't far, but it was long enough. Jeff would have to cover the distance like Linford bloody Christie if there were troops under the canvas. It was imperative they stayed off the radio, much less got behind the wheel and buggered off.

Another beat of silence. Our 110 was like a man-trap on a hair-trigger. The slightest thing could have set us off.

The driver's door opened and caught the wind, banging against the side of the jeep. Two Iraqis got out. I took the guy who'd been on the passenger side and watched his eyes through my sights. The eyes' reactions give you a split-second warning what the brain behind them has clocked. Though I couldn't see his insignia, something instinctive told me he was an officer, a senior one.

I watched him glance between the two net-strewn

vehicles in front of him. His driver had moved off towards Tony's, the third in our cluster, but the officer was faced with another choice: Taff's or mine.

I knew that the boys in the other 110 had these guys in their sights, too, but it didn't make it any fucking easier.

He took a couple of paces towards us, then stopped. My finger tightened on the trigger. He swung round and said something to the driver. Now he, too, stopped and turned. They looked at one another, then turned back to the GAZ.

Shit. Maybe they'd sussed us. I felt a momentary rush of indiscipline. An urge to spray the whole bloody lot of them with automatic fire. But I held off. This thing wasn't played out yet.

They reached their respective doors, opened them, then bent down and grabbed something.

I fully expected the officer to come back up with a gun in his hand; or worse, a grenade.

Instead, he produced a battered-looking helmet. So did his pal.

Cold relief in a situation that was worsening by the second. I thought: You're gonna need more than a bloody helmet, mate. This guy was a second or two from meeting his maker and he was worried about his appearance.

The two soldiers put their helmets on, adjusted them, then resumed their former courses. The officer made straight for the front of our vehicle.

For a moment, I was struck by our predicament. It summed up in a single instant the sheer brass balls of our operation. We were 200 klicks behind enemy lines. A handful of scraggy-looking vehicles holed up in the middle of a vast and hostile desert.

What else could we be to these people but their brothers in arms?

Maybe they thought we were sleeping. Maybe they thought we were playing games. The last thing that would have ever crossed their minds was that we were a search and destroy team from the Special Air Service come to wreak havoc behind their lines.

I heard my heart beating in my ear, felt a thin sheen of sweat beneath my trigger-finger. I followed the guy's eyes as he reached the net. He was now no more than three feet away. A moment of doubt passed behind them, but it was simply indecision: he was looking for an entrance.

I steadied my breathing, then stopped it.

The Iraqi bent down and lifted the cam-net. He stooped as he pulled it up and over his head, muttering some oath to Allah as he did so. He was inside the LUP, when he straightened, saw me staring at him down the barrel of my 16 and froze.

That was when the shooting started.

ONE

I heard about the Iraqi invasion at 23,000 feet. A lot of people remember where they were on 2 August 1990. Me, I was hanging off the side of a mountain, close to fulfilling a lifelong ambition – standing on the roof of the world. The SAS had given me leave to join a civilian expedition. I was a keen mountaineer and determined to earn myself a place in the team picked for the final assault on Everest, which was scheduled for the spring of the following year.

The assault itself held an interesting twist – one that particularly appealed to me. It involved a three-way attack on the summit, a moment's reflection at the top, then a parapente off the roof of the world. Basically, the plan was to unfurl our parachutes and step off the side of the mountain into the abyss.

As practice, the summer expedition I found myself a part of in 1990 involved back-to-back attempts on mounts Schischapanga and Choyo – the latter is the third highest peak in the world.

On that second day of August, Everest was close. I could see it. I wanted more than anything to be a part of next year's climb. But that was before Saddam developed plans for Kuwait.

The day started normally by Himalayan standards: I was up, fed and brewed before the snow had softened and the sun had begun to track across the slopes. I threw the dregs of my tea over the cloud-filled canyon below my tent and turned to the summit.

The last section of the route looked a bitch: hard ice with a steep angle; the only run-out, should anything go wrong, an 800-foot ice-cliff that fell away into a bunch of ugly crevice scars on the rock slope below.

The six hours before my return to base camp required every ounce of concentration I possessed. The order of the day was to hump stores up the mountain to Base Camp 2 that was being established short of the summit. I'd come close to jeopardizing my place on the expedition already. I didn't want to blow it again.

We'd been at around 22,000 ft and a week into the trip. At first, it crept up on me. Tiredness, leading into a fatigue like I'd never known. I felt absolutely bolloxed, but I'd been tired before and figured I could beat it. Then the water retention cut in. It's one of the most excruciating feelings of pain I have ever known. You feel the need to pee so badly it makes you want to cry. But you can't even do that, because your body is conditioned to hang onto every drop – sweat, piss, tears, whatever. They put me on oxygen and within a day or two I was fine again. The prognosis was simple. Altitude sickness. I'd been pushing too hard before my body had acclimatized. Bloody stupid. No one was angrier about it than me. My overriding concern was that I had dropped my place on the following year's climb.

I looked down the ice-cliff. One slip and I'd be a permanent fixture in the glacier. I'd been mountaineering for years and for some perverse reason falling had never held any fear for me. I glanced up at the towering crag above me and the outline of Everest beyond and allowed myself a moment's indulgence. After my early mistake, things were beginning to look better. With luck, I thought I had a reasonable chance of making it to the next round.

I was tired when I finally got back to base camp and turned on the news. Listening to the World Service was part of the daily ritual. A reminder of things at home. And, occasionally, that there were still some mad fucking people in this world.

My first reaction to news of the Iraqi invasion was shock. My second was a yearning to be back home. I could picture the activity at Hereford, the speculative conversations in the interest rooms, the buzz, the excitement.

This was a chance for a good work-out. An opportunity to put into practice all the training I'd received. I'd always regretted missing out on the Falklands, but it didn't take a rocket scientist to figure that, potentially, this was bigger.

There was, of course, one tiny problem. I was stuck. All of a sudden, I forgot Everest. To hell with the Himalayas; I needed to get back home.

If it hadn't been for Harry Taylor, I'd have gone nuts. Harry was the leader of the expedition and a former SAS sergeant. He'd been a mountain-man all his adult life. His fattish face and slight build belied a fitness that was rare, even in the SAS. Harry had been in B Squadron until his departure from the Regiment five years earlier. He was only in his late twenties, but already had amassed a wealth of experience on and off the mountain. He'd been on a couple of expeditions to the Himalayas before, once with the Regiment, once as part of a civilian trip. On the former, a couple of the guys had been very badly injured and two had died. The civvie trip had failed to get to the top. So, now, Harry was driven. You could see it in his eyes. Harry will probably die on a mountain, because, like an addict, he can't give the damn things up. Once he's finished a climb, it's onto the next summit, and then the next, and then the one after that.

Maybe because of his own addiction, Harry understood something of my pathological need to be back;

to get on with the job I had been training to do since joining the Special Air Service eight years earlier.

Over the next few weeks we talked a lot of shop, going over all the military options we reckoned would be available to the planners in Whitehall and the Pentagon. Drawing up our own plans was an interesting mental exercise, but more importantly for me, it stopped me from going mad.

The weeks passed agonizingly slowly. When, at last, the time came to say goodbye, Harry's parting shot was simple and to the point.

'You lucky bastard, Cammy. Have a good one, mate.'

We shook hands and I turned towards the steep, scree-lined path that led eventually to Hereford.

'See you when you get back,' Harry shouted after me.

Six months later, those words would come back to haunt me. But right there and then, as I forced myself from breaking into a jog down the mountain, I could think only of what lay ahead, not of the men who wouldn't be coming back.

It was good to be back with the boys. But it was weird, too. Two days earlier I'd been breathing the rarefied oxygen of the Himalayas. It had taken twelve hours to descend the mountain on foot and by yak; a further fifteen hours to get to Lhasa by four-wheel drive. From there, it was a day-long plane journey back to London and thence a bus journey to Hereford. Eventually, three weeks after Saddam's troops trampled over Kuwait, I was back at Stirling Lines and raring to go.

Only it wasn't quite that simple. For twenty-one days the Regiment had been a hive of activity as preparations were made to meet the Iraqi threat. Saddam's troops were still pouring into the tiny, oil-rich state and from there they could have gone anywhere in the Gulf. Saudi Arabia, the lynch-pin of Western interests in the Middle East, could be the next to fall. Never mind that I'd seen none of my mates in almost two months. The shit was flying and I had to fit in around it.

There was a squadron photograph at three and I was told to be there, beard and all. After a month's worth of growth on my face I looked worse than a tramp. In the meantime, I made myself busy, handing back my mountain kit to stores and snatching conversations with as many of the lads as I could.

There is usually a sense of purpose in the way people move around the base, especially at exercise time. But this was different. Everywhere I looked, the boys were involved in little projects all connected with Kuwait. I moved between them, looking over their shoulders, trying not to be intrusive. Nigh on a month of waiting and already I was feeling like a spare prick at a barmitzvah. It was Steve, the head of Freefall Troop, a big guy who looked like a throwback from a Sven Hassel novel, who summed up how I felt.

'Back of the queue, Cammy,' he said, slapping me between the shoulder blades as he headed off to another briefing. 'You've missed this one, mate.'

There are four troops in the SAS: Mountain, Free-fall, Mobility and Boat. As a sergeant in Mountain Troop, I couldn't really allow this to pass unchecked. 'I didn't expect to see any of you Aldershot boys on this call, Steve. Saddam's army must be a bigger bunch of poofs than I thought.'

He laughed. 'Yeah, well, you crap-hats would know, eh?'

Fuck. First round to the Paras.

I decided to go check my mail: I'd been putting off opening the Access bills and all the other crap that accrues when you go away for long enough. As I crossed the centre of the compound, the activity continued. Every spare patch of ground was occupied by the big, brown bulk containers that stores our kit for ninety-nine per cent of our existence. It takes a war to break it out. Wherever I looked stuff was being stockpiled and readied.

It was then that I saw a couple of familiar faces through the organized mayhem; Tom and Jeff cutting across the compound, each with a clipboard under his arm. From the direction they were heading, I guessed they were making for the Kremlin, the most secure part of the Regimental enclave. This is where it all came together when we were planning something big.

Tom looked up, saw me, and nudged Jeff. They came over. 'Fuck me,' Tom announced, an evil smirk on his face, 'we're preparing to go knock the shit out of the Iraqi Army and they let one of their spies in for a gander.'

Tom was an excellent soldier, one of the best I'd ever seen. Four years earlier, I'd helped train him for the Regiment. His chief faults were his bloody awful taste in clothes and the fact that he was an ex-Para, something he never let you forget, especially if your parent regiment was infantry, like mine.

They started to look me up and down. Tom tugged at the growth on my face. Jeff lifted his nose and pretended to gag. I'm pretty dark – I guess it's the Celtic ancestry – so I let Tom's remark go. But I clipped Jeff around the head. In my years with the Regiment, there'd been times when I'd smelt a hell of a lot worse.

Both of them dissolved into laughter. We shook hands. It was good to see them again.

You tend to hang out a lot with the guys in your troop. Professionalism, I guess, if nothing else, binds you together. But there's also another gaggle of blokes; people who are both popular, because they're witty and amusing or whatever, and highly professional. Tom and Jeff weren't in Mountain Troop. They slotted into the latter category. Jeff was a Kiwi I'd met several years earlier while on exchange with the New Zealand SAS. Jeff, like me, was a 'crap-hat' – that is, his parent regiment was infantry, too.

They couldn't hang around long. They were due in the War Room for a target-attack assessment briefing at any moment. These, I found out, had been going on relentlessly since the invasion. The list of targets was a long one. Power-stations, leadership sites, command bunkers, airfields – any key establishment inside Iraq of any strategic worth had been singled out by the Regiment intel planners for special attention in the event we got word to go in there and take them out. Tom and Jeff weren't giving away any trade secrets when they told me that their target-pack for the day was a hydro-electric dam somewhere in the mountains north of Baghdad.

My sense of isolation deepened and I guess Tom must have seen it, even though I'd done my best to keep it light.

'Don't worry,' he said, 'there's plenty more of this stuff to go round. Go home and scrape that shit off your cheeks. It'll be show-time soon enough.' He turned to jog after Jeff, who'd resumed his trek towards the Kremlin, then paused, adding: 'Oh, by the way, crap-hat . . .'

I grunted wearily, preparing for another string of jokes about my 'swan' through the Himalayas.

'Welcome back, mate,' he said.

*

9

That evening, I saw Jade again for the first time in two months. We're not married, although we have been together for a good many years and plan to get hitched one day. She has two children – Aaron, eleven, and Jamie, five – from a marriage that didn't work out. They're smashing kids and I love them like they're my own. They were both awake when I finally extricated myself from Stirling Lines and walked through the door. For the next few hours, until way past their normal bedtime, we sat up and chatted about what they'd been doing, then about what I'd done and seen over the past few months. Finally, Jade issued the order to go to bed and after a flurry of shrill remonstrations, the house was filled with silence.

Jade is five foot six, of medium build, with long brown hair. She is Welsh and very beautiful. We'd had our ups and downs over the years, but she was my best friend and I loved her and she knew it. For me, the Army has been a way of life for as long as I can remember. I joined up as a boy-soldier at sixteen and enlisted in the Queen's Regiment as soon as I could. I passed selection for the SAS soon after the Falklands campaign in 1982 and from then on found myself on call for deployment to any God-forsaken spot in the world at a moment's notice. On top of that, there's a load of exercises, many of them on foreign soil, that we get sent on every year. For me, it's half the reason I do this job. But for someone who's married into the system it's not easy and I guess it accounts for the high divorce rate among Regimental personnel. At least, Jade came from a military family, so it wasn't all new to her. No matter how good the work-out I've been on, though, it is always great to get back.

We talked and made out and talked some more until we fell exhausted into bed sometime in the small hours.

During the night, I awoke in a muck-sweat, clutching my stomach and clawing for air. I never know when I'm going to get the dream that has lived with me for a decade or so now, but each time, it's as vivid and as shit-awful as the last. As ever, I was convinced that I'd been gored through the stomach by a thick wooden stake. I wake up with the bloody thing sticking right through me, staring at it, half in amazement, half in absolute horror. The dream has never reached its ultimate and logical conclusion – I wake up before that, thank Christ – but in the course of time, no doubt about it, I had come to see it as some kind of premonition of death.

After that, sleep didn't come easy, so I got dressed, kissed Jade lightly on the forehead, took a last look at the kids, who were still asleep, and drove to camp. It was starting to get light as I made my way through the barracks towards the Squadron Interest Room. It was a glorious morning; one of those dawns that you know presages the onset of a good day. Roll-call was still a couple of hours off when I walked into the

Interest Room and turned on the lights, relishing the silence after the bustle of the day before.

The Interest Room is A Squadron's work room. Each active duty squadron – A, B, D and G, the four Sabre Squadrons – has its own, making four at Stirling Lines. The plaques, shields, photographs and other mementoes on their sixteen walls contain pretty much the entire history of the SAS over the post-war period. I panned past souvenirs from Malaya, Borneo, Oman and the South Atlantic until my eyes came to rest on the far wall, which always contains charts and data in support of the issue of the moment. Needless to say, it was filled with material on Kuwait and Iraq. There were threat assessments on tanks, surface-to-air missile systems, helicopters, aircraft, you name it. Confronted with this for the first time, and in the silence before the day's activity, the reality of the situation we were facing hit me for the first time. I knew our intel on the Iraqi orbat, or order of battle, wasn't what it could be, but the sight of all those flags dotted around Kuwait and Southern Iraq – each one representing one of Saddam's key military units – said that if it came to a fight, we were going to have our work cut out for us.

My feelings of excitement were marred by another reality. In the late summer of 1990, A Squadron, my unit, was doing its stint on the counter-terrorist watch. The lads earmarked for deployment to the Gulf were the stand-by team. We weren't ready to go stand-by until the end of the year. I was still ruminating this fact, when a huge hand landed on my shoulder.

'Relax, Cammy, it'll all be over by fucking Christmas, mate.'

I turned around to find myself confronted by a giant, genetic fuck-up. Nick was six foot plus with more muscles than a Grimsby trawler. He'd come to the SAS from the Paras via the RAF Regiment, which was unusual. Somewhat ponderous, he used to get the piss taken mercilessly, but he was a hell of a bloke, an extremely hard worker and had a heart of gold. Being a dems man par excellence, he was also bloody good at blowing things up. We exchanged pleasantries.

'Nick, you're getting fat,' I said, never missing a chance to rub an ex-Para up the wrong way. 'Eased off on the training, mate?'

'Round the fucking back and I'll show you, Cammy, you wanker.'

Before it degenerated, a couple of other lads walked in and I started having to fend off a torrent of comments about the so-called doddle of a freebie I'd been on for the past eight weeks. After this, I thought, a major fucking conflict might turn out to be a bit of a holiday.

Roll-call, as ever, was at ten past eight. From there, we went to Squadron Prayers in the Interest Room. Prayers were presided over mostly by Robert, our sergeant major, and Graham, our OC. Robert was a hell of a bloke. Tall, well-built and dark, whatever he did, he did well. He boxed and played football for the Army and spoke a couple of languages fluently, including Arabic.

I had particular cause to remember him. A couple of years earlier I'd been taking a group of eighty students, as we call SAS hopefuls, on a 30 km hike at Penn-y-Fan in the Brecon Beacons as part of their selection training. These things are done at a hell of a lick and are, frankly, gut-busters. As leader of this thing, I had to set an example – beat everyone to the finish or suffer smirks from the students for the rest of the course. I had a technique for this, a simple one: once I started, I didn't stop and I didn't look back. For the first ten klicks you hear the trample of boots somewhere behind you, but after a while the sound falls away and you can throttle back a bit, take it a little easy and admire the bleak scenery. But on this occasion, somebody was sticking to me like glue; what was more, he had this problem getting air down his nose – it sounded like I had a raging, snorting, demonic bull on my heels. So, I kept pounding that fucking hillside, hoping to shake this monster off, but however hard I pushed, it remained there, never more than a few feet off my right shoulder. Eventually, just when I thought I was about to die of heart failure, I broke my golden rule and turned. There was Robert, a hundred or so pounds on his back, grinning at me like a demented monkey. Summoning all my strength I tried to make believe I'd known it was him all along

– and that he ought to watch himself, as it looked like he was getting a little unfit. Robert was a good friend and commanded immense respect from everyone on the Squadron. When he got up there, you knew you were in good hands.

I wish I could have said the same about Graham. Graham was a major and, strictly speaking, wasn't one of us. He was on exchange from another unit, but maybe they didn't want him back or something, because he'd stuck with us for a year and showed no sign of buggering off. While we lolled in the tatty armchairs of the Interest Room listening to Robert, Graham hung around behind him, smoothing back his wispy, sand-coloured hair and looking pensive. He was an OK guy, but getting a decision out of him sometimes was like squeezing blood from a stone. For some reason, though, the powers-that-be must have thought the sun shone out of his arse, because he could do no wrong. Like a lot of Ruperts – officers – he was good socially and that counts for a lot in the upper reaches of the Army. That's just the way it is; it's the system and, unlike some people, I don't let it bother me.

Squadron Prayers broke up and we moved into Troop Prayers. This is where you find out in some detail who's doing what. For the bosses, it's a good time to get feedback from the troop sergeants. For me, it was an opportunity to get the official view of what was going on in the Squadron.

Eventually, the formal briefings finished and the room emptied except for me and Alec. Alec was a fellow sergeant and another bloke for whom I had a lot of respect. 'OK,' he said, the moment the last person drifted out, 'you heard the party line. You want to know how it really is?'

I nodded. In the corner of the room, the TV that stayed on throughout the day so that blokes could keep abreast of events was pounding out a diet of Gulf developments courtesy of CNN.

I'd already familiarized myself with the Iraqi build-up. How there were over 300,000 Iraqi troops inside Kuwait and neighbouring areas in southern and western Iraq. They were accompanied by 3500 tanks, over 2500 armoured vehicles and 1700 artillery pieces.

'This is serious shit,' Alec said. 'Whatever you may have seen or heard, the prognosis here is that this isn't some other raghead army, but a sophisticated opponent. The guys we've got to watch are this mob' – he tapped the map behind him – 'Saddam's Republican Guard. While much of the regular army is composed of conscripts, these guys are hard-core, the real thing. Green Slime says that if push comes to shove, they're liable to give our boys quite a time of it.'

Green Slime – the Int Corps – provided us with the bulk of our intelligence. 'Where does the Regiment come into it?' I asked.

'G squadron, as you know, is about to deploy to theatre and D Squadron will head out a few weeks later. There's a base being set up for the Regiment somewhere in the United Arab Emirates.'

'And A Squadron?'

Alec shook his head. 'Not a chance. For the moment, we're staying put.'

I swore. With so much happening in the Gulf, it was frustrating beyond belief that we were being held back on counter-terrorism (CT) duties.

'Maybe it's not so bad,' Alec said, trying to sound upbeat. 'There's talk that terrorist groups sympathetic to Saddam may be mounting plans for hijackings in the coming weeks. As far as our training goes, aircraft have moved up the priority list and Tube trains go to the back of the queue. Time to break out the black kit and bone up on some new entry techniques they've been working up for us.'

We were always able to get our hands on civilian passenger aircraft to play around with when we needed to.

'Alec,' I said, 'if the balloon goes up, we might miss out on the whole thing. Is that what you're saying?'

'Bottom line. Yes.' He fell silent for a moment. 'Until G Squadron return in late November it's going to be tough. We've got to keep two heads on our shoulders: One that's full of CT shit and another that's clued about the latest moves inside Iraq and Kuwait. Bet you wish you stayed on that mountain now, eh?'

I glanced towards the television and saw a US Army

M1 Abrams main-battle tank battling through the desert sands of Saudi Arabia. The latest news from 'theatre' was that Saddam had just moved another 50,000 troops into the fifteenth and newest state of Iraq.

TWO

As the stalemate between Iraq and the Coalition over the occupation of Kuwait dragged on, the weeks drifted into months and before we knew it, we were well into November. Having thought at the outset that there was no way we'd be a part of the action, we now began to see a glimmer of hope. The political situation looked as intractable as ever, although with US, British, French and Arab troops pouring into the Gulf in their thousands every week, the sense that this was leading towards something big was unshakable. What had changed was the rapidity with which G Squadron's return to Stirling Lines now began to loom before us. For weeks it had seemed like it would never happen. Now it was writ large across the calendar that hung in the A Squadron Interest Room.

What we gathered from G Squadron's early returnees was highly encouraging. Our own 8000-strong 7th Armoured Brigade was almost ready for offensive operations, we had helicopters out there, fighters, bombers and surveillance aircraft. In addition, the government had just elected to send a second armoured brigade to Saudi Arabia. By the end of December, we, the Brits, would have 30,000 troops in place. But if you think that's impressive, the G Squadron guys told us, you should see what the Yanks have deployed. And then they left, heartily dejected; because, even if this thing went down tomorrow, that was it, they weren't going back.

In a way, you had to feel sorry for them, but I reckoned I'd seen everything, when I caught Nick, in a rare moment of compassion, putting a huge arm around a downcast G Squadron oppo and offering warm words of consolation over the opportunity of a lifetime he'd just missed out on. 'You can always ask the CO for a transfer to A Squadron,' he said, looking up to give me a wink as I walked past. 'But if I were you, I'd hit him with the request after you've bought him a few drinks at the bunfight.'

The bunfight was our end of year knees-up. It was good advice, except for one thing – given half a chance, the rest of G Squadron would be doing the same thing.

We handed over the CT role to G squadron, one hacked-off bunch of bunnies, at the end of the first week of December. From then, things really started to hum. At Squadron level, there were some interesting developments on the kit-side. One morning, a bunch of evil-looking guns turned up in the main compound. These were 20 mm Giats that the Regiment had been evaluating before the Gulf crisis blew up. The evaluation was not yet complete, but somebody, somewhere had decided we should take them out to theatre anyway, just in case. When it came to support weapons, all we really had to rely on was the heavy Browning .50 machine gun. It's a brute of a weapon, but temperamental, having a nasty habit of jamming just when you need it most. Even so, I had my doubts about the Giat. I'd had a go with it soon after it arrived at the Regiment's Ops Research Wing and didn't like it much then. Twenty millimetre is great. You can punch holes through almost anything with it. But in the case of the Giat, the system fires electrically and experience said that if a complex bit of equipment like this could go wrong, it would. But somebody higher up the chain of command said they went and they did.

I busied myself with kit matters of no less importance. I went and paid a visit to Mary.

Mary is a tailoress at Stirling Lines, in her late forties, I suppose, and an amazing woman. I'd first met her when I was undergoing selection. When you start out, they issue you berets that are so stiff they're good for nothing, unless you want to go around looking like Fred Scuttle, the Benny Hill character. I'd been 'working' my beret for a while, bending it and shaping it so it'd look well worn when the time came for me to don it officially. I figured, while I was about it, I might as well have my winged dagger sewn on, too, so I went to the tailor's and encountered Mary for the first time. Mary pronounced this move somewhat cocky, but for the price of a cup of tea, she put it on anyway. We've worked pretty much the same way ever since: I make the tea, while Mary sews.

Ever since we'd known we were heading for the Gulf, I'd spent time boning up on the weather and the terrain we might expect when we got out there. Much of the region is rocky and sandy – shit that can be murder on the knees and elbows if you're spending hours at a time keeping some enemy convoy or outpost under observation. Most of the lads accept the clothing and webbing they're given without question. Me, I leave nothing to chance.

With Mary's help, I customized wherever I could. Extra thick pads went on the elbows and knees of my fatigues. Perfectly good zips were ripped off jackets and Velcro substituted. Mary made me sand-gaiters that'd keep all the crap you find in a desert from entering my boots and giving me blisters, a soldier's worst enemy. And finally, I asked her to add pockets to the calves of my trousers that were just the right size for a shell-dressing. When the shit hits the fan and you're lying there with your guts hanging out – or staring at somebody else's – you need kit like that to be instantly accessible.

Mary knew where I was coming from. She understood. 'S'pose I were to make that dressing pocket just a touch bigger, Cammy,' she said, a needle clamped between lips on one side of her mouth and a knowing look in her eyes. I didn't get it at first. Then, she placed a packet of Silk Cut over the area she'd marked out with tailor's chalk and I saw the light. Like I said, a remarkable woman is Mary.

For the most part, the period between our hand-over to G Squadron and our end of term wash-up or cross-brief, a week before Christmas, was one big back-to-school session. The learning was relentless and when we did have the odd break, most of us used the time to go around making sure we had absolutely everything we'd need for a sustained operation in the Gulf.

The odd training course reminded us, if ever we had cause to doubt it, that a lot of people were pulling together to take the fight to Saddam. One day, our laser target designators, or LTDs, were removed for modifications that would allow us to take part in combined operations with the Americans. The LTD is a neat bit of kit that helps ensure accurate aerial bombing. Once a target has been earmarked for attack, we work our way to within range of it, point the laser beam and wait for the sound of jet aircraft above. The next thing you know, a voice over the radio is telling you to squeeze the trigger and a few seconds later the target evaporates. We'd been working the system for some time, but only in conjunction with the RAF. Now, after a bit of tweaking, and some small changes in procedure, we'd be able to designate for the USAF, too.

As a bloke with extensive demolition training, the LTD was part of my bag of tricks. Taking a leak-break from one of our training sessions one day, I wandered into the bogs to hear the most atrocious wailing sound coming from one of the cubicles, then a silence followed by what sounded like the worst case of coughing and expectoration I'd ever heard. For a moment, my blood froze, then I remembered that Ian and Keith had Arabic class that day. I could tell it was Keith from the grunts and straining sounds between bouts of recited vocab. You get to learn almost everything about your colleagues on prolonged exercise, right down to the most unpleasant of details. 'Don't forget,' I called to Keith on my way out, 'that the Bedouin doesn't use bog-paper, but his hand. Or, if he's lucky, a stone.'

I speak Arabic, not fluently, but well enough to catch the gist of his reply. His phraseology was coming along nicely.

It was at this time, too, that we familiarized ourselves in even greater depth about the enemy's strengths and weaknesses. The Int Corps went into overdrive, preparing briefs day-in and day-out on what we might expect when we went into Kuwait and Iraq. Having succumbed to the secure belief that the Iraqis were nothing but a bunch of ill-disciplined ragheads, I was shocked by some of the stuff that I heard during those sessions in the Interest Room. I started, for instance, to develop a healthy respect for the Republican Guard. These boys were billed by Green Slime as fiercely loyal and battle-hardened, following their extensive combat experience during the 1980–88 Iran–Iraq war. Remoulded in the 1970s to act as Saddam's personal bodyguard, they developed into a fully fledged fighting force during the fierce and bloody war with Iran, achieving heroic status in 1988, when they were instrumental in the recapture of the Fao peninsula, the engagement that broke the Iranian war effort and persuaded the Ayatollah finally to sue for peace.

'Respect them,' our Int Corps briefer said, 'these bastards are vicious and without remorse. In the Fao peninsula, they used their chemical weapons expertise to lay down a barrage of nerve and cyanide agents that killed everyone and everything it touched. The Iranians didn't stand a chance.'

Tom, lolling in an armchair beside me, nudged me and whispered: 'That's because they were trained by crap-hats, you know. Stick with the Paras, Cammy, and you'll be all right. Promise, mate.'

I thanked him for his concern and suggested he might like to extend his offer to every non-Para member of the Regiment at the cross-brief in a few days' time.

The cross-brief is the Regiment's formal review of the past twelve months as well as a glance forward to what we might expect the following year. Given the way things were heading, nobody was too concerned with the past. All eyes were on the weeks and months ahead. The cross-brief is always slated for a week late in the year. It starts on the Monday and lasts all week. It's a bit like a convention. Everyone attends, including non-badged members – drivers, storemen, cooks and armourers.

The week is punctuated with presentations on the Regiment's past performance and future commitments: the exercises and such like that are earmarked for the year ahead. You're expected to attend just about everything, but in practice you pick and mix, asterisking those talks that are only directly relevant to you or your unit. On this occasion, for instance, I skipped the padre's chat, but made damn' sure I didn't miss the Int-Corps' final wrap on the Iraqi armed forces' fighting capabilities. I'm not prone to religious sentiment, but given the hand that the Almighty could be playing in the proceedings, I couldn't help thinking afterwards that I might have got my priorities wrong.

When it was all done and dusted, and we'd filled ourselves with as much gen as we could stand, we gathered in the gym at the end of the week to receive our final pep-talk from the CO, Colonel Harry Rollings. He started by asking the hall to be cleared of non-badged members. Then, he told those of us that were left to close up. The Regiment is not a big fighting force. All in all, it comprises about 600–700 people.

But when the non-badged personnel left the room, and with our complement depleted by the two squadrons out in the Gulf, barely 50 people remained.

We drew close and waited. You could hear a pin drop. Rollings looked about as grim as I'd ever seen him.

'Fellers,' he started, 'there's no turning the clock back on this one. As you know, Saddam has until the 15th of January to get out of Kuwait. But if you want my opinion, and those of my superiors, he's not going to budge. This thing is going down. And when it does, we're going to be there.'

He went on to give his personal assessment of the threat and in what capacity he saw the Regiment being used. In essence, it wasn't that far removed from the concept of operations devised by David Stirling, the founder of the SAS, whose Long Range Desert Group had fought so successfully against the German Afrika Korps forty years previously. The vehicles might have changed a bit, but the tactics were much the same: find out what the enemy was doing, report back and, where appropriate, take him out with extreme prejudice.

Then, Rollings said something I didn't expect. 'You should also prepare yourselves mentally for the worst.' He paused while glances were exchanged among members of his audience. 'You know the calibre of the threat you face. You know what the Republican Guard is capable of. Gentlemen, if the proverbial shit hits the fan, you will not be coming home. It's as well you square up to that now.'

Only then did I realize what he was saying. Rollings wasn't talking about body-bags. He was talking about what the Iraqis would do to us if we got captured. A silence descended on the room. There were no quips; no cracks about Paras and crap-hats. On the one hand I was taken aback. It was like being asked if you've remembered your maggots when you go fishing. Of course, we knew what the enemy might do if we were captured. Yet, it drove home in me something else: in all the months of preparation for deployment to war, I never once even considered the possibility of being taken prisoner. Maybe, that was what had prompted Rollings to say it. Maybe, we all needed a little reminder that, for whatever reason, some of us wouldn't be here at the next cross-brief.

There were no long faces when we filed out of the gym and headed for our final engagement of the week, our end of year bunfight in the mess-hall, but you could sense a definite change in the atmosphere.

A few minutes later, we were downing tinnies in the mess-hall like they were going out of fashion. You get a speech like the CO's and you don't dwell on it; it's onto the next thing. In the 'green army', Rollings' words would have devastated your average eighteen-year-old and probably sent him AWOL at the end of his next leave. Nick, Tom, Alec, Jeff, Tony and I crashed cans and drank to the same toast: death, glory or the rest of our lives as eunuchs in one of Saddam's palaces.

The party broke up at two the following morning after a crawl around Hereford's finest hostelries. Some of the guys had their wives or girlfriends come and pick them up. My girl had already joined the proceedings. After we said our goodbyes, we headed off in our separate directions for ten days' leave. Jade and I walked slowly home, arm-in-arm through the empty streets, each with our own thoughts. Mine drifted back to what the CO had said earlier. As a squadron, we'd done everything in our power to ready ourselves for whatever lay ahead. But on a personal level, I knew I still had some work to do before we embarked en masse for the Gulf on 29 December.

When I hit camp, it was a shadow of the place it had been over the past few months, with just the odd few people going about their business. I went straight to my room and laid everything out. Each of us is allowed to keep our own room at Stirling Lines. It's nothing fancy, just a place to store our kit. Now, in the silence of the camp, two things were uppermost on my mind: first, every item had to earn its place on the trip. With only 80 lb of weight allowed per man, this didn't leave much leeway. Second, if I got it wrong, nobody would be bringing whatever I'd forgotten into Saddam's backyard – if, indeed, that was where we were headed. So, I put aside my jungle and arctic kit and set to work preparing the things I'd need for the desert.

First things first: webbing. This carried two magazine pouches, two water bottles and a utility pouch, the last holding stuff like the hexamine tablets we use for making fires, some spare medical kit and essentials like tea-bags. My webbing had served me well over the years, but it had never gone to war. Even in Northern Ireland, you're never more than a few miles from the nearest phone box. If I had to go on the run inside Iraq, however, the stuff in my webbing might mean the difference between freedom and capture, life or death. I weighed it all up and came to a swift conclusion. Basically, it wasn't good enough for where we were headed; so, I'd have to do a little customizing. I made a quick call to a bloke called Dave who runs a specialist kit and clothing company in Devon. It wasn't the first time he'd got a call from me requesting some weird bit of gear in a nigh-impossible timeframe. Dave had a good understanding of military equipment. If I told him I needed a pouch on my webbing big enough to hold four double-16 mags, I didn't then have to spell out the vital statistics. He just got on with it. And he never asked awkward questions.

I drew up what I wanted on the back of a fag-packet and faxed him the spec. When it came back, it'd include special pouches on the chest for grenades, medical dressings, morphine and cylume sticks, plus all the usual stuff. What's more, Dave's astute enough to turn it out in desert cam without my having to tell him.

Now I'm happier. If I'm in the shit, I reckon I've got everything I need to get me home.

On day two, I set about packing my Bergen, the back-pack we all carry with us on active service. Into this went all the regular stuff: sleeping bag, NBC (nuclear, biological and chemical warfare protection) kit, spare boots and clothing, a small stove and some extra water containers. Our standard water containers hold only one pint, which is fine under normal conditions, but when you're under stress, your water intake goes up. I took another look at the situation and wondered what could be done about it. Too many water bottles clutter up your Bergen and leave you with no room for anything else. So, I removed the nozzles from several plastic water containers and super-glued each one onto a plastic bag. I now had a kind of water bladder that when shoved into the Bergen full, moulded itself into the nooks and crannies, making it maximum room-efficient.

On day three, I fine-tuned the Bergen's inventory, adding some of the smaller, but nonetheless essential items I'd need to take with me. These included my compass, a short-wave radio – the BBC World Service was vital listening if we had to go on the run, telling us everything from whether we'd won or not to the small matter of if the war had gone nuclear – and a special E&E kit of my own making that'd contain a number of essentials if I ever had to escape and evade inside enemy territory. Into this small baccy tin I managed to pack around forty items as diverse as hacksaw blades, anti-shit tablets, water sterilizers, a candle stub, razor blades, a scalpel, tweezers, needles, an animal snare, plastic bags, chocolate, two oxo cubes and a durex. The last is good for keeping the muzzle of your rifle dry when you're up to your ears in water. In our case, though, the real enemy was going to be sand. In the desert, the bastard stuff gets into everything. Sand and weapons do not mix well.

Finally, I looked at my personal weaponry. We all carried an assault version of the M16 called the Commando, which was usually accompanied by a 203 grenade launcher. This was a well-proven combination and required no special attention. I was less happy with the kit that went with my 9 mm Browning pistol. Not that I ever thought of myself as Wyatt Earp, but there might be a time when I needed to draw the thing in a hurry and under the present arrangement that was an impossibility. I looked at three or four different models of holster and in the end elected to go for a shoulder type which I then played around with to fit my belt harness. It was good and accessible, but wouldn't shed the Browning when it wasn't meant to. I also went and bought myself a 20-round magazine to replace the standard-issue 12-rounder. All these add-ons are at your own expense. Special forces or not, the army issues you with stuff it considers sufficient for the job. Trouble is, in our line of work, sufficient can wind you up dead.

By the afternoon of the third day, I had everything ready. There was just one last thing to do before I could go back to the Christmas break. I sat down and wrote letters to my parents, to Jade and the boys, plus one to the senior NCO or officer charged with entering my room if I failed to make the clock. I'm a meticulous son of a bitch and wanted to be sure that everything was squared away before we set off for the UAE. I propped the letters next to my Bergen against the wall on the far side of the room, took a last look around to make sure I'd forgotten nothing, then turned off the light and shut the door.

With Christmas just a few days away, it was busy enough for both Jade and me not to have to think about the countdown to war. On Christmas Eve we helped Jamie prepare for the arrival of the Bearded One by putting out mince-pies and carrots next to his stocking. Carrots, as everyone knows, are what reindeer like best after a hard slog around the globe. On Christmas Day the kids tumbled out of bed early, of course (Jamie having happily observed that a reindeer had taken a nibble out of one of the carrots), and it was full-swing into the festivities. We always have Christmas lunch at Jade's twin-sister's. Frances has got two girls, with whom the boys get on well, and we spent the rest of the afternoon getting slowly pissed and doing our best to avoid projectiles launched from Action Man's various new weapon systems.

And then, all of a sudden, the final day was upon us. Saying goodbye to Jade wasn't easy. I tried to play the Iraqis down as a piece of piss, a load of amateurs buggering around with the premier league. But it was all a bit half-hearted. I told her I might be able to call her when I got to the UAE, but neither of us liked the phone, so it seemed pretty pointless. We also agreed that there wasn't a whole lot of point in my writing since all our letters would be censored and I didn't like the idea of some quasi-intelligence sleazo reading out my innermost thoughts. So, we agreed that I wouldn't phone and I wouldn't write; that it was much better, all in all, if we just left it until after the whole thing was over.

After the kids were asleep, I found myself getting dangerously sentimental. She reminded me that it was Frances I'd first tried to ask out, not her, and we both laughed. It helped break the tension, by now almost unbearable, between us.

But it didn't alter much. I knew she was hoping that the phone would ring and I'd be told to stand down – that by some miracle the whole thing was being called off. Needless to say, it didn't. Instead, we tried to forget everything by spending our last hours together screwing like teenagers.

Sometime in the small hours I had the dream again. As with the other times, it was vivid as hell. I woke, as ever, convinced I'd been gored through the stomach by a thick wooden stake. Strange as it may seem, on the morning of my departure to the Gulf, my conviction that the dream was some kind of premonition provided Jade with some small shred of comfort. Where I was going, wooden stakes weren't half as plentiful as Iraqi shells and bullets.

THREE

Standing on the tarmac at Dhahran next to the giant fuselage of the Galaxy, I surveyed the scene. I'd seen aircraft in my time, but this was something else, it was brimming with transports and fighters as far as the eye could see. There was a sense of urgency and threat about the place: soldiers wearing flak-jackets, helmets and NBC kit. Though still a long way from Baghdad, we had entered the battle-zone. Dhahran was well within striking distance of the Iraqi Air Force and Saddam's Scud ballistic missiles.

The evidence was everywhere. Until now, no one had really pointed up the Scud threat. It was always billed as a nuisance, but tactically worthless, a bit like Hitler's V-2s, but I couldn't help wondering if we weren't going to hear more about Saddam's Scuds.

There was no knowing how long we would have to wait for our ground transportation, so I took a wander. I found Nick sitting on a trolley parked beneath the wing of a nearby aircraft. He seemed deep in thought.

'Homesick already, mate?' I asked.

He shook his head pensively, which, in Nick's case, is a worrying sight. 'Next time we see this much kit let's hope it's on the other side, eh, Cam?'

'Yeah,' I said, not quite sure if he was serious or not. You could have nuked Dhahran and still had to have come back to mop up. The coaches arrived and we left for our training base in the United Arab Emirates. The journey lasted about six hours and it was dark when we finally arrived. The camp was extremely spartan. There was a cookhouse, an armoury-cum-storeroom and an ablutions block. As for the rest, everything was tented, but since the climate was temperate we couldn't have given a shit. Since we'd been on the move for the best part of thirty-six hours, we crashed as soon as we arrived, lapsing into unconsciousness to the put-put rhythm of the camp electricity generators.

The next morning we got cracking. Dawn gave us a chance to get our first good look at the area. It seemed perfect for the kind of training we had to do in the run-up to the deadline that had been set for Saddam's withdrawal from Kuwait, approximately two weeks away. By 12 January, three days before the deadline expired, we had to be fit, acclimatized, fully trained and ready to ship out to our forward mounting base.

Time was going to be tight. I drew comfort from the sight of our vehicles lined up in the early morning sunshine. They appeared none the worse for wear after several months of abuse at the hands of G Squadron.

All four squadrons in the SAS follow the same order of battle. Each is composed of the four sixteen-man troops – boat, freefall, mountain and mobility – but all members are cross-trained in the methods of the other troops. Because no soldier has the same degree of other-troop skills he has acquired in his own, the next twelve days would be devoted to bringing us all up to speed in one essential area: mobility operations.

It was a time for going right back to basics: understanding the vehicles, how to do emergency repairs, driving over difficult terrain, navigating by dead reckoning and GPS. We never totally relied on our sat-nav systems. In case they went wrong when we were in Iraq, we practised as we had before the arrival of GPS – using the old time, distance and speed formula.

For the first few days, we trained individually, mainly in the use of the support weapons we'd be taking with us. These were the Mk19 grenade launchers, .50 calibre Browning heavy machine-guns and Milan missiles that were fixed to our vehicles. We also spent a lot of time working with a selection of Iraqi weapon systems we reckoned we might encounter, if – when – we slipped across the border: nobody, as yet, had said that that was where we were headed. But since it was what we did best, it was a foregone conclusion that when the shit hit the fan we'd be into Iraq like Flynn. We pored over the enemy's small arms and heavy machine-guns with the same attention to detail we'd devoted to our own weapons. If things went tits-up over there, an Iraqi gun would do the job as good as any other.

In addition, we received extensive demolitions training, something I'd always enjoyed, as dems was a strong back-up skill I'd acquired during my time with the Regiment. We practised right on the edge of our normal safety limits. Our mock attacks and skirmishes were fully live, using every type of explosive and ammunition in our inventory. We blew up fac-similes of targets we reckoned we might be called upon to attack. We devised numerous new techniques for maximizing the effects of our explosives. We were restricted only by the limits of our imagination and, when it came to some of the devices we built, were often only a fag-paper's width from death.

Two days before we left Manama, we broke out of our troop affiliations and formed up into our fighting orbat. We divided ourselves into two half-squadron convoys of approximately thirty men each. The personnel in our half-squadron convoy consisted of the following: half of Mobility Troop, half of Freefall Troop and all of Mountain Troop. The other half-squadron convoy got the other half of Mobility Troop, the other half of Freefall and all of Boat Troop. The dynamics were dictated by the need to disperse

Mobility Troop, the guys with real experience of fast, roving ops behind enemy lines, between the two convoy groups.

Our convoy would consist of six fighting vehicles, one Unimog mother support vehicle and four bikes. The little four-wheeled fast-attack craft that had offered promise in the early stages of our training would be left behind. They turned out to be quite unsuitable for the boulder fields that we looked set to encounter in northern Saudi, Kuwait and Iraq. We also spurned the Giat 20 mm cannons. We'd brought about fifteen of them with us to the UAE, but in the end considered them too much of a risk. Even if the electrical firing system worked as advertised, we were still lumbered with the fact that they didn't have any night optics. We tried gluing them on, but every time we fired the damned things, the vibration shook them off. As temperamental as it was, we'd just have to rely on the .50 instead.

Each of the six 110 Land Rovers consisted of a commander, a driver and a weapons systems operator, plus a fourth guy who'd take turns with the rest of them riding on the bike that was attached to each vehicle.

The Unimog crew comprised a driver and co-driver. This squat mechanical dinosaur would carry all the supplies we couldn't manage on our Land Rovers. Since it had no real fighting function, the idea was to 'scab' it onto a pair of vehicles at any one time for its own protection. The six fighting vehicles divided into three of these pairs or patrols. Each patrol would contain a weapons expert, a dems man, a medic and an Arabic speaker. The patrol system gave us the option to divide into three distinct working groups if we needed to, although our feeling this side of the border was that we should stay together, at least in the initial stages. Dividing us up, we figured, increased our chances of compromise. As it happened, events in the lives of the other convoy members were to prove us right.

The composition of the vehicles sorted, we then had the task of dividing ourselves into groups. This wasn't easy. We all got on reasonably well, but inevitably some people got on better than others. One of the attributes the Regiment is looking for during selection is the candidate's ability to co-exist with his fellow man; and when someone does piss him off, the ability to tune it out so it doesn't affect his judgment. While this is all well and good for training, operations would provide the ultimate test. Looking around our gaggle of blokes, I couldn't see any obvious rift lines. But that didn't mean they weren't there.

Within an SAS Sabre Squadron, all decisions are made using the Chinese Parliament system: that is, the boss and the four troop commanders or 'head-sheds' – air, boat, mountain and mobility – all offering views that allow the boss to arrive at what is hopefully the best decision. Chinese Parliaments are unique to the

Regiment. When we're on CT duty, the system works a little differently, but the principle is the same. We are split into teams – assault, sniper and special method of entry – as opposed to troops. Here, also, in the desert, we were being broken out of the troop system and put into teams, comprised, this time, of individual vehicle crews.

As one of the head-sheds, I had some influence over who was assigned to mine: Big Nick, Tom and Jeff, the Kiwi. Having helped select and train them as an instructor, I was pleased I got them.

The other head-sheds were Tony and Alec. Tony was the senior mobility man and a terrific bloke. Ex-REME, he was also one of the most professional soldiers I had ever come across. The great thing about Tony was his coolness. His catch-phrase was 'slowly, slowly, catchy monkey', and it summed up everything he did. He was a highly educated bloke, with enough qualifications to be a Rupert any day. Six foot four and slim, he had an officer's bearing, too, but none of that occasional pomposity you get, thank God. His reputation as a thinker, someone who worked out all the angles before coming to a decision, had earned him a great deal of respect. If I could have picked anyone from the Regiment as a fellow head-shed, I couldn't have done better.

Alec was less my cup of tea, though I had no real complaints. He was the antithesis of Tony, I suppose. Both were bright, switched-on guys. But while Tony was quiet and methodical, Alec was brash and ambitious. Not that there was anything wrong with the latter. We all had ideas of where we wanted to be in five years' time. But there was something about Alec I couldn't quite put my finger on. I remember voicing it once to a former troop sergeant, a guy I very much respected, the day Alec switched from Air Troop to Mountain Troop; a move that was widely construed as an ill-concealed attempt to jump the queue in the troop leader stakes. My buddy, a wise old bird who'd left the Regiment some time earlier, had worked with Alec a lot. He'd lifted his head from his beer and with a knowing look, said: 'Watch that one, Cammy. Alec's a career soldier and he doesn't fucking care who he climbs over to achieve his aim.' I felt a little guilty for recalling those sentiments now. Behind enemy lines we'd all have to pull together as a team or we'd be lost. Besides, I knew that if it came to a fight, Alec would be as good as the next man.

What none of us had any say in was the bloke who'd be leading our half-squadron convoy. That job fell to Graham.

Before I could stop it, my memory scrolled back to a different time and place altogether. It was a month before Christmas, and we were on our final counter-terrorist exercise in Scotland. These exercises revolve around some kind of incident, such as a train hijacking, or a siege situation, and are totally realistic. So much so, that if you're not careful, the stress can really get to you.

Graham was not one of us. He was an exchange officer, an outsider. This particular remount could not have been more crucial. If we fucked it, we could have discounted any ideas of going to Iraq. The target on that day was probably the most challenging of all the hijack situations we encounter: an airliner, with 150 passengers on board. Within minutes of our arrival at the airport, we convened the Chinese Parliament and got to work. We needed to carry out a recce. I asked Graham if he wanted to come with us.

While 150 poor bastard volunteers were freezing their nuts off in a clapped-out old plane in a remote corner of the airport, Graham sucked his pencil.

'Maybe it's better if I wait here for the others,' he said. We were the advance party that had arrived by helicopter. The main CT force was still burning up the M6 from Hereford in the Range Rovers.

I heard Buzz groan behind me.

'Boss, you know the form,' I continued. 'The others aren't going to be here for at least another four hours. And in an hour and a half you've got to brief the Chief Constable.'

'Or the CO'll be eating our fucking bollocks with his bacon and eggs tomorrow,' Buzz whispered audibly enough for Graham to hear.

'Right,' said Graham. 'You go anyway. I'll stay here just in case.'

We moved off. We couldn't afford to hang around any longer. 'In case, fucking what?' Buzz panted, as we ran across the rain-spattered tarmac. 'We get invaded by space sodding aliens? Jesus, you need a crystal ball to read that bloke sometimes.'

The Chinese Parliament is a good system. It gives the person who has to make the final decision a chance to utilize the experience amassed by the head-sheds in his charge. But at the end of the day, it was only successful if the boss made that decision. Graham could listen all day and still not make up his bloody mind. On that day in Scotland, we blew a few doors and shot all the right people. We got a slap on the back and then we went home. But this was the real thing. Wars had a habit of bringing out the best and the worst in people. To be honest, I had no idea which way Graham was going to go. But then, the same could have been said of any of us. Not least in that line-up of suspects, I firmly included myself.

Trained and fully tooled-up, we made our move on the afternoon of the 12th to join the rest of the Regiment at the forward mounting base; a place designated as Victor. We moved north in attack formation: fighting vehicles to the front and rear, Unimog in the middle, bikes all around and fast-attack craft following up behind. We swept through the desert as the day dragged into night, looking like something out of *Mad Max*. We were an aggressive and unruly looking bunch. Any Westerner who might have encountered us would have been in little doubt as to who we were, although, at a pinch, we could have just as easily come over as a bunch of Iraqis on a penetration mission as a unit of the SAS. The fact of the matter was, though, we had no other way of getting all our vehicles, weapons, ammo and kit to the forward mounting base. I prayed we didn't run into any of the British press corps that was rumoured to be marauding the desert looking for us.

We pressed on, finally reaching Victor sometime in the small hours. It was some kind of garrison town and huge. We kept driving until we reached the edge of an airstrip. This was progress. We knew we had been allocated a hangar somewhere on the base, so we had to be close.

Across the runway, we could see a clutch of large buildings. We headed towards them, amazed at the size of the place. It was lit up like Harrods on Christmas Eve.

We pulled up at the first of three giant hangars and got lucky. There was nothing inside except a load of camp beds, but somebody told us we'd got the right place, so we parked the vehicles and strolled in. As with the rest of Victor, nobody was worried about the electricity bills. After the night drive, the suspended ceiling lights burned into our brains like lasers. The hangar echoed to the sound of our boots as we wandered around and surveyed our new home. You could have put a 747 in it and still had room for a couple of Learjets.

Nobody had to be told. Each of us grabbed a bed and dossed down. Within minutes, the entire squadron was out for the count, snoring like pigs.

The following morning, we caught up with the boys from D Squadron who were decked down in the next-door hangar. The one beyond that had been allocated to B Squadron for when they arrived. Over the next few days we shot a lot of shit with blokes we hadn't seen for months. It was good to catch up.

The difference between the training base and Victor was dramatic. Everybody was here. We had all the support bods we needed under three roofs. So, it was an ideal time to make good some of the deficiencies we'd encountered during our training period. I caught on early that you had to grab these logistics people when you could as they were in hot demand. One of the things I wanted to do was to weld extra hooks on the side of our vehicle so we could hang things like jerrycans and our Bergens on the outside to make precious room on the inside for the hundreds of items we'd be taking with us into Saddam's backyard. I found a guy from the REME who said he could do it, no problem, then wandered outside for a smoke, feeling pretty pleased with myself.

By the second night of our arrival at Victor, we were getting bored. The big picture was still hard to read with all kinds of desperate diplomatic activity going on in Baghdad, New York and Moscow. We had no idea how long we were supposed to be here, but figured that we'd get our orders from commanders in Riyadh soon enough. Whether war was inevitable or not, it made sense for us to slip across the border before tension escalated into full-blown conflict. If and when the balloon did go up, we would then be in place to do all the things we were supposed to do on Day One. Apart from packing and repacking the vehicles and running nav exercises in situ on our GPS systems, there really was bugger-all else to do.

Until, that was, we found Paddy.

Paddy was from the British Army's Small Arms School and had been attached to the Regiment for a couple of years. He was the resident expert on big support weapons like the .50, the Mk19 and the Milan; and, age aside, the closest I'd ever come to a personal meeting with Q, SIS's eccentric weapons inventor from the Bond movies. During our training period, I'd become increasingly concerned with the performance of the .50 heavy machine-gun, which was showing an alarming tendency to jam. Paddy was a busy man at Victor, but I managed to collar him one day for a more in-depth appreciation of our weapons' quirkier habits. If the .50 was going to jam when we needed it most, I wanted to know about the warning signs.

'It's a sound thing,' Paddy told me, earnestly. 'You've got to listen to the .50 all the time. Once it falls out of tune, it's too late. It'll jam up and then you're . . . er, basically, you're fucked, Cammy.'

'How do I recognize the problem?'

Paddy sucked his teeth. 'Practise,' he said, owlishly. 'I'm afraid it's the only way.'

I looked at my watch. It was mid-morning. 'What are you doing for the next couple of hours?' I asked him.

Before he could even reply, I frog-marched him into the hangar and made the introductions to Tom, Nick and Jeff. 'Boys,' I said, 'we're going into the desert for a music lesson.'

For the next few hours we listened to the timing and tuning of the .50 as it spat out thousands of rounds into the dunes till we were satisfied we knew what we were supposed to be listening for.

While we had Paddy there, we decided to ask him about the Milan. The SAS is renowned for asking weapons to do things the manufacturer never intended in a million years. Paddy kept our feet on the ground. If you wanted to take a bunker out at 200 metres with the Milan, you could forget it, he explained patiently, because the Milan seeker only acquires – picks up – its target at 300 metres.

'Shit, Paddy, that's no good,' Tom said. 'What's the point of having the bloody thing if it doesn't work when you want it to?'

'It is good for trench-work, of course,' Paddy offered. 'Then you don't have to worry about target acquisition, you just aim and fire. Iraqis see that coming and they'll not be back in a hurry, you mark my words.'

'I don't suppose you'd like to come with us?' the BFG asked.

'I would, actually. Not that it's an option.' Paddy sighed. 'Too bad. Never mind.' He looked genuinely despondent for a moment, then shook himself and perked up again. 'Now, while I'm at it, I might as well tell you how you can cut a few corners on the Stinger.'

We'd not had the Stinger long, having got it in short order barely a month or two earlier. The Stinger is a great weapon, as any Soviet fighter pilot who had to fly over Afghanistan in the 1980s will tell you, but it takes a while to get the measure of its target-acquisition process. Even when you're practice perfect, if you do it by the book, the chances are the Iraqi MiGs are already gone and you're dodging bombs. In a few short minutes Paddy told us how we could shave valuable seconds off the intricate build-up to the moment you got IR lock-on to the target. Then, like a doctor writing out a prescription chit, he told us to go away and practise till we got it right.

Heaven.

Over the next couple of days we went into the desert and shot off a total of around thirty Stinger rounds – cost to the tax-payer about 30,000 quid a shot. We fired at radio-controlled model aircraft called MATS and then, when we'd used all them up, we popped off some lume rounds into the sky from the 81 mm mortar.

'You can't get enough of this hands-on shit I always say,' Nick said, as he squinted through the Stinger's sight and loosed off the cost equivalent of a Merc or a BMW at the flare dangling gently on its parachute in the blue sky above us.

'Fucking A,' Tom agreed, a moment before – whoosh – he, too, launched. Between them, they severed the strings connecting the flare pot to the chute. Then, a split-second later, the missile exploded.

Claps, wolf-whistles and cheers all round.

Towards the end of our week at Victor, we'd defined exactly which weapons would be coming and which would stay. Apart from the support stuff, we'd also be taking 66 mm anti-tank rockets – which are crap at taking out tanks, but good for trenches and soft-skinned vehicles – and 94 mm anti-tank. The 81 mm mortar had a nine-kilometre range, which was excellent, but the weight of the ammo wasn't so good. We had to take at least 80 rounds with us or it wasn't worth the effort. But in terms of laying down fire in-depth, the 81 mm was indispensable. If the enemy got through that lot, the next thing he'd face would be 51 mm mortar fire and the Milan anti-tank missile. Thereafter, it was the Mk19, which had a range of over a thousand metres, the .50 and our GPMGs. This General Purpose Machine-Gun was lethal at its optimum range. At around 500 m it could lay down a one-metre wide by 20 m deep 'beating zone' from which next to nothing would walk away. Understanding the science of the beating zone and how multiple GPMGs could combine to produce a bigger and even more fearsome killing ground was essential for survival behind enemy lines. Luckily, we all understood the score pretty good. Then, there were the 203 grenade launchers which were fixed to our M16 assault rifles and the M202, an incendiary that could get the sand burning at 300 metres it was so awesome. We also took a couple of sniper rifles, bar-mines, slab charges, anti-personnel mines, electrical timers, radio-command switches and a host of other bangers and squibs.

What we didn't have, but needed, we foraged and scrounged.

While the boys tinkered with the vehicle, the head-sheds of our half-squadron convoy – Tony, Alec, Graham and I – gathered in a corner of our hangar to do some serious map appreciation. HQ in Riyadh had shipped over some pretty low-grade aerial shots of the Saudi–Iraqi border, which was where we would make our insertion as soon as the order came down to move. We knew by now that our objectives inside Iraq were the main supply routes (MSRs) between Baghdad and Jordan along which Saddam was moving a lot of his war material.

As piss-poor as the aerial shots were, they did

highlight one significant problem: stretching east–west along the border was a berm, a mound erected by Iraqi engineers soon after their invasion of Kuwait to deter entry into Iraq.

The resolution of the shots made it impossible to tell how high the damned thing was, but those who'd been out along the border to take a look at it said it varied from a handful of metres to maybe a dozen. We figured it wouldn't be an insurmountable problem – it was, after all, only a pile of sand – and pressed on with the rest of the appreciation, plotting likely routes towards the MSRs and feeding way-points and possible rendezvous (RV) points for helicopter resupply flights into our GPS systems. It was good to get our teeth into some proper planning at long last and gratifying to see how well we three NCOs worked as a team. Graham, our OC, always the outsider, remained pretty quiet throughout, watching our moves intently. I just couldn't the figure the guy out.

January the 15th came and went much like any other day. We carried on as we had before: planning, plotting, sleeping, foraging, waiting. The trouble was, there was no TV at Victor to catch the latest on CNN, so most of us relied on the good old World Service of the BBC. Sometime during the afternoon of the 16th I wandered outside to peddle some scuttlebutt with the boys and pick up the latest news – whoever was working on the Land Rover at the time usually had the radio tuned to the unfolding developments.

There were some worrying reports coming out of Washington and the Arab capitals that Saddam might, in the event, be getting extra time for the intermediaries to try and pull an eleventh-hour deal out of the bag.

When I got there, Jeff was putting the finishing touches to the vehicle. Some wise-guy in the regimental supply-chain had decided to make a fast buck by importing a bulk load of rubber rats – the toy kind you get in joke-shops. By lunch-time, every vehicle in the regiment sported a rat on its bonnet and our vehicle was no exception. This, of course, was our nod and a wink to the LRDG boys who'd been doing the business out this way forty years earlier against the Afrika Korps. The trouble was, the rats looked like a mutant strain of Biker Mice From Mars.

The other in thing among the crews was to paint names on the vehicles. This had been a particularly vexing exercise for us. We'd tried Pegasus, Road Warrior, Avenger and a bunch of other stuff, but it all ended up looking naff as hell. As I drew close, I could see Jeff applying the finishing touches to some new monicker. He sat back and dusted his hands. 'There,' he said, in that New Zealand twang of his. 'Waddya think?'

I squinted in the bright afternoon sun. 'Tarakiwa,' I managed, mouthing each syllable deliberately. It looked like some Kiwi anagram for something disgusting. 'What the fuck does that mean?'

'Maori god of war,' Jeff replied, still admiring his handiwork. 'Neat, eh?'

I shrugged. It was better than anything else we'd come up with. So, Tarakiwa it was. 'Just don't go getting us to do the haka every time we run into a bunch of ragheads,' I said.

That evening, all badged members were summoned to a Scale A parade in the mess hall. A Scale A means everybody in the Regiment and is extremely rare. The rumours started flying. They covered everything from missions to go assassinate Saddam to 'endex' – a dread fear that we were going home without having fired a single shot. We were a subdued lot as we gathered in the mess hall and waited.

Suddenly, Brigadier Massey strolled in and jumped onto one of the long tables. He was renowned for being a bit of a showman and came over as being pretty pleased with himself. He started by telling us there was still no word from London or Riyadh on the latest diplomatic moves, but all the signs said it wouldn't be long before we were heading off to war. He then gave us a brief synopsis of the Regiment's desert exploits in the Second World War and the Omani campaign. Finally, he got to the point.

'You're the best-trained, best-equipped, best-organized SF organization in the world,' he told us. 'The area that has been assigned to you inside Iraq is yours for the taking. Seek, locate and destroy enemy targets and personnel as and when they present themselves. Create havoc and confusion throughout the enemy's lines of communication and supply.' He was walking up and down the tables, clearly enjoying himself. 'What lies before you is an opportunity in a soldier's lifetime. Take your equipment, take your training and use it well.'

He paused, gazing briefly around the room, before adding: 'The Iraqis have presented you with a theme park. Get out there and bloody well enjoy yourselves.'

When he had finished, we all left. There was a definite purpose in our strides as we moved back to our hangar. It had little to do with the pep talk we had just been given. We had a more pressing need – scoff.

I turned and saw Jeff skulking by the door. I asked if he was coming.

He shook his head. 'No, mate,' he said, patting the top of his head. 'I'm full up to here with bullshit pie. I'll see you later.'

Nick was more prosaic. 'What's that arsehole on about, anyway?' he said, barging his way disgustedly through a set of double doors. 'Last time I went to a theme park I spent the whole day in shagging queues.'

For the next half an hour or so, the mess-hall echoed to wise-arse comments like: 'Where's the big dipper?' and 'anyone for bumper cars?' There was a lot of laughter, but behind it, I knew everyone was thinking the same thing. We'd just been given carte blanche to do whatever we wanted. It was one hell of a directive.

All we needed now was the word to move out.

It came in a way none of us really expected. A bunch of us had gone over to D Squadron's hangar on the night of 16 January to find out if they had been assigned better missions than us.

I walked in and heard the usual cry from within: 'Careful, lads, A Squadron's on the ground. Watch your kit!' On this occasion, a few of the boys from B Squadron had also come over from their hangar, so there was quite a party going. One of the first people I ran into was a 'cockney-sparrer' type with an impish grin and an iron handshake. Despite being on different squadrons we'd known each other for a while and got on well. 'Andy, give us a couple of grenades, will you,' I said, getting into the part.

'Why? You lot must have hundreds.'

'I know, mate, but for where we're going, hundreds just ain't going to be enough . . . really.' I sucked my teeth, giving the performance some extra welly. 'Love to tell you more and all that, but –'

McNab's face cracked a smile and he delivered a well-aimed rabbit-punch in the vicinity of my solar plexus. 'Fuck off, Cammy,' he said. 'You guys wouldn't even know where to find the pin.'

I moved on and ran into another mate, a Welshman and ex-Para called Shug. Shug had done a lot of time in Northern Ireland, was a seasoned professional and very popular, in part because of his capacity for being a hell of a wind-up merchant, both on the giving and the receiving side.

About six months earlier a bunch of us had broken into his room at camp while he was away on exercise. It was always a bit shabby, so we decided to do a bit of DIY about the place. We filled in all the cracks in the wall behind his radiator with some ultra-mature Stilton, turned the rad up full, then switched off the lights and locked the door again. Three months later, Shug got back from the Middle East and proceeded straight to his room to dump off his kit before heading home. He opened the door and it hit him in the face like a Mike Tyson left-hook. We were all stood about six feet away, trying not to piss ourselves, but he still didn't get it; just told us meekly he had some things to tidy up and he'd see us later. An hour later, having turned the place upside down, he found the source of what had now become a serious bio-hazard. The truth was a great comfort to him, since he'd been convinced it was a pair of his unwashed socks that had been the culprit. He got his revenge on me by priming his big, 'wake-the-dead' alarm clock for 3 a.m. and leaving it outside my room after particularly heavy exercises.

It was sometime after midnight when we got the news off the World Service that the air war had started. Our reaction was mixed. On the one hand, we were glad the waiting was over; on the other, we were pissed as hell that the Americans had steamed in there before any of us had got into Iraq.

'Let's drag old Stormin' across the border and see how he likes it,' Tom said, 'breezing into a place that's been stirred up like a bloody hornet's nest. Christ, the Yanks can get on my tits sometimes.'

But it was a half-hearted admonition. The fact was, the war was on. We were headed for the biggest work-out the Regiment had faced in decades. Sure, there was some trepidation in our boots that night, but not half as much as the sense of relief that we were finally getting on with the job.

FOUR

The war was a little over twenty-four hours old, when word arrived at Victor that Saddam had launched Scuds at Israel. After the euphoria of the past day and night, when the news kept on coming that target after target was being taken down in Iraq for next to no losses on our side, it came as a sobering wake-up call. The Iraqi rockets fell on suburbs of Tel Aviv and Haifa. Initial reports said that no one had been killed but that there were injuries; also that, despite the warnings from Saddam, these warheads, at least, had not contained any chemical agents.

Most of the Scuds flew westwards, but one blasted off to the south-east. This had been shot down by a Patriot missile as it streaked towards Riyadh, the Saudi capital. As people woke in the nations of the Western Coalition, they greeted the news with alarm tempered by some relief that this major potential escalation of the conflict had, for the moment, been contained. But no one doubted that Saddam would try again – and that next time, maybe, the Scuds would be tipped with chemical or biological warheads.

First thing on the 18th A Squadron was pulled into a briefing by the CO. Our directive, he said, had changed. The news from Israel was extremely serious. President Bush and Prime Minister John Major had both telephoned the Israeli Prime Minister Yitzhak Shamir to plead for Israel's restraint. Everyone knew what was at stake. If the Israelis launched any kind of strike against Iraq, the Arab coalition, already fragile, would probably split apart. And after the Syrians and the Egyptians buggered off home, there was the very real prospect that Saudi Arabia would throw up its hands and say *khalas* – it's all over.

Without the Arabs, the Western Coalition was useless. It was essential that Israel was kept out of the war.

The CO gave us the run-down. Bush and Major had promised Shamir that a large percentage of their military air assets would be diverted wholly towards the Scud threat. Finding the missiles' fixed launch sites had been relatively easy; and in the small hours all of these silos were believed to have been destroyed. It was the mobile launchers that were the problem. Saddam was reckoned to have about 40 of these eight-wheel monsters, the transporter-erector-launchers, or TELs, we'd first been briefed about back at Hereford. Some had been destroyed on the first night. But the rest, perhaps as many as 20 to 30, had scattered to the four winds of Western Iraq, along with Christ only knew how many missiles. Right now, the CO said, just about every airborne recce aircraft the Coalition possessed was hunting them down.

But it didn't look good. The latest news out of Tel Aviv was that the Israelis were planning for the next contingency. They'd apparently told the Coalition army commander, General H. Norman Schwarzkopf, that if the US and British jets couldn't hack it, then they'd put a couple of army brigades of their own into Western Iraq to hunt down the Scud launchers for themselves. Schwarzkopf had had to do some fast thinking. In reiterating the pleas of his President not to get involved, he'd asked the Israelis what on earth they could do in Iraq that the British SAS weren't already doing. 'The Regiment will achieve what you are trying to achieve,' he was reported to have told them. 'This is the way ahead.'

So, that was it. We were now directed to hunt down Scuds, Scuds and more Scuds.

Preparations were made immediately to get our half-squadron convoy to our forward operating base (FOB) in north-eastern Saudi Arabia. For the foreseeable future, it was to serve as the Regiment's head-quarters and the nerve-centre from which all directives would go out and all information from the various groups and convoys operating inside Iraq be proces-sed. The plan was to ship us all there – vehicles, bikes, men and material – in the RAF's already overstretched C-130 Hercules fleet. Half of our group left later that afternoon. We followed twenty-four hours later.

We let down in the clag of a mid-afternoon rainstorm and taxied to our dispersal point. As we drove off the back of the C-130's ramp, evidence of the conflict was everywhere. We manoeuvred our vehicles around trenches, bomb shelters and rows of attack aircraft bombed up and waiting to fly against targets deep inside Iraq. We made our way to a tented area away from the flight operations.

Here we found the Regiment's senior NCO, a big bluff bloke from Yorkshire called Roger. Roger was the RSM, the Regimental Sergeant Major, and nigh on twenty years with the SAS. The RSM epitomizes any regiment. He is its backbone. Roger had seen action in Oman and the Falklands and a host of other places besides. He could be an awkward sod, but he was a hell of a character. He was a popular figure, but I imagined that fighting with him would be a nightmare. Rog was so laid-back that I couldn't really see him going to war. I guessed he'd been pulled down to the FOB as a spare watch-keeper; someone who could lend a hand in the ops room. Given his quirky demeanour, I reflected that it was probably the best place for him.

'Bloody hell, Rog,' I said, looking around at our spartan surroundings, 'they got Sky TV down in the UAE, but not here. What are you going to do?'

Roger was a sports freak and a betting man. He'd bet on bloody anything. But first he needed to be plugged into a game.

'Don't you foockin' believe it, mate,' he replied. 'There's bloody Yanks everywhere. They don't foockin' go nowhere wi'out bloody television. I'll find something to have a punt on, don't you foockin' worry.'

If Roger said it, I didn't doubt it.

With the rain spattering on the canvas above, me and the other head-sheds gathered in the inner sanctum of the nerve-centre, surrounded by powerful transmitter-receivers and various other pieces of specialized comms kit. Our orders were to give our vehicles a final once-over, check for any last provisions we might need, then head north to the border.

On my way back to the Land Rover to give the boys an update, I ran into Phil, our RQMS. Phil was a thin, wiry, straight-talking cockney and smart as hell, which you need to be when you're in charge of an entire regiment's supply operation.

'Everything all right, mate?' he asked.

I nodded. We were as ready as we'd ever be.

'Listen,' Phil said, 'if there's anything you need while you're over there – anything – tell me, and I'll bust my balls to try to get it for you.'

'Thanks, mate. Good of you.' I took a pace forward, then stopped. 'There is one thing you could do for us.'

'Shoot, mate.'

'Keep the fags coming in on the resups, eh.' I reckoned I had enough Silk Cut for two to three weeks. Thereafter I was down to an assorted bag of Marlboros, B&H, local Saudi stuff and, if I became really desperate, some Embassy Regals. As back-up, I also had a tin of baccy, but seeing as I couldn't roll-up to save my life, I didn't count on it lasting long. I'd leave that duty to Tom, my only other smoking ally on the vehicle, and an expert roller.

Phil gave me a wave. 'I'll see what I can do. Promise. Good luck, Cammy. Give 'em hell, eh?'

'I'll do my best,' I said, before carrying on back to the vehicles.

After dark, Alec, Tony, Graham and I gathered in the main ops room for a final pep-talk from the Two i/c. After we sergeants left, Graham remained behind for a few more minutes for some last words of wisdom, before rejoining us at our vehicles. Then, after a brief check on our route, we saddled up and set off, our ears filled with the deafening blast of jet engines as another wave of fighters clawed into the sky en route to bomb more enemy targets.

Ahead of us we had a 200 km drive, routing via another big Saudi base at a place called Arama. Then, after a short 50 km leg along the road parallel with the Saudi-tap oil-line, the idea was to cut north across the last 80 km of desert to the Iraqi border.

The drive was a bitch. The weather was unusually

cold, but there was no stopping. We were in a race against time. As soldiers, we felt the need to cross into Iraq and get our hands dirty before the politicians got cold feet and pulled the plug on Desert Storm, as the operation to liberate Kuwait was now called.

At times, visibility was down to twenty or thirty metres. The clag was a combination of fog, dust from the vehicles in front, low cloud and drizzle. As our vehicles were open, it wasn't long before we found ourselves slowly freezing to death.

Tom, who was driving, started to rap a beat out on the steering wheel before launching into vintage Foreigner at the top of his voice.

He turned to look at Nick and me, as if egging us on for a sing-song. I was sitting up front in the passenger seat, Nick was behind, manning the Mk19. Jeff was out on the road, riding the Cannon. Under normal conditions there was only room for three on the vehicle. The fourth team-member took it in turns to ride the bike.

Tom rocked on.

'Christ,' Nick shouted above the slipstream and the racket to my right, 'are we going to have to endure this till Saddam chucks in the towel?'

'Not if I've got anything to do with it,' I grinned, patting my sidearm. I hadn't considered Tom's love of music when I engineered a place for him on my crew. Tom played guitar. He was no Eric Clapton, but he wasn't that bad either. I wish the same could have been said for his dancing. The odd night when Jade managed to drag me down to the disco, there was old Tom, with his Hawaiian shirt, going through the most extraordinary contortions in the middle of the dance floor. If he was looking for a little harmonious accompaniment on this beano, then he was hanging out with the wrong crowd. I've never been able to sing a note and Nick isn't much better.

Jeff was the dark horse. I knew him, but not as well as Tom and Nick. I didn't doubt, though, that before this thing was out, we'd all know each other as well as our wives or girlfriends.

With that disturbing thought, I flashed a glance at Nick. The Big Fucked-up Giant had just stuffed a whole Mars bar into his gob.

'What?' he enquired tenderly, his teeth smeared with chocolate.

'You're an animal,' I said.

'Do you want me to start singing?'

'Anything but.'

'Then, shut the fuck up, Cameron.'

The songs tumbled thick and fast for the next hour. It was like being next to a nuclear-powered Wurlitzer. But at least it helped us forget the cold. We stopped in the small hours and did a fuel replen by the side of the road. We needed to cross into Iraq, of course, with maximum fuel, but it was also a chance to get ourselves sorted.

Hot brews were handed round while the bowser

crew went about filling our vehicle tanks and jerry-cans.

The brew is an important ritual in the SAS. Each bloke has a flask which he fills with tea just before we leave an LUP. On the principle, each to their own taste, we fix our own. I knew from experience, though, that it's handy to have blokes share your taste in tea, because after a while brews get passed around and mixed up. Tom and I had a predilection for the same kind of tea: brown enough to stain your tongue and sweet, too. We'd already managed to educate Jeff, who'd arrived in theatre an aficionado of your piss-weak variety. But with Nick we had a real problem. For some reason, the BFG, who was the biggest scoff guzzler I'd ever come across, didn't like sugar in his tea. We spent ages trying to convince him it was sensible to get a bit of sugar down his neck, but he just wouldn't wear it. Tom and I made a pact with each other that before this adventure was out, we'd have him gagging for a hot mug of sweet tea. It became something of a challenge.

We cupped our brews and sipped them gratefully beside the road. We were wet through, but it was a problem we could do little about. Every item on our wagon was essential and loads and weights were critical. There was no room for luxuries and extra clothing would have fallen into this bracket. There was, however, one more layer we could use and that was our NBC gear – a jacket and trouser combo designed to protect us in the event of a nuclear, biological or chemical attack. Within a short space of time, we were all lumbering around in our noddy suits.

Once the replen was completed, we headed north to the border. Gradually, the cold and wet even succeeded in penetrating our NBC kit.

We pulled up at the base of a small depression about an hour before sunrise. The border and our crossing point were about five kilometres ahead. We needed time out to conduct a recce. It was also essential that we had a complete night ahead of us so we could penetrate deep into Iraq before sunrise.

With an hour till first light, Graham signalled the start of our LUP drill. We parked the vehicles, covered them with cam-nets and put sentries out. Then we waited for daylight and the start of our covert scan of the border area so we could select our final crossing point. All being well, we would do the insertion when night fell.

To establish an LUP, or Lying-Up Position, that kept us concealed during the day took time – it always did. To the casual observer, it might have looked like a simple case of parking our vehicles and throwing some camouflage nets over them. But in reality, an LUP had to be extremely secure and provide us with the means to defend ourselves if we were attacked. The routine was well established: a few dog-leg manoeuvres back on ourselves to our final position; a quick appreciation of the lie of the land and careful consideration of possible avenues of enemy approach; identifying weapon arcs and killing fields and fully interlocking them between vehicles and individual weapons; the deployment of sentries and, finally, plotting our emergency 'bug-out' or escape routes if things turned nasty.

Preparing an LUP was always done at the end of the night's work, no matter how tired you were. You only got one chance to get a hide right. If you cocked it up, once daylight came, looking for another was out of the question.

By sun-up, the LUP was complete. Our infiltration point was roughly in the middle of the area we had been assigned to patrol. This was a considerable chunk of turf in Western Iraq – equivalent, say, to Scotland.

Prior to our arrival at the LUP, the information we'd been given on our crossing point was basic. We knew only that the Iraqis had erected a large berm and that in front of it was a large trench running as far as the eye could see. This prevented a vehicle taking any kind of a run-up.

Graham decided to check out a couple of areas we had selected from our reconnaissance photographs as potential crossing points. The pictures weren't great, but we didn't figure it would be a problem. Our int-people at Victor had got onto their American counterparts in Riyadh and plugged them for more info – and, if possible, some better stuff. But they didn't get a whole lot of extra help. So, we were forced into taking pot-luck.

The recce team consisted of two motorbikes supported by a Land Rover. The final approach to the mound would be carried out on foot. While we knew about the position and general strength of the Iraqis' brigade and divisional groupings, the exact deployment of individual units was largely unknown. Saddam moved his military assets around constantly, making our task a hard one. It was paramount that no one knew where we had entered Iraq.

While the recce teams deployed to their respective areas, the rest of us settled into our normal LUP routine: constantly checking the security screen, rotating sentries, maintaining a post on the radio, encoding and decoding the vast amounts of two-way traffic we had to process.

The recce teams returned shortly after four o'clock, nearly ten hours after they departed. It had been a hard work-out. They were covered in dust, with rivulets of sweat streaked across their skin.

Keith Norman was the first of them I got a chance to talk to. Normally quiet and reserved, he was thoroughly pissed off.

'I'd like to get my hands on the boss-eyed fuckwit who gave us those photographs,' he said, throwing his helmet onto the sand. 'What a load of fucking bollocks.'

Deep down, we'd known they hadn't been up to

much, but we'd always hoped we could salvage something once we got on the ground with eyes on.

I was filled with a sense of foreboding.

We held a debrief thirty minutes later around the back of one of our Land Rovers. Maps and photographs were spread out. All the head-sheds were present.

As I listened to the reports, my spirits sagged. From what the recce-ers were saying, it was pretty bloody obvious there wasn't going to be any crossing tonight.

They had driven, walked and crawled in excess of 50 km, checking and re-checking the border for crossing points.

The berm was doing exactly what it had been designed to do – deterring, nay, denying, entry into Iraq. A sizeable chunk of the border was uncrossable. After the recce teams left, me and the three other head-sheds got down to some serious talking. Guided by our mobility rep, Tony, we went over the various options, laying each in front of Graham so he could come to a decision. These ranged from moving to a different location to manhandling our Land Rovers over the berm. In the latter case, there was no doubt we could do it, but not in one night; nor without leaving evidence.

Graham mulled his choices in excruciating slow-time. He could not reach a decision. In the end, we made it for him.

We decided to move somewhere else.

'Tony, is it me?' I asked the mobility king on the way back to our vehicles. 'Why do I get the feeling Graham's not firing on all cylinders?'

'He's under a lot of pressure, Cammy. Give him time.'

'The war'll bloody be over, mate, if we give him much more.'

Tony smiled. 'Slowly, slowly, catchy monkey, mate. Don't worry, we'll get our hands dirty soon enough.'

When I returned to my vehicle, the look on my face must have said it all. The boys gathered round and I gave them the short version: crossing the border here was a non-starter.

As the sun began to set, hot meals were prepared, flasks filled, kit stowed, night optics broken out, the route ahead checked and RVs pre-plotted into our GPS systems. It was decided that we'd pull back from the border and head north-east, eventually cutting back in to relocate ourselves close enough for another scouting mission the next day.

A final fag in the darkness, a last pull of tea as we sat in our vehicles and we shipped out. The lead 110 slipped into the prearranged route. The remaining vehicles slotted in behind. The running order of the convoy was now firmly fixed: fighting vehicles in front, mother support craft in the middle, more fighting vehicles at the rear and our motor bikes at the flanks and to the fore. A total of seven vehicles, two bikes and thirty men. We stopped at irregular intervals to swap positions. At first light, after twelve hours of this, our eyes and various other parts of our anatomy were feeling the strain.

We established our LUP and once more went into the routine.

When the recce teams arrived back that afternoon it was the same depressing story. The berm was still unbreachable. It was at a time like this you needed your sense of humour. We were by now cursing the lack of information available to us on this section of the border. Tony, Alec and I were also feeding Graham with loads of options, but we weren't getting a whole lot back. This was not how it should have been. We considered sending a flash priority signal back to regimental headquarters that read: 'Required urgently for crossing – eight sets of fucking wings.'

At last light we set off for a new location to start the whole process again. In the course of the following day, we received word over the radio that the other three convoys had made it across. We were glad for them, but it made us feel like right bloody idiots.

'I can hear the slagging at the next cross-brief,' Nick said, shaking his head. 'A Squadron, beaten by a poxy sand castle.'

'I shall take great pleasure in pointing out,' Tom said, 'that we didn't leave thirty per cent of our fighting vehicles behind. When we get across, that is.'

The Hereford drums were rapping out a constant beat of gossip, fact and rumour that kept us in touch as we monitored our communications systems. We heard that one particular group had successfully infiltrated the border, but in the process had burned out a couple of vehicles through the sheer effort of crossing the berm. The vehicles had had to be abandoned and hidden. Whether it was a hundred per cent true or not we didn't know, but it sounded good enough to use in evidence against them later when the banter started and we were defending our corner.

Nick got to his feet and kicked the nearest tyre he could find. 'This has got to be some kind of wind-up. HQ's idea of a joke. Anyone seen Jeremy sodding Beadle?'

I went over to Tony's 110 and found him bent over the map, looking at the border. 'I thought you said these vehicles would go over anything,' I said to him.

It was a poor joke. As the mobility man, Tony was more pissed off about the berm than anyone. He confided he'd just come from a meeting with Graham, then he went quiet for a moment. Finally, he said: 'Listen, Cammy, the berm's crackable. The berm isn't our real problem, here.'

'What are you saying?'

He folded up the map and put it away. 'Let's just leave it at that for the moment, shall we, mate?'

I turned away and headed for my vehicle. To say I was troubled was an understatement. Up till now, we'd been kidding ourselves. But for Tony, Mr Implacable, readily to finger the source of the trouble, even indirectly, meant that things were worse than I thought. And to cap it all, I couldn't begin to see how we were going to sort it out.

And then, later that day, thank Christ, the prospect of some action.

We received instructions via radio detailing some preparations the Iraqis were making for a Scud launch inside Iraq. A Scud site requires highly accurate tri-angulation to enable the launcher to be programmed and the rocket to fly to its target. We knew that a number of launch sites had already been pre-surveyed and marked for future use by Iraqi missile crews. We checked the coordinates and saw that this site was about 40 km to our north. It was one we hadn't plotted before.

We came up with a plan of attack. We didn't know if the launcher was already at the site or if it was shortly due to arrive. We planned for both contingencies. In the latter case, a couple of concealed bar-mines would provide a nice surprise for the launch crew as they backed the transporter-erector-launcher, or TEL, into position against its pre-prepared berm.

Because of the ongoing problem with *our* berm, one thing we had already decided: if necessary, the whole mission would be done on foot.

Planning the attack was complex, but exciting. A Scud convoy consists of a number of vehicles accom-panied by a large group of soldiers and defensive weaponry. Going in on foot would affect our speed, especially in the withdrawal phase. Men on foot are no match against fast-moving vehicles.

The distance would also restrict what we could carry in – for example, the Mk19 grenade launcher with ammunition weighed well over 150 lb. The same thing went for the .50 Browning.

It was also imperative that when we destroyed the missile we were at least 800 metres away, preferably upwind, as the fuel and any biochemical warhead posed a serious threat. Heavy, cumbersome NBC gear would be required clothing.

Because it was recognized that the war could turn chemical at any moment, we were given a pill known as a NAPs tablet that was meant to give us some protection if we were caught out in a nerve agent attack. These tablets were supposed to be taken once every day, but a lot of us looked on them with deep suspicion. In the end, I reckon the half-convoy was divided fifty-fifty between those that took their NAPs tablets and those that didn't. I was in the latter category, figuring I'd take my chances in the Sarin cloud with my NBC suit on, sooner than pump my body with a chemical that nobody had told us a whole lot about. The joke of it was, those of us who'd let our beards grow were supposed to smear our faces with a special navy-issue lubricating cream that was meant to seal our NBC masks tight when the old chemically tipped Scuds started to fly. Since space was tight, this was one of the first items to have got canned from the wagons back at base. Instead, somebody had figured that the axle-grease and other vehicle lubricants we had with us would do the job just as well. Now, as I listened to the options for taking the missiles out, I tugged thoughtfully at the several days' worth of growth on my chin and wondered where I'd put the bloody stuff.

The two obvious plans of attack were: one, close with and neutralize the threat from enemy soldiers before blowing the missile and sensitive components on the launcher; or two, get into a position where we could use our Milans and mortars.

It was going to be a long night, but a kill was in the offing. There was a new mood afoot.

When the recce teams returned, it was the same old story. The berm was uncrossable.

Our frustration was offset by the knowledge that the Scud mission was on whether or not we took any vehicles. While we continued to plan the attack, others worked on the berm problem. Eventually, someone requested permission to move to a part of the berm that had been successfully infiltrated by one of the other convoys.

It didn't take long for headquarters to come back to us. We received a transmission ordering us to a new RV point – a place where we could infiltrate into Iraq with a reasonable degree of certainly.

'What about the attack?' somebody asked.

We checked the coordinates. Moving would take us further away from the Scud site.

It was then that we learned the mission had been scrubbed.

'Jesus, Cammy,' Tom said. 'This can't get any worse, can it?'

I tried not to let my frustration boil over. Thirty of us, keyed up and ready to go. Only to find ourselves trapped on Saudi soil by a mound of fucking sand.

We were in disconsolate mood when we shipped out that night to the new RV point. There was a general feeling, however, that if we ever did make it across the border we were so wound up with suppressed rage, the Iraqis wouldn't stand a bloody chance.

The RV turned out to be an old Saudi fort, something straight out of *Beau Geste*. It was manned by a small platoon-sized contingent of Saudis whose task was to monitor this key section of border.

We arrived, as ordered, at last light, and parked our vehicles out of sight of the border. It was no more than 200 metres away and gloriously free of anything that remotely resembled a berm.

As we approached the fort, we were met by our liaison officer. Dave was a major and a highly experienced member of the Regiment.

'What are you doing here?' I asked him. 'I thought you'd be in Riyadh, living it up on expenses?'

He grinned broadly. 'When – if – you lot finally fuck off across the border, I might just get the chance.'

I laughed. It was good to see him.

He took us up onto the battlements. We studied the border through our night optics and received details on the lie of the land and some of its inherent problems. The main one was an Iraqi border post about 500 metres ahead and to the flank. I studied it through a night vision pocket scope. It turned out to be a large box-like construction on a metal stand, about fifty feet above the desert floor. Although there was no knowing how many Iraqis were inside, it gave a commanding view in all directions.

The second problem was the terrain. There was little to no cover to conceal our move across the border. We spent time carefully scanning every metre of the ground ahead and eventually found what looked like a small depression leading into a wadi about one and a half to two kilometres inside Iraq. It wasn't perfect, but it would have to do. If we could get into the start of the wadi system that led deep into the heart of Iraq, we were away. But it was vital that our infiltration went undetected.

'What about that lot?' I asked Dave, indicating a huddle of Saudi guards in the courtyard below. 'Are they above board?'

Dave shrugged. 'Who knows? They've been briefed, obviously, but you can't tell what they'll do once we're out of here. For all I know, they're out there swapping fags with their Iraqi cousins when there's nobody else around. If we were the Yanks, of course, we'd have quarantined this place for a month. But we don't have the resources. I'm afraid, Cammy, you're just going to have to keep your fingers crossed.'

For the next few hours, we kept our eyes glued on the Iraqi position – every optic we had scouting for signs of a patrol. There was nothing that gave us any real cause for concern except for the moon, which was for the most part tucked behind the clouds. We hoped it would stay that way. We'd already made up our minds. We were crossing tonight, shit or bust.

It was decision time. Did we take out the Iraqi border post? If we did, then a hundred per cent sure it would draw somebody's attention to the fact that something was going down in this area. We decided in the end to take a gamble and leave it alone, hoping that the ragheads didn't spot us as we inched across the two kilometres of bare ground to the start of the wadi system.

There was little more to be gained by hanging around. We returned to our vehicles and double-checked that all our equipment was stowed correctly. The merest rattle or bang of a loose item and we could be in deep shit. For the next two hours – from the moment the first vehicle left the sanctuary of the fort to the last entering the wadi – we were going to be in silent running.

I felt more than a twinge of nerves as I went around the vehicle checking that everything was where it should be. Nick, Tom and Jeff, were there, too, each making sure that nothing was out of place. One of the big things about working at night is you have to know where everything is, so that if you do need it in a hurry, you can lay your hands on it instantly without fuss-arsing about.

Scanning ahead from the top of the fort, we could see that the terrain was pretty typical: flat and featureless with the odd scattered clump of vegetation sprouting up from the rain-drenched sand. Hidden, we knew, amongst this sparse carpet of scrub were boulders, lots of them. Tony went around the vehicles reminding drivers not to grip steering wheels with thumbs on the inside. You hit a boulder, even doing a few miles an hour, and the spokes could pull a thumb right out of its socket. Normally, Tony would have been greeted by a fair bit of banter, words to the effect that he should stop being an old mother hen. But this was no normal night. Everyone worked in silence. Evidently, I wasn't the only one who was caught up in the drama of the occasion.

On our wagon, Tom was to do the driving. He and Nick had the most experience behind a wheel, even though each of us had had plenty of practice at driving across the desert at night. The trick to our night moves were our PNGs – passive night-vision goggles. These were probably our fourth most important commodity, after bullets, water and our GPS navigation systems. To help us see at night, we had a number of options.

The first was our pocket scopes, which resembled a medium-sized pair of binoculars. These we hung around our necks, raising them to our eyes whenever we needed to take a quick look-see at something that had piqued our interest. Pocket scopes worked by magnifying the ambient light from the moon and the stars. The Coalition strategists of Desert Storm had picked the night of 16 January for the beginning of the offensive against Iraq because it was the first moonless night after the expiration of the deadline to get out of Kuwait. A week on, however, and the moon had reappeared as a thin sliver in the sky. With no light pollution out here in the desert, even this small crescent of luminescence removed much of the shadow you would normally count on for a covert border crossing.

Because he was engrossed in his task, a driver required something a little more substantial than a pocket-scope to see where he was going. On a good night, PNGs were good out to about 200 metres. On a bad night, they were pretty awful, but still marginally better than your average mark one eyeball.

I didn't envy Tom this first stint on the PNGs. They were big heavy mothers that were strapped to your head with the aid of something that looked like a rugby scrum-cap. After an hour, your neck muscles began to ache like buggery from the strain of supporting the equivalent of a couple of bags of sugar in front of your eyes. On top of that, the optics, which bathe everything in a fluorescent green, make your head throb. Sometimes, it's so bad, it feels like your eyes are going to pop right out of their sockets. This is because the eye's viewing rods are working overtime to adjust to their synthetic environment. And while those of us who are using pocket scopes are careful only to view the scenery through one eye so as to preserve night vision in at least one side of your head, the driver has no such option. If things go tits-up and he loses his PNGs or has to shed them in a hurry, basically he's fucked. For the next three or four minutes, he has no night vision and is stumbling around the desert like a blind man. Until, that is, he's cut down by a bullet cued by a sniper's thermal night-sight, or run down by a tank that he never even saw.

On top of all this, working with PNGs gives you no depth-perception either. You may clock a boulder up ahead, but it takes a hell of a lot of practice before you get a feel for how far away it is. Before you bloody know it, you're on top of the damn thing, grounded like a beached ship, with a bloke in the back who's compressed a vertebra or two. The other problem, is short distances. Because you focus your vision to infinity when you're driving, your near-term vision is hopeless if you suddenly have to call upon it. It's so bad, that if you want to pass the guy a brew, you literally have to grab his hand and direct it to the cup. The scope here for wind-ups is pretty obvious, of course, but as we each prepared mentally and physically for our cross-over into Iraq, spoofs involving PNGs or any other bloody thing were very far from our minds.

We started to make the crossing with the vehicles spaced a hundred metres apart. On a full-moon night, we might expect to double this distance between vehicles. On a bad night, with no moon, full cloud cover and driving rain, we would probably bunch up, with no more than fifty metres between us. Tonight was pretty average in terms of light density, but it took a bit of discipline to see it that way. Because of where we were and what we were doing, it felt like we were going in in broad daylight.

We kept our speed down to the equivalent of a slow walk. Every effort was made to suppress the noise of our engines and the dust generated by our tyres. The bikes were lashed and secured to our support vehicle.

Our 110 was half-way across when the moon broke through the clouds. Tom brought us to an abrupt stop. It felt like somebody had a searchlight trained on us.

I caught Tom's grim expression out of the corner of my eye. The clouds were zipping across the sky at a seemingly impossible rate. Tom evidently was thinking along the same lines as me – the shit-awful conditions we'd endured on the drive from our forward operating base: mist, fog and visibility down to thirty metres. Murphy's law was dogging us every step of the way.

The moon went back behind the clouds and we decided to keep going, inching our way towards the imaginary line in the sand that was the border. Helmets worn, flak jackets on, weapons trained in every direction, we finally crossed into Iraq soon after midnight on 24 January.

Our rate of progress from the border to the edge of the wadi was dire.

None of us was in any doubt that we were committed. It was a strange feeling, also, because we had no idea what lay ahead. As relieved as I was that we had finally got the show on the road, there was no time for celebration. Our crawl from the Iraqi border post to the wadi was as uncomfortable a feeling as I'd ever had. We kept our eyes trained on the observation tower through our optics, looking for signs of activity, but saw none.

On the face of it, this was good news. But every cloud has a shitty lining and the fact that the Iraqis weren't firing star-shells or popping shots off at us came as little consolation. All of us were consumed with the same thought: what if these muppets had tracked us and were now relaying the information ahead to a welcoming committee of the Republican Guard?

I turned to Tom, who'd had an unlit roll-up welded to his top lip ever since we'd crossed the border.

'If they've got comms, then we could have fucking problems here,' I said. 'Maybe, we should have spent more time keeping them under observation before we took the decision to go.'

Tom gave an involuntary shrug as he concentrated on the terrain ahead. 'Well, mate,' he said, 'I guess if it starts raining shells, we'll know we made the wrong decision.'

I squinted at him through my PNGs, trying to read his expression. 'Well, if we have to leave the vehicle in a hurry, the baccy tin's wedged behind the gear-stick.' Under the circumstances, it was all the bravado I could manage.

At last, we reached the edge of the wadi and stopped. It was not deep, but it would keep us well below the sky-line. At this point, the dried-up river bed was wide – perhaps as much as 400 metres across – but the maps said it narrowed ahead.

A quick recce, a last look behind us, before seven vehicles in line-astern inched into the wadi and uncertainty. Our charts – the best we had was a pilot's map of only moderate detail – showed that we ought to be able to stay with it for around 15–20 km, heading due north, the direction we needed to go to intersect the MSRs and start looking for Scuds. In the meantime, we just had to pray that our ingress hadn't been observed and the Iraqis weren't lining the sides up ahead.

Within an hour, it had narrowed considerably. We

found ourselves in a canyon with sides so steep it would be impossible to get up and out if we needed to leave in a hurry.

After an hour of this torture, we stopped and convened a head-sheds' meeting. It was now four in the morning. We'd pushed our luck long enough. It was time to look for somewhere to establish our LUP. We had to be holed up and hunkered down an hour before daylight – anything less was potential suicide.

We drove for an hour and covered around fifteen km of some of the flattest landscape I'd encountered in my life. The sodding rubber rat on the bonnet would have had difficulty finding a place to hide. We now faced the unenviable task of concealing an entire patrol in this country, and on our first night, when we were all jumpy as hell.

By five it was still as flat as a pancake and we were all starting to get just a tad concerned. We'd now gone beyond any prospect of finding a classic LUP feature – a ravine, say, into which we could disappear under the cover of our cam-nets – and were now looking for something, anything, that might offer a little protection.

Five-thirty – twenty minutes before first light – and still an endless flat landscape. Even after we'd decided to relax our normally stringent rules for LUP selection, we'd seen the square-root of fuck-nothing. The head-sheds gathered round again and decided to send out two bikes and a Land Rover in a 360 degree spoke. Tony, as our lead mobility man, took the 110. The rest of us switched off, perched nervously on our vehicles and watched them disappear into the black ether that lay beyond the range of our night-scopes.

And then, we waited.

I had to square up to the possibility that they wouldn't find anything. Then, what? Did we sit there on the plain like lemons? Did we turn back? Or did we carry on driving? I turned to Tom, who was sitting behind the wheel and puffing on a roll-up.

'Take your pick, mate,' he said. 'It's a hell of a way to start, isn't it?'

When things are bad, and look like getting worse, you expect your leader to work on a bit of a command and control. If Graham had gone on the recce and led from the front a bit, he would have been doing both us and himself a favour. I'm not saying that the rest of us had any better idea than him of what to do; but at times like this, the OC needs to be seen, at least, to be doing something. If nothing else, the activity stops you dwelling on the world that is rapidly turning to rat-shit around you. But Graham just sat there in his vehicle. He looked like he was praying.

After ten minutes and still nothing, all any of us could hear was the wind whistling across the jagged tops of the Land Rovers. Then, suddenly, I caught the first hint of an engine noise on a particularly strong and persistent squall. I felt my body tense. It was impossible to tell if it was a bike or a Land Rover – or some other kind of vehicle altogether.

For what seemed like ages, we listened to the sound of first one engine, then several getting closer. Then, Nick, on the back of the vehicle, like a look-out in a crow's nest, rasped: 'It's OK, it's a bike. And there's the other one.'

Within a minute, the two bikes and the 110 were back. Graham, Alec and I grouped around Tony to hear the verdict.

'It's a fag-paper job,' he said, 'but I think I've found something. A bit of a depression. Christ knows, it's not ideal, but it's something.'

'Then let's fucking do it,' Graham said, shrilly. 'Lead the way.'

As soon as we reached it, we saw what Tony meant. There, in front of us, was a barely discernible hollow. We'd already put in our deception loop, a ploy that was designed to spoof any Iraqis on our trail just long enough to give us time to scarper or engage them on our terms. Then, with one eye on the eastern horizon, we got down to the job. It takes about an hour to make an adequate LUP. We'd have to do it in half that if we were to make good before sun-up.

It seemed that Murphy had upped and followed us right across the border, the bastard.

Setting up an LUP is a science in itself. First, you have to put guys out on stag or watch. Then, you deal with the vehicles. The trick is to space these as far apart as you can within a relatively compact radius of, say, 150 metres. Where each vehicle went depended on its support weapon. These have to be positioned to provide maximum protection. The Milan, for example, is ineffective under 300 metres, so you plot the most likely vehicle ingress route and – as vehicles are what the Milan kills best – train it in that direction. Then, other weapon arcs are linked in, each crisscrossing the other so that, in the end, you're left with a seamless security system. When the 81 mm mortars are included, this can extend to eight or nine kilometres. The mortars are placed in the middle of the LUP and trained on likely approaches. If necessary, we could be mobile and scattering to the four winds while the first rounds were still in the air.

Sometimes – in a wadi, for example – you need to increase your arc of observation, so you put extra blokes out. At others, it might be sensible to head back down the track and lay a bar-mine, just in case someone's picked up your trail. A bar-mine can turn over a Challenger tank, so you tend to hear it when it goes off. This can also help buy you time if you need to get away in a hurry. In this case, because we were so exposed, it was hard to know where to train everything. There were no obvious ingress routes. The threat was omnidirectional. The Iraqis could have come from bloody anywhere.

The activity proceeded at a feverish pace as we raced to beat the sun. In an ideal world, we'd have doubled up some of the LUP sites so as to cut down on the acreage of camouflage netting. It also paid sometimes to share assets, such as sentries. But on our first night in Iraq, and with the light upon us, we just wanted to get hunkered down as quickly as possible, never mind sorting ourselves into bloody pairs.

As each of the seven vehicles found its allotted space and arcs of fire were interlocked, each crew went about securing and camouflaging its vehicle. We were all positioned approximately thirty metres from our nearest neighbour, spacing that ensured, with any luck, that if we did come under fire, a direct hit on any one of us wouldn't take the others out, too.

Somehow, on this flat, tabletop expanse of hard sand, we had to make ourselves unremarkable to the casual observer. The best we could hope for, looking at our surroundings, was that we might be taken for some sandstone hillocks, or an aberrant cluster of vegetation. The one thing you can't count on, however good the terrain, is that you'll be invisible. The camouflage nets we carried were good, but they couldn't perform miracles.

Nick and I went into the routine. The idea was to make a kind of garage out of the cam-net, so that if we did need to make a fast exit, we could drive straight out and away without dragging the bloody thing with us. The amount of time it took to set up was in direct proportion to the care and attention you'd taken to stow the net away last time. Nick took one end and

I grabbed the other. We braced ourselves and lifted. I got a face full of sand and cursed my fucking mouth off. Because the net is stowed on a couple of hooks attached to the roll-bar, it tends to attract a lot of dust and grit while you're driving through the night. In the rush of the moment, I'd forgotten this and taken a sand-shower. Next time, Cameron, I told myself, keep your bloody mouth shut.

To create the garage-effect, we carry six poles with us that make up the frame over which the netting is laid. Having partially unfurled the cam-net, Nick and I now assembled the frame, by first creating the two inverted u assemblies that would go at either end of the vehicle. We then spread the net over the horizontal poles, each of us working like madmen to ensure that there is sufficient clearance – but not too much – between the top of the vehicle and the cam-net. At the best of times this is a frustrating procedure because the net tends to snag on everything: bits of protruding equipment on the vehicle, the support weapons, even your own webbing. And while you're grappling with this unruly monster, all the time you're getting this sand and grit shower as the net yields its deposits from the night's drive.

With the net in place, we then run around the base of the vehicle and peg the sides down like boy-scouts on speed. You don't have time to stand back and admire your handiwork, but if you did, you'd take in the overall box-like effect of this man-made scab on the landscape, with its flattish roof and its gently tapering sides. What you're left with is something that you have to live, work and sleep in all day. Visits between other vehicles are permitted, but it's best to restrict movement to the minimum, certainly at this stage in the proceedings, when we were all looking to acquire that nose for trouble you need to develop when you're behind enemy lines. We didn't have it yet and probably wouldn't for several more days.

Under the cam-net, you're pretty much cut off from the rest of the world. Living within this atmosphere takes a fair amount of battle discipline as there is very little clearance between the netting and the vehicle itself. The space below the roof is effectively off-limits since there is barely enough clearance for the wagon. This means that your living space is restricted to the sides, and because of their angle of taper, it isn't exactly roomy here either. My mind had conveniently chosen to forget how claustrophobic it was in this environment, but it came back to me in a rush, as I shuffled in an undignified half-squat between the bonnet and the 'administration' area at the back. This is the part of the wagon where we prepare our brews and our meals. It's created by pulling down the tail-gate and locking it in position with chains to create a table effect. Here, too, all brewing and cooking is done in the half-crouch and after a while it becomes murder on the back.

Sleeping is done at the side of the vehicles; your

best bet for any semblance of rest being to snuggle around the wheel-arches or – luxury, this – to grab one of the seats up front and kip in the upright position. The golden rule is, nobody sleeps until everything's done. On this occasion, we were all so keyed up that the prospect of shut-eye was out of the question. It'd be a while, I knew, before I'd purged enough adrenalin to rest, even though I was dog-tired. The relentless drama with the berm meant that none of us had really slept for the best part of three days.

As soon as we'd made the position secure, we got on the radio. I crawled over to the next vehicle as Harry, known as H, the designated radio operator of the watch, was setting up the comms link.

We use two methods of communication in the field, satellite and HF. The former is used for transferring low-grade information, the latter for all our secure stuff. For the sitrep, which contains our position, our progress and our intentions, all the data is keyed into a ruggedized laptop and dispatched to the Forward Operating Base in a quick, coded burst of HF airtime. This was essential for the smooth operation of the SF campaign in Iraq, since the potential for confliction – two patrols bumping into, and firing upon, each other – was not inconsiderable. Through the sitrep, reported in by each patrol after every night move, RHQ knew where everybody was and issued advisories on the progress of neighbouring patrols. Our coordinators would also put an imaginary box around us and forward these to the air campaigners in Riyadh. The last thing any of us wanted was to find ourselves in the gunsight of some over-zealous F-16 jock looking to paint another vehicle on the side of his cockpit.

'Zero, this is Alpha Two Zero,' H said several times into the satcom handset. 'This is a radio-check, over.'

There was a crackle of static on the ether, then: 'OK, Alpha Two Zero. Receiving you Strength 5, over.'

H gave me a glance and a thumbs-up.

'Ask 'm how the other lads are doing,' I said.

H nodded. 'Zero? How's Alpha Two Zero-Alpha, over?'

'Last we heard . . .'

The voice that came back to us was lost in some momentary atmospheric distortion.

H flicked a switch and pressed one of the headset bins to his ear. 'Say again, over.'

There was a pause. Then he glanced up again. 'They're doing OK,' he said, one ear still tuned to RHQ. 'Still heading north.'

I nodded, satisfied, and moved back to my vehicle to share the news with the lads. Nick was squeezed between the top of the vehicle and the roof so he could get the dust out of the Mk19 after the night's drive and Tom was checking the tyre pressures, his fingers oil-stained from a recent session under the bonnet. Jeff was somewhere on the perimeter, doing his stint on stag. Tom had already seen to it that he had a brew to keep him company.

I ran over everything we were supposed to have done, nagged by an uncomfortable feeling that something wasn't at all right. RHQ was cool. We'd got the LUP established. We'd fixed our position on the GPS and plotted our bug-out routes and emergency rendezvous points. In short, everything was as it should be, except for our location: we were seven very obvious mounds on the face of a flat and almost blemishless plain in the western Iraqi desert.

'Christ,' I said, moving round to the back of the vehicle where Tom was crouched over the tail-gate in the throes of getting together another brew, 'if it's going to be like this for the rest of the time we're here we're going to be in the shit.'

Tom grunted. 'It's early days, mate, we're all on edge.' Bang on cue, Nick swore as his finger snagged on some awkward part of the Mk19.

Tom handed me my brew. 'Get this down you. What about breakfast? I could break out a bag-ration.'

We work on a basis of three meals a day: breakfast, dinner and tea. Breakfast consists of a boil-in-the bag 'menu' such as beans and sausage, beans and bacon or a bacon grill. Dinner, our mid-day snack, is either a tin of corned beef, a meat pastie or some cheese-spread on bread. There's also a small packet of biscuits for good measure. Tea is another boil-in-the-bag number: either meat balls, or a lamb or chicken stew.

Pudding is a small tinned fruit-cake or some fruit salad. There were slight variations on the theme, but that was essentially it.

'No,' I said, 'let's save it and double up later.' I lifted the cam-net and found Nick still wrestling with the grenade launcher. 'That OK with you, big man?'

He nodded grimly. Poor Nick. Tom and I were all right. We could subsist most of the day on brews and fags. Jeff didn't seem to require much swill either. And when he did, he wasn't fussed how he ate it. Several times on the trip up to the border he'd tucked into his ration of nosh stone-cold straight from the can or the bag. A diplomatic incident almost ensued when Nick asked him whether gas and electricity had arrived in New Zealand yet.

When it came to food, no doubt about it, Nick was the guy who suffered most. His capacity to put away grub in camp was legendary, but as soon as we went out on ops a big meal and seconds became a memory, something to salivate over in his dreams.

We lived on stews in the desert – at least, that's what we euphemistically called them. These we concocted from our daily ration allocation. When it came down to it, every meal was a different shade of brown mush, with beef, lamb or chicken somewhere at the centre of it. What there was, was high in calorie content. It had to be if we were to have the energy to keep going at night. Without energy, the unusually cold winter would sap our strength on the long night drives. In no time, we'd be next to fucking useless. That was why we'd taken to saving our breakfast rations for the meal that we prepared before we moved out at the end of the day. The man who usually cooked it was Tom, who loved good food and was determined to give us some variety, at least, during our time across the border. Marco fucking Pierre White he wasn't, although he fancied himself enough to get a little petulant if you asked him to pass the salt. Tom's so-called *pièce de résistance* was his curry, into which obscene quantities of spices and unidentified herbal sprinklings disappeared. Had any of us ever had the balls to test it with a biological warfare detector, it would probably have red-lined off the scale.

'For Christ's sake, grab some gonk,' Tom said. 'It's going to be another long night.'

Ten minutes later, I lay down, my mind buzzing with images of the last three days: Victor, the FOB, the fort, the border, the wadi, here . . . Sleep wouldn't come, partly because I was too wound up, but mainly because the ground was so fucking hard I'd have been better off sleeping on a bed of nails. Contrary to its romantic image, the desert isn't endless stretches of rolling sand – at least, not here, it wasn't. The ground was basically rock, with a thin top-soil and a hefty scattering of little rocks. Whenever you reckoned you'd cleared these away, there was always one more, and, nine times out of ten, it unerringly found its way to a part of the body where it could inflict the most pain: the small of your back, your neck, your pelvis, even up the bloody arse . . .

It was in a bliss-state such as this, that I eventually lapsed into sleep.

Two hours before dark, the drill started all over again. We grabbed our hot meal, then packed away our day optics and replaced them with starlight scopes and PNGs. I gathered with the other head-sheds for a final brief on the route we were planning to take that night and what we hoped to achieve. We were closing on what looked like a minor MSR running north–south to the border. It was important that we check it for any Scud-related material, before proceeding northwards again to the principal east–west MSRs, where, we were informed, all the enemy's main convoy activity was concentrated.

Thirty minutes before dark, all the cam-nets were removed, our Bergens packed and everything stowed. Having checked we had no last-minute priority signals from RHQ, we sat in our vehicles, cupping our brews, waiting for darkness to descend, each man left with his thoughts on what our first full patrol might bring.

It didn't take long for the weather to close in: it was cold like I'd known in Brecon in the depths of the foulest of Welsh winters, but not here, in the heart of the Middle East. It had been persistently cold since we'd left Victor, but this was something else again. All of us were wearing our NBC suits for extra insulation, but there was nothing much we could do about our hands and faces. Because we'd departed our forward mounting base in the comparative warmth, none of us had thought to pack any serious glove wear. We were all feeling the effects, but no one quite as bad as Frank, one of Tony's drivers, who'd resorted to rubbing vehicle lubricant into his hands to keep them from cracking asunder. It hadn't worked. They were a mess. He had splits along his fingers like fault-lines and they were seeping. But Frank was a big boy. Somehow, he just managed to grin his way through it.

Humour gets you through bad spells like this and sometimes it helps to have a comedy partner. Mine, I guess, was Tom, with whom I went back a long way. Frank's was Buzz, a big lumbering six footer, with feet that seemed to go on for ever. Buzz was built like a battleship and had a character to match. Very much a country boy, his special hobby was poaching. It was not uncommon for Buzz to turn up at Stirling Lines with the remains of a dead deer in the back of his truck. When somebody made the big mistake of asking him why he'd brought a large animal carcass into work with him, Buzz would tell them the truth: he was half-way through skinning the bloody thing and, besides, it helped him to relax at break times. That was usually enough to ward off the unduly curious.

Frank and Buzz left an indelible stamp wherever

they went. If it were possible, Frank was the more cerebral of the two, while Buzz, with his big hands and feet, was the clutzy one; if there was a mug of tea or coffee within a six-foot radius of the bloke, chances were he'd knock it over before it was drunk. They were the original Dumb and Dumber, constantly arguing and bitching amongst themselves, pulling each other's legs and generally game for fucking about and sod the consequences. This had got them into trouble on more than one occasion.

I remembered one time, when we were tasked with playing the bad guys during some exercise that was designed to test the defences of an RAF airfield back home. Buzz suddenly found himself cornered in his jeep at the end of the main runway. The horizon was wall-to-wall RAF Regiment soldiers, advancing towards him, weapons raised. But Buzz wasn't finished. Faced with the 'for you the war is over' routine, he jammed the jeep into reverse and shot out backwards through the perimeter fencing. He removed a whole section of it and was last seen weaving his way across a field pursued by twenty irate RAF soldiers and trailing enough wire to encircle an Australian sheep station. But Buzz never stopped. He left them to pick up the tab and what little fencing remained. Needless to say, our CO took a dim view of it when the truth came to light.

It was this same capacity for bluntness and aggression that made me pretty sure Buzz and Frank would be good blokes to have around in the thick of a fight.

Within a short space of time, on that score, I'd be proved right.

The rain was coming down in sheets. Nick and Tom swapped places behind the wheel every few hours. It made seeing through the PNGs even more testing. Staring through these things was a bit surreal at the best of times. Now, to keep the convoy together, we'd closed right up. The next vehicle was probably no more than forty metres away. Our one consolation was knowing the enemy would have as hard a job spotting us as we had maintaining a watch on each other. That, of course, could cut both ways, so those of us not in the driver's seat spent the night scanning through our hand-held optics for signs of Iraqi life. It was a time for concentration and silence. Humour took a rest that night.

We'd been driving for around five hours in this shit, when, all of a sudden, the convoy stopped. There's always a good reason for a stop – usually it's to allow a change-over in the drivers or for someone to take a leak.

I jolted out of my stupor. We'd stopped barely ten minutes earlier to do both of those things. So this time, it could only mean something else.

Trouble.

The four of us focused to the front, each of us checking the ground ahead for signs of enemy activity.

Nothing.

With seven vehicles stretched out nose to tail it's

difficult to tell what's happening down the line. We were travelling third from the front, so we had a good view forward, but next to no knowledge of events to our rear. We'd been warned not to use the radios, as the Iraqis were rumoured to have a good electronic surveillance measures (ESM) capability. The belief was they'd be able to home in on us in next to no time if we used the radio for anything other than our vital calls to RHQ and for emergencies.

We were still scanning for signs of the enemy, when Joe, one of the outriders, pitched up on his Cannon.

He singled me out in the darkness. 'Cammy, we got us a fucking drama, mate.'

My heart began to quicken. 'We've been scanning our heads off and can't see jack,' I said.

He shook his head. 'Not enemy, mate. It's Keith. He's hit the back of the Unimog. Jesus, what a mess. You'd better get down there and see for yourself. I've got to go up front and tell the others.' And with that, he gunned the bike and drove off.

I left the crew and ran back down the line. I was wondering what to expect. My mind conjured up images of terrible injuries. I knew the guys in the Unimog would be all right. A huge, brute of a thing, it could hit a tank and still come out right side up. But for the guys in the Land Rover . . .

I got there to find a cluster of blokes around the two vehicles. The moment I stopped, my feet mulched down into the wet sand. The 110 looked like it had been welded to the Unimog. As the group parted, I saw how the whole thing had happened. The 110 had ploughed straight into the back of the mother support craft, which, being high off the ground had all but removed the 110's radiator with its diff.

Tony was under the 110, calling out a register of the damage. Even in the depths of a drama like this, his voice managed to maintain its customary cool and unruffled authority. Interpreting his words, however, it was quickly apparent that not only was the steering bent to buggery, but the engine looked like it was a terminal wreck, too.

The only good news was that there were no serious casualties, just cuts and bruises among the four guys on the Land Rover.

In retrospect, it was a disaster waiting to happen. We were all tired. And the cold and the rain didn't help either. They'd probably only been doing 20 km/h when they hit the then stationary Unimog, but it must have felt like they'd run up against a charging rhino.

You didn't need a degree in mechanics to appreciate that this 110 had reached the end of the line. It was, to use the vernacular, an ex-Land Rover.

Alec, Tony, Graham and I chewed the options. We were now extremely vulnerable. If we got a contact, we'd lose our supply vehicle. And without fuel, ammo and water we all might as well go home.

Somebody fixed some chains to the 110. Another

vehicle dragged it from the Unimog. It was already two in the morning. We'd chanced our arm once with our first LUP and had got away with it. Now we were facing not just another setback, but a catastrophe.

'What do we do?' Graham asked Tony.

The mobility king didn't hesitate. 'Nothing else for it. We got to dip the fucker.'

Graham swore. 'We can't leave it here. It'll stand out like a sore thumb.'

Tony remained impassive. 'I'm not suggesting we leave it in the open. I'm talking burying it, Boss.'

Graham looked at his watch. We could almost hear the tick of the second-hand as his brain moved in slow-time over the correct course of action to take.

'OK,' he said to Tony at last. 'Tell the bikers to get out there and find a hollow. Fast.'

The Cannon riders came back ten minutes later. They'd got something.

We towed the Land Rover 500 metres, until we reached the spot. Then, we got to work. Everybody moved quickly. We were in another race against time. We had less than three hours in which to strip and bury a Land Rover, then put up to 40 km between us and the burial site – anything less just wouldn't have been safe.

Everyone not on stag got stuck in. First we cleared the depression of boulders, then we moved everything out of the wrecked 110 – weapons, optics, ammo, supplies, the lot – and transferred it to the Unimog.

Next, we rolled the vehicle into the dip, deflated the tyres and chucked the cam-net over it. The last part was the ball-breaker: gathering boulders and piling them high until the vehicle was no longer visible. The whole thing took us a little over an hour.

The time was coming up to four when we shipped out. The four guys who'd been on the 110 hopped onto the Unimog. We drove as far and as fast as we dared, finally stopping after about an hour and a half. It was only 25 km from the crash site and far from ideal, but we had no choice. In next to no time, it'd be light.

This LUP was especially challenging because we had to redistribute all the kit from the wreck through-out the rest of the convoy. After all our careful packing at Victor and the FOB, this was not easy. We were already brimming over; now we had to find more room. It would have been easy to be furious with Keith and his co-driver, but none of us were. Several times I'd nodded off and hit my head on the GPMG and if it hadn't been for Tom and his nicotine sticks I'd have probably succumbed to sleep myself. Tom and I made a pact there and then that during those dead hours between three and four we'd talk to each other and keep talking. We couldn't afford this kind of thing happening again. If necessary, we decided, that might even involve us having a bit of a sing-song to keep us from nodding off.

Keith was still walking around in a bit of a daze.

He kept mumbling about how he was sure he'd hit a mine.

I saw Nick's brow furrow. In a rare gesture of compassion, the BFG laid a supportive hand on Keith's shoulder and said: 'If it had been a mine, you wanker, they'd be looking for your genitals in Syria.'

Keith went and mumbled somewhere else.

The next big test would be RHQ's reaction when we reported the events of the past night in our morning sitrep.

As it turned out, they were surprisingly philosophical. No one attached any real blame to the drivers – like the rest of us, they knew that these things happened on ops. They merely requested the precise lats and longs of the dead vehicle's location, apparently with a view to mounting a Chinook flight that would remove all the evidence, Land Rover and all.

It never happened. Unbeknownst to us, RHQ was contemplating weightier matters. Somebody had decided we'd had more than our share of bad luck for one mission. People in high places were looking for a cause, an explanation. It turned out they'd had their suspicions for a while.

Events over the next few days were to confirm them comprehensively.

FIVE

After the setbacks of the past two nights, we set off on our third patrol with a distinct feeling that we were about to see action. It had stopped raining around dawn, giving the ground time to dry out. Our task was to proceed to a point about 25 km to the east where, using the map, we had earlier identified a minor MSR. We needed to check it out before resuming our course northwards en route to the main east–west MSRs that ran between Baghdad and Jordan.

There was a definite air of anticipation amongst the blokes as we left the LUP. All our weapons had been checked and rechecked. Though our initial carte-blanche directive, spelled out in the 'theme park' speech, had been revoked, there was a general agreement amongst us that if we saw a convoy that night we'd splash it, whether it was Scud-related or not. In the Q&A that would follow, we'd plead a well-worn excuse – sorry, guv, at that range it *looked* like a Scud convoy, honest – and bugger the consequences. We needed to get blooded.

With visibility good, the convoy, now minus one vehicle, spaced out. Tom drove, while I sat up front beside him, scouting every which way for trouble. The wind, which was bitter, was blowing directly in our faces, making this night move a bitch. The standard technique is to drive around 100 metres behind the driver in front, maintaining his line across the sand. This turns to rat-shit, however, when the wind blows, because you end up with half the Syrian Desert in your face. After less than a week of ops, my hair was so stiff and matted it felt like someone had thrown a bucket of starch over me. For this reason, some of the blokes, I'd noticed, had taken to cutting their hair right down to the wood, national service style. Others – lads like me, I suspect, who were getting a bit thin on top and were worried it wouldn't grow back – let theirs grow, adding to the overall Mad Max ambience.

Tom pulled off-line and the dust content in the wind dropped appreciably. I turned around and did a quick scan and noticed that the next two vehicles had done the same. We were now offset and driving in a diagonal line across the desert, which is fine if you don't like dust in your face, but adds to the workload considerably. When you're following the vehicle in front, it's a pretty safe bet you're not going to get any nasty surprises. Now, however, we were cutting a virgin swathe through the sand and we had to be extra vigilant. Having just lost one vehicle, we couldn't afford to dispatch another by grounding out on a boulder or, worse, ploughing over the side of a wadi.

We drove and kept driving. The scenery was unrelentingly dull – wide, sweeping desert from horizon to horizon – but at least it gave us plenty of warning time should the enemy appear. We stopped for nothing, except occasionally to swap drivers. We'd all made our brews before leaving the LUP and these were poured from their flasks and passed around at regular intervals. But still the cold got to us. It felt every bit as cold as the times I'd been in Norway, where the temperature dropped down to around twenty degrees below. The reason was the wind-chill, which was proving to be a killer.

When at last we pulled into the MSR after four hours of this torture, we emerged from our seats clutching our backs and hobbling around the vehicles like doddery old men. My hands were so cold, I'd long lost the feeling in them. In order to refuel the wagon, Nick and I spent twenty minutes trying to remove the top of a Jerry-can with our wrists. Looking around, I saw that we weren't the only ones. Blokes were picking cans up with their forearms and holding them in place with their chins. Fuck knows what we'd have done if the enemy had rounded the corner at that precise moment. Until the blood flow came back to my hands – and experience said that could be half an hour or more – I couldn't have changed my underpants, let alone a magazine.

Other than that, the journey to the MSR was uneventful – so uneventful, in fact, that when we finally hit the road, we almost missed it. 'Road' or 'route' was something of an exaggeration for what we found ourselves standing on. It was more of a dirt-track. We double-checked the coordinates on the GPS and concluded that this had to be it. It looked monumentally unspectacular, but there were lots of fresh tracks on it, so we decided to stay and check it out.

We pulled back about five klicks and set up our observation post. Vehicles were dispatched 15–20 km in either direction to give us due warning of any enemy approach. It was a drill we had practised many times during our training in the UAE. In effect, we had 30–40 km of road under observation, with a designated killing zone of around five to seven kilometres in the middle. We ranged this stretch with the laser and made sure that the mortars were accessible if we needed them.

The laser is a neat bit of kit. Essentially, it's a laser-beam generator built into a pair of large binoculars. You line up the binos on the target, make sure no one's in the way, and energize. A two-second squirt at the target would result in a red digital print-out of the distance being projected at infinity on the lens. The distance was recorded and passed on with bearing information to RHQ for possible assimilation in the daily target packs for the fighter-jocks. Our one laser ranger was kept in Tony's wagon, but anyone with a bit of dems experience was expected to use it.

If we got a contact here, the plan was to attack any convoy of five trucks or more, melt into the darkness, then dog-leg back and hit the road somewhere else on the next night; and then the next and the next, until we shut the whole bloody thing down.

We settled down and waited, everybody keyed to a man. With the adrenalin pumping, we soon didn't notice the cold. I kept one ear tuned to the hiss of the radio for the low crackle of static that would precede the call from one of our picket vehicles that we had a contact.

The minutes ticked it into hours . . . five of them. By three o'clock, after we'd remained there considerably longer than was sensible, we came to the inevitable conclusion that there was nothing moving on this particular MSR at all. As we headed north towards our LUP for the following day the sense of anti-climax was palpable.

The maps said that the terrain up ahead was good LUP country. They lied. At 06.00 we pulled up in the midst of another enormous stretch of flat, featureless desert and stared in disbelief at our GPS systems. There was no doubt that we were where we thought we were. The map showed us to be in an area thick with rocky outcrops and wadis, but it was like the proverbial fucking billiard table. If it were possible, this was the worst area for a daylight hide yet.

In what was rapidly becoming a nightmarish routine, we sent out bikes and vehicles, Tony eventually finding something that was one per cent better than the surrounding environs for our LUP. It was a case of either dossing down here or carrying on in broad daylight, an option that we all considered a suicidal act of madness this early on in the game.

And so, with the sun breaking above the eastern horizon, we got to work, setting about constructing yet another hide in world-record time.

Toiling hard and with the sun on my face, I soon worked up quite a sweat. Even the presence of a cold morning breeze was insufficient to cool me down. All it succeeded in doing was covering me in yet another layer of sand. Every time I wiped the sweat off my forehead, it felt like I was swiping myself with sandpaper.

The fucking sand was starting to get everywhere. I drained my brew and found a millimetre of grit down in the dregs. Whenever I tucked into a meal, I heard the sound of sand grinding in my teeth. We learned to eat our food quickly or face the prospect of a gritty, damn' near inedible meal. I don't know what effect it was having on my innards, but it was doing terrible things to my arse.

Now, after a brew and a fag, I felt the first stirrings of a package. Even in the desert, and without my All

Bran, I found I was dumping regular as clockwork. Normally, this might be the source of some pride, but out here a crap meant another torture session.

As soon as the hide was constructed, I went for a stroll to shouts of 'man walking with shovel'. Crapping is about the most personal function we might ever hope to perform in life, but you can discard any thought of dumping in privacy when you set foot in the desert with a Sabre Squadron. Whenever we went for a crap, the rule was: keep it short – the length of time spent doing the deed, that is, not necessarily the package itself – and keep it close. Because we lived in the constant expectation of an appearance by the enemy, wandering off half-way to Baghdad was not a luxury we could allow ourselves. Not that it would make much difference at this particular hide, which was only marginally less flat than the one before. The one other golden rule was: keep downwind of the rest of the LUP or expect to face the wrath of the entire unit when you returned.

I found the tiniest of inclines about twenty metres from the vehicle and looked around for a suitably soft piece of ground, so I could scrape a hole and drop the package straight in. It is essential that we remove or hide all evidence of our presence at an LUP. As revolting as it sounds, a turd can be analysed and its perpetrator identified by his diet, even out here in the boondocks. And while our MO in Iraq required discipline, it wasn't half as bad as some other operations I'd been on. If you're in an observation post, or OP, in Northern Ireland, for example, you shit right where you're living and sleeping, which is probably under a bush or a bracken thicket. Under these circumstances, cling-film is essential. You spread a sheet on the ground, dump right onto it, which is not as easy as it sounds, then wrap it up and hang onto it, until you can sneak away from the OP, usually at dead of night, and bury the bastard. Since you can be in an OP like this for days on end, you learn to pray for a mild case of constipation.

With this consoling thought in mind, I found a suitably soft patch of sand and started to scrape with the shovel. To my horror, I found a freshly laid log a couple of centimetres below the surface. I shouldn't have been so surprised, but then it'd been a while since I'd been this long in the desert. Given the constraints on us, there are only so many places around an LUP where you can go and do the deed. With thirty guys all looking around for the best spot for a quiet crap, and with our training, it was almost inevitable that I'd walked into a ceremonial dumping ground.

I moved on and settled down. Because we only got a limited amount of bog-paper in our ration packs, we learned, too, to get pretty sparing with the stuff. If you failed to do everything in two or three swipes, tough – your undies acquired some interesting designer motifs. And God only knew when you'd next get into a clean pair. Luckily, I'd got my action down to two sheets, every time, no exception.

After I was all finished, I ambled as nonchalantly as I could back to the wagon, but it's hard to disguise that John Wayne lope – the gait of a man whose rubbed-raw buttocks have just received a fresh infusion of sand.

I was about to slither under netting over the 110, when I heard a voice calling to me from the next door vehicle. I turned and saw Taff's face peeking through a gap at the base of his cam-net. Normally replete with Welsh cheek and humour, it now radiated anxiety. I crawled over and slid under the netting of his 110. 'Yeah,' I said, 'what's up?'

He glanced at my shovel. 'Excuse the question, Cammy, but have you just been for a dump?'

I looked at him suspiciously. Taff was an ex-Green Jacket, a short-arse from the Valleys and king of the bloody wind-ups. He was one of the most popular characters on the squadron, but he'll go to any lengths to stitch up an unsuspecting victim. 'Maybe, maybe not,' I replied, hesitantly. 'Why?'

'Well, it's kind of personal, like.'

'Try me.'

He took a deep breath. 'All right, then. What colour was your shit?'

My face broke into a grin. 'Excuse me?' I laughed. 'What colour was my shit? What kind of a question is that?' I started looking around the huddled confines of the vehicle, expecting to see Dean or some other member of Taff's crew taking notes. These, no doubt, would be used in evidence against me in some stitch-up of *Candid Camera* proportions back at Hereford.

When I turned back, Taff's round face was purpling with embarrassment. He raised his finger to his lips. Only now did I become aware of a terrible lesion on the side of his mouth. I'd previously taken it for some mottling effect from the cam-net.

I pointed to it. 'What the fuck is that?' I asked. It looked like the worst case of herpes I'd ever seen.

'Well, that's just it, you see? Ever since I started taking those bloody NAPs tablets, I've been coming out in these.' He touched the scab self-consciously. 'And that's not all.'

I urged him to go on.

We were tucked down by the side of his vehicle, sitting on our haunches. There was no room to do anything else. It's that cramped in an LUP.

Taff leaned forward conspiratorially. 'My shit's turned fucking black.'

I pulled a face. 'Black?'

'Shh, for Christ's sake. I don't want the whole convoy to know, do I? I just wondered if you'd been suffering from the same affliction.'

'No, mate,' I said, trying to make my face a picture of sympathy and concern. 'But then, again, I ain't been taking those bloody tablets. I didn't much like the look of them to start with.' This was true. I was one of those who'd decided to chance my arm against Saddam's chemical warfare arsenal.

'What do you think I should do?'

I sucked my teeth. 'Dr Cameron says stop taking the bloody medicine, if you haven't already. Listen, I know you're only thinking about that wife and those kids of yours, but if we do get hit by a chemically tipped Scud, it can't do you any more harm than that.' I nodded towards the thing at the corner of his mouth.

'Thank you for that,' he said, patting me on the shoulder. 'I feel so much better.'

'Pleasure,' I acknowledged, ducking the sarcasm. 'Anything else? I must be away on my rounds.'

'You won't tell anyone about this, will you?' he hissed after me, as I rolled out from under the cam-net.

I held two fingers up. 'Scouts' honour, mate. Honest.'

A minute later, I was round the back of our wagon. Tom was making another brew on the tail-gate. Nick had moved onto the GPMG, checking its action and removing as much sand as he could from its working parts. I ran over what we had done on this LUP and what we were still left to do. The 110 had been checked for oil and water; its tyres gauged for pressure. The weapons were almost squared away. We'd allocated bag-rations for the day's meal and we'd set up our sentry rosters for the remainder of the day. This was made easier by the unusual way in which we'd grouped the vehicles at this particular LUP. Because the terrain was so shit-awful, we'd thought it best to divide the convoy. Tony's wagon, mine and Taff's were bunched in one group; the other three had gathered 200 metres away in a protective circle round the Unimog. As a result, our three vehicles were able to share forward sentries, which meant more gonk all round. A forward sentry goes forward a little way from the vehicles to get a slightly better view of the approaches and so provide a little extra warning time in case of an appearance by the enemy.

Despite the poor terrain on which we'd pitched our daylight hide, I began to relax.

What we did for the next few hours was largely down to us. After we'd drunk our brews, Jeff went out to do his stint on stag; Tom announced he was going to get some kip. He unrolled his maggot, climbed in and curled himself around the rear off-side wheel, on the leeward side of the vehicle. Within seconds, he was asleep.

The sense of fatigue shared by the convoy was palpable now. The hassle of getting across the border and the fraught time we'd spent looking for LUP sites had ensured that. Tired as we all were, there were certain dos and don'ts of sleeping al fresco. The cam-net doesn't really cut out much light, so most of the time you sleep with the sun's rays beating down on your eyelids. Even though it's broad daylight, you daren't bury your head to block out the light because you lose your sense of hearing, a fatal mistake when you're in the enemy's backyard. Instead, you lie down, head exposed, and immediately get hit by a carpet of shifting sand – millions of little pin-pricks in your face, whipped across the desert by the eddying wind. Wheel arches offer some protection from this affliction, and though it would be nice to crawl under the vehicles and shelter from the sun and the sand, this is to be resisted, if possible. If you're under the 110 and need to get out of your maggot in a hurry, you can't. Besides, a few years earlier, when I was still in the Queen's Regiment, three of our guys had decided to shelter their heads from the rain under a Chieftain during a big NATO exercise in Germany. In the middle of the night, the tank began to sink. It had happened so slowly that nobody had clocked what was going on until it was too late. Lessons like that tend to stick in the mind.

At long last, Nick finished working on the weapons and slithered down from the top of the vehicle to the tiny living area where we had to subsist in a permanent crouch – unless, of course, we were otherwise tucked up in a sleeping bag.

I needed to talk a few things through with Tony. As I slipped out from under the cam-net again, Nick announced he'd be sleeping alongside the next-door wheel-arch to Tom. It's essential we know seemingly inconsequential details like this. The last thing needed by a dog-tired guy who's got three hours' sleep allocation ahead of him is to be woken up by some clot who mistakes him for the bloke whose turn it is to go on watch. A guy curled up in a maggot looks indistinguishable from anyone else. When you've been driving all night, sleep is a precious commodity. It's another reason for the golden rule of silence that reigns over an LUP.

I tabbed over to Tony's vehicle to find Buzz and Frank in a slanging match. Buzz, true to form, had just spilled tea over Frank's bollocks as he'd attempted to manoeuvre past his maggot.

I found Tony poring over a map at the back of the vehicle. I don't think I'd ever once seen the mobility king asleep. Somehow, he was managing to tune out the cross-fire of whispered invective that was going on just a few feet away. 'I don't know how you put up with it,' I said, nodding at Tweedle-Dum and Tweedle-Dee.

Tony just shrugged. 'They're good men,' he said, simply. 'If we ever get to meet the enemy, I know I'll be damn' glad they're on my side. Want a brew?'

I nodded. If Frank and Buzz inflicted half as much damage on the Republican Guard as they did on our own side, we'd be home and dry. I remembered one occasion after an exercise in Belize when Buzz decided to practise his dems skills by blowing up a bar where several of us had gathered. Tony laughed when I reminded him of it.

Frank, who was inspecting his scalded tackle within the privacy of his sleeping bag, looked up and said:

A Squadron, 22 SAS

The author feeding a camel during the build-up in Saudi Arabia.
They were a bit of a problem on the practice ranges as they'd turn up
whenever we stopped for food or a brew.

Sorting out the stores to split up among the vehicles. On the ground are Claymore anti-personnel mines, C2 high-explosive grenades and 66 mm anti-tank rockets. The rest of the boxes contain more ammunition and explosives.

During the build-up training. From left to right are the Unimog support vehicle, the 110 Land Rovers and the Cannon motorbikes. At the far right are the fast-attack vehicles which we chose not to take into Iraq.

Testing the .50 on the ranges. The Arab boys were interested in collecting and selling the empty cases left behind after firing.

The Forward Operating Base in Saudi. The helicopter is an RAF Chinook like the one used for the resupply when our C/O was flown out. In the background is an American F14.

Moving north towards Iraq for the final preparations before going over the border.

Forty-eight hours earlier this Wadi had been completely dry and had been for over twenty years. Here it's almost uncrossable, giving an indication of the kind of weather that patrols had to contend with.

MMBD. Miles and Miles of Bloody Desert. If you're stuck on a plain as flat as this and it's nearly dawn you do start to get a bit concerned about how you're going to hide during daylight.

A typical LUP. Cam-nets are all up and the position is in a small depression. The photo also shows some of the terrain we had to cross. The small boulders were a pain in the neck for the guys on motorbikes.

Buzz in the captured GAZ. This shot shows the flatness of the LUP where our first enemy contact took place. The blood above the wheel is seepage from the bodies we had to dump in the back.

The start of a night's patrol. The cam-nets removed, we would sit having a last brew and smoke, waiting for complete darkness before moving out.

Showing off our new outfits. Wearing the bedou coats brought in during the resupply that flew Graham, our C/O, out of Iraq.

A member of the mobility troop checks a 110 engine. The grenade-launchers on the bumper were for laying down a smokescreen when in contact with the enemy. The plastic desert rat on the bonnet, meanwhile, was just for a laugh.

A good shot showing the amount of kit that got draped over the 110s. There are 7.62 mm GPMGs front and rear. The cam-nets are rolled up and tied to the roll bar, the sand channels are over the back wheels and above them, looking like dumb-bells, LAW 90 light anti-tank weapons.

'Yeah, and then the bastard had the nerve to whinge when he got barred.'

'I bloody never.'

'Yes, you did, you liar. You whinged like a baby. That place didn't have a roof after you'd finished with it.'

Sometimes, it was like they were bloody married to each other.

I took a pull of my tea and asked Tony what the plan was for the night's move.

Tony looked thoughtfully at the map. 'We keep moving north and hope for better terrain up ahead.'

'Christ, whoever issued these maps should be shot.'

'It's uncharted territory,' Tony said phlegmatically. 'Besides, a winter like this can change the landscape out of all recognition. There's wadis where there was sand yesterday and vice versa. The rain and the wind are redrawing the map daily.'

As if on cue, the wind blew against the side of the cam-net. Particularly hard gusts could rustle and flap the netting so hard you could barely hear the guy next to you. Through a gap in the netting, I watched a dust devil spiralling its way across the LUP site towards us. It struck the vehicle and a cloud of stinging grit spattered the map, us and the tea we were drinking. Frank and Buzz, both of whom had now settled in the narrow living space beside the vehicle, both swore in unison, then rolled their separate ways and settled down to sleep.

'And we've still got another 200 klicks to go to the main east–west MSR,' I said, with more than a tinge of frustration.

'Slowly, slowly, catchy monkey, mate. We're a hundred klicks in and we're still alive. Things could be worse.'

That was Tony all over; unflappable and master of the half-full cup, unlike Graham, whose own pint pot always seemed to be half-empty. If only their roles had been reversed, I'd have felt a lot more comfortable about our position. But that was fantasy-land. As it was, we were heading for the teeth of the enemy under the charge of a bloke who seemed like he really didn't want to be here at all. It was down to the rest of us to make the best of it.

For the next hour, Tony and I went over the route that lay ahead of us – and some of the problems we might expect along the way. Thirty kilometres ahead of us lay another east–west MSR. This wasn't as big as the Baghdad–Jordan artery further to the north, but still plenty sturdy enough – if these maps were to be believed – to convey the odd Scud convoy. If things went to plan, we'd probably be on target at the main MSR in around three nights' time.

I spent another hour shooting the shit with Taff, whose vehicle was so close to ours you could almost reach out and touch it. When I walked around to our wagon, I roused Nick with a kick in the ribs and a hot brew. Tom was up, preparing lunch. I took a sniff and pulled a face. I'm renowned for not eating much and declined this delicacy, which looked like corned beef and goat's dung hash. Besides, I was tired and needed some gonk. Before I turned in, I refilled my cup and leaned back against the tail-gate, sharing one of my precious Silk Cuts with the chef.

After a couple of drags, Tom looked as if he was about to make some deep pronouncement about the fragility of life or how much he missed the texture of his girlfriend's skin. But instead he said: 'Cammy, why do you smoke this crap?'

I looked at him. 'Fuck off. I'll smoke the whole thing myself if you don't want it.'

He shook his head. 'I meant, mate, what's the point of smoking bloody Silkies, which are meant to be good for you – or less bleeding worse – when at any moment you could cop a round of Iraqi high-velocity. It doesn't make a lot of sense, does it?'

'So who turned you into a doctor-cum-fucking-philosopher all of a sudden?'

'You crap-hats are all screwed up,' he said, tapping the side of his head.

I laughed. 'Put a sock in it, will you? You're wrecking my Marlboro moment.'

'Ah, now there's a real fag . . .'

I sat there, taking my time over the smoke and the brew, until I felt my eyelids dropping. After three days and nights with scarcely a moment's shut-eye, I staked out my own patch around the forward wheel that

Tom had vacated, ticking off those last few things I needed to know before I could sleep. Jeff was getting some kip at the next wheel. The visibility was good – out to ten kilometres, a mixed blessing. We were just about set for the rest of the day. All Tom had to do was clean his M16 and he was done, too. Buzz had taken the forward sentry position. Everything was as it should be. I adjusted my webbing under my head, got comfortable, and within seconds had lapsed into sleep.

After what passed for five minutes – I later found out it was an hour – I heard Buzz's voice go off in my head. He could only have whispered the warning, but it sounded like a fucking siren going off in some deep recess of my brain. The words tumbled over and over. There was something faintly hypnotic about them. For a moment, they held me in the grip of a dreamy kind of paralysis. Then, Tom was shaking me.

The words came back to me and I knew it was no dream.

Stand-to, stand-to. Enemy.

Fuck. A pang of fear hit me in the gullet, followed by a weird moment of doubt. Could this be some kind of wind-up? The fear re-doubled and hit me again. Nobody, not even Tom or Buzz, would pull a stunt like this on our third day. This was for fucking real. I was up and out of the sleeping-bag in a second, fumbling for my Bergen and my M16. For a few seconds more, chaos reigned, then we were taking up position.

Suddenly, a vehicle appeared. It slowed, then stopped, sitting there 700 metres out; watching us, watching them. And then, it came towards us, and kept coming, until it drew up right outside our cluster of cam-nets. Two Iraqis got out. They paused to pick up their helmets, then divided. The driver moved for Tony's vehicle, the commander headed straight for the front of our Land Rover, where Tom and I had taken up station. The officer bent down and picked up the cam-net. That was when he saw me.

The last thing I remember thinking was that it shouldn't be like the fucking movies, but that's how it was – the whole thing moved in excruciating slow-time like a Sam Peckinpah Western.

I had a moment to register the look of blank surprise on the Iraqi's face as he came up under the cam-net and twigged me. He started to raise his weapon, but I fired, quick double-tap – *ba-bam* – and he went down. As he fell, his body was hit by at least six more rounds – bullets from other weapons that had been trained on him from the moment he'd got out of the vehicle – and he pirouetted in a macabre death-dance before hitting the dirt, face-down.

I heard more firing and saw bullets striking the second man. Several punched into his chest. One all but removed the side of his head. A voice in the back of my head started telling me over and over that I'd killed a man – bam, just like that. But it was a small voice. And it was rapidly drowned by a chorus of other thoughts. What about the GAZ? Who else was in there? Had Jeff made it with the phosphor grenade?

Training, thank God, takes over. You're not left long with the moral consequences of your actions.

I was out from under the cam-net before I even knew it. As I moved towards the still twitching body of the man I'd shot, I could see a flurry out of the corner of my eye as Buzz and Jeff tore into the back of the GAZ. Your training doesn't allow you to look, even though your instincts want to. I was on the body in a second, pulling it over, one hand tugging at his arms in the search for firearms, grenades, knives; you never know what the fucker might still have up a sleeve, even in his death-throes.

Secure.

I looked up and saw a similar scene being played out around the other body.

No doubt about it, they were both dead.

And then there's a blood-curdling cry from the GAZ.

I spun around to see Buzz and Jeff dragging something – someone – out of the Iraqi vehicle. Another man had been in the back, but they'd got the drop on him. As far as I could tell, the guy was uninjured, but he was squealing like a stuck pig all the same.

Jostling, blurred action as Buzz and Jeff threw their captive to the ground, both of them yelling at the top of their voices: shut the fuck up.

The Iraqi doesn't get it and starts jabbering and wailing louder than ever. And then he opens his eyes and sees the muzzle of Buzz's Commando a moment before it grinds into the thin skin between his eyebrows. At the same time, Buzz is shouting again, only now the tone is different. The shrillness that had been there in the initial adrenalin rush is gone. There's depth and authority in his words. Be quiet, he's telling him, or he'll blow his fucking brains to Babylon.

This time the Iraqi makes the connection and zips it.

Silence.

In the stillness that followed, there was a fraction of a moment in which my heightened senses registered the blueness of the sky and the sound of the cam-net flapping in the wind behind me. And then it started all over again. Shouts, movement, oaths, orders, as blokes from the other vehicles pounded over to our two 110s to join the fray.

I left a group of the boys to go through the uniform of the body at my feet as I searched the scene for Alec, Tony and Graham. It was time for a fucking head-shed meeting, the fastest we'd ever had. Two, maybe three minutes had elapsed since the first shots had been fired. Everybody recognized the situation for what it was. True, we had things under control, but you could hear traces of panic in the shouts and rasped commands around you.

The situation had turned to rat-shit and no mistake.

I spotted Tony and Alec in a huddle beside the second 110. As I jogged towards them, the interpreters began to go to work on the surviving Iraqi. First, they had to get him to calm down. The guy had gone into prayer mode and I couldn't say I blamed him. He was convinced we were going to slot him, too.

While the interpreters told him he'd live if only he kept his bloody mouth closed, a couple of other guys continued to work on him. The handling was rough, aggressive. You want to maintain that sense of shock a prisoner goes into after an engagement like the one we'd just been through. The two handlers were tearing through the prisoner's uniform, looking for anything of potential use. You don't know exactly what you're looking for, but you know it when you've found it. It could be a notepad, or a regimental badge, a diary or some briefing notes scratched on a fag-packet. We are religious about destroying anything that we write down on ops, but I'm always amazed how ill-disciplined other people are. Anything we do write down we destroy, usually by turning our pockets out and burning any extraneous paper whenever we have a brew.

Graham arrived at the head-shed meeting at the same time as me. He was visibly flustered: his cheeks were flushed and he was breathing heavily. Because his vehicle had been some distance from ours, the finer points of the engagement had eluded him. He demanded to know what had happened, asking questions like: 'Who the fuck opened fire first?' What the hell difference did it make?

We told him everything. It was now a good five minutes since the shooting and we were all starting to get nervous. In all, we'd fired between twenty and thirty rounds. Anyone within a radius of two kilometres would have heard those shots.

Graham went deathly quiet. We stared at him, waiting for a response – or at least a sensible question or two. Tony was the mobility man, the guy with all the answers in his head. Graham should have been in there, getting Tony to spell out our options. But he never asked. Graham wasn't saying shit. It was as if he was holding some deep and meaningful conversation within himself. And while he was gone, off travelling in some distant corner of his mind, half the Iraqi army could have been heading for our position.

We had two dead Iraqis on our hands – one of them a half-colonel officer. I dreaded to think what the Iraqis would do to us if they caught us with their blood on our hands. Again, I saw an image of the CO making his speech at the cross-brief; the part where he was telling us about the consequences of capture.

'Boss,' Tony said, some urgency in his voice now, 'what are we gonna do?'

'We've got to move,' Graham said, turning around with a vacant look in his eyes. For an instant, I thought I saw the demons that haunted him. I'd seen them, too, in the dream that has me gored through by the stake. But, thank Christ, my demons had never haunted me in broad daylight, or on ops.

'Move where?' I said.

The seconds ticked by.

'Move where, Boss?' I asked again.

'North, no, south. Fuck, I don't know. How did we get in this shit-awful mess? We can't stay here. We've got to get out of here.'

I looked at Tony and Alec. This needed to be deliberated. But quickly. 'There's three more hours of daylight,' I said. 'If we move, there's a good chance we get compromised.'

'We can't stay here – not with them here, like that.' Graham jabbed a thumb at the two bodies behind him.

'Right,' Alec said. 'Even if we buried them. We still got the prisoner to contend with. And the GAZ.'

'OK,' I said, 'so we move. But where?'

'North or south, Boss?' Tony added. 'Which is it to be?'

Graham shook himself out of his torpor. 'We go south,' he said, with some conviction this time. 'We clean up here and go fucking south. We've got to cut the distance between us and the border.'

Tony and I looked at each other. I could see what he was thinking. Our thoughts were the same. 'Boss,' I said, knowing I was speaking for both of us, 'if we're going to move, let's go north. It's the last bloody thing the ragheads would expect. These guys wandered over to us, because they thought we were Iraqi, for Christ's sake. Let's triple the distance from the border and really get into the part.'

'Bingo,' Tony added. 'We take the prisoner and the GAZ and whistle up a Chinook when we're holed up somewhere quiet up north. We don't have to be close to the border to do an exfil. We could be 300 klicks from Saudi and the chopper could still reach us, no problem.'

I nodded. This not only made tactical sense, it also spared us from going through the whole bloody rigmarole of infiltrating Iraq from the border again.

'No,' Graham blurted. 'These guys aren't a couple of toms out touring the countryside. They're officers. One of them is a half fucking colonel.' He stared at us, in a half-pleading, half-glaring kind of way. 'We're going south and that's bloody it. Now, let's get this place cleaned up and move it. God only knows, they could be coming for us right now.'

And that was it. The Chinese Parliament is there for a purpose; a means of allowing us – senior NCOs and officers alike – to go through the issues and offer our OC a menu of sensible, well-crafted options. Well, for once, Graham listened to what we had to say and did something about it in reasonably short order. The only trouble was, it was the wrong decision. But, in retrospect, what did we expect? He wasn't one of us. He was an exchange officer and an outsider. As OC, he didn't have to take our advice. That was his prerogative. He was holding it together, but only just. I don't think he was scared so much as gripped by an inability to be decisive. He didn't like being deep inside Iraq. It was alien to him and the way he had been trained for the majority of his career. So be it. Somebody at RHQ liked him. But right from the start he was the wrong guy for the job.

I jogged back towards our vehicle and gave the news to the boys. They were split on the issue of staying or leaving – that one was a tough call. But you didn't have to be a field marshal to know that the course of action Graham had decided for us – moving out and heading south – was wrong.

Tom gave vent to his feelings as he helped Nick and Jeff pack up the Land Rover, ready for the off.

'Hey,' I said, 'I'm on your side, mate. You fucking tell him to go north.'

He stopped for a moment, a dark expression on his face. Then, he cracked a half-smile. 'There's only one thing worse than a crap-hat, Cammy, and that's a fucked-up Rupert.'

'Well, we're stuck with it. And that's that.'

It took a lot to rile Tom. I knew then that we'd crossed some kind of threshold with Graham. It was an insoluble mess. But I couldn't see any way out of it. Somehow we just had to press on and make the best of a bad lot.

I turned back to the killing zone. The prisoner was being trussed. A gaggle of blokes were bundling the corpses into the back of the GAZ. Another group was cleaning the ground around the vehicles, retrieving spent bullets and pieces of skull; sprinkling sand over the blood that stained the spot where the two soldiers had fallen. Packing up an LUP is as much a science as creating one. Normally, the little things are put away first – brew-kit, cooking stuff, day-optics – and so forth. Then we move on to the main radio equipment before finally setting about the cam-nets and the poles.

Now, we shoved things in any old-how in our haste to break camp and get out of here. We would organize everything later, when – if – we made our next LUP.

In amongst all this frenzied activity, I noticed a couple of guys clutching freebies. One of them, Rob, was holding a neat-looking Russian sidearm and an even neater pair of artillery-spotting binoculars. I knew the kind. They had in-built graticules and were brilliant for ranging.

'You jammy bastard,' I said, nodding at the binos.

Rob shrugged. 'You know how it is, mate. First come, first served in this business.' He held out a khaki-coloured sack with a strap on it. It took me a moment to recognize it as the satchel that had been hanging by the side of the senior officer as he had stepped out of the GAZ. 'You'd better take a look at this, Cammy. It could be something.'

I opened it up and saw the corner of a map. I riffled past it and found more charts. I pulled them out and opened one of them up. It was a map of the area we were in. And it was littered with pencilled symbology – stuffed full of it, in fact. I felt a lump in my throat, brought on by a cross between fascination and horror at what swam before my eyes.

I called Tony over and spread the map out on the bonnet of the 110.

He studied it for a moment and then looked at me. 'Jesus Christ,' he said. 'They're all around us.'

And so it seemed. We appeared to have stumbled into an entire regiment of artillery. There was a lot of Arabic scrawled over the topography, but the symbols – depicting gun pieces and armour, HQs and so forth – told their own story. You didn't have to be an intelligence muppet to figure it out. The enemy was spread out in depth 360 degrees around us. It was a miracle we hadn't bumped into any of these positions during our night move.

'Hang on,' Tony said, 'there's no date on this thing. We don't know what the state of play is with these charts. These could be today's positions – but they could equally be yesterday's or tomorrow's.' He swore under his breath. 'We'd better talk to the prisoner.'

While Tony carried on looking at the map, Chris, one of the interpreters got to work. Chris was a bit of a smoothie – we used to call him gel-boy because of what he did to his hair – but he left the Iraqi in no doubt about what we'd do if he didn't sing. The Iraqi didn't need any persuasion. The maps, he said, were current. So, we decided to use them – albeit with some reservation. There was no way we could trust them absolutely, nor him, but they were better than nothing. If we really were surrounded, then the charts spelled our only real chance of making safe passage south to the border.

It took around fifteen minutes to formulate a plan. Tony was in charge of plotting the route. We had to work our way through scattered artillery positions to a point where we could RV with a helicopter and get this prisoner out. A Chinook was big enough to accept a GAZ, so we figured we should take the vehicle with us and have both man and machine removed by the helicopter while we were about it. Buzz was assigned to drive the GAZ to the RV, a job he accepted with relish since he'd already discovered it had a heater, a luxury that was a distant memory to us after our freezing night drives in the open-topped 110s.

'Oi, Buzz,' Nick yelled, as he jogged past the GAZ, 'if we drive by any airfields, try not to snag any bits of Saddam's fencing, eh? We got enough bloody problems already.'

Buzz was rearranging the two bodies in the back, manhandling them with the same ease he loaded and off-loaded deer from the back of his truck. I only hoped he didn't forget himself and start skinning them. Because of the restrictions on space, the plan was to truss the prisoner and shove him in the back of the GAZ, too.

'Piss off, Action Man,' he shot back at the BFG. Things were cooking and Buzz was happy. In the hell-hole that had become of our world, I found it strangely reassuring.

Half an hour after the firefight, we were ready to move. Tony had marked out a route for us through the Iraqi positions, plotting each waypoint, or turn, on our GPS systems. It was going to be extremely tight, because, if the maps were anything to go by, on a number of occasions we'd be passing within several hundred metres of the enemy. The GPS/Navstar system is good to within a metre and as long as we used the cover of darkness to slip by the closest of the enemy units, we reckoned we could do it.

We took a last look around for things which could give away our presence at the LUP, but everyone had done a good job. There was nothing to signal we had been here, let alone dispatched two enemy soldiers, except for our tracks. But since the Bedouin themselves in these parts weren't past crisscrossing the desert in their four-by-fours, we reckoned we could get away with leaving them untouched.

The convoy left the LUP in the full glare of the afternoon sun. Tony led us out. We were second in line. Buzz, in the GAZ, was third from last, just in front of Graham's vehicle.

Nobody said anything as we swung south for the border.

*

For the next few hours we moved slowly, stopping every 500 metres or so to scan the horizon for trouble. Every step of the way, we checked and double-checked our position on our GPS receivers. Either Tony had done a great job in steering us with the utmost precision through the enemy positions or the Iraqis had buggered off completely. For the two and a half hours of daylight driving we had to endure, we saw no sign of the enemy.

Come nightfall, it was a different story. We pulled up and set up our comms. It was now imperative to get word of what had happened to RHQ. As H rigged the comms link, we noticed headlights in the distance. My first thought was that at least we'd done the right thing in moving. Now we were away from the LUP and were static, we had the drop on these characters. From the concentration of lights, I reckoned there were a half dozen vehicles out there, all looking for us.

I raised a night-scope to my right eye and trained it in their direction. Then, I blinked. The desert bloomed with lights – at least twice as many as I'd seen with my naked eye. It took a moment or two for my sleep-starved brain to get it. These muppets were using night optics just like we were. Only their stuff wasn't passive, but IR. We could make out the pathway of the infrared beams though our passive night-scopes. And then, a fresh pang of fear hit me. What if they were using passive night-optics, too? With kit like ours that magnified the ambient light of the moon and the stars, they could be on top of us and we'd never even know it – until they got within range of our optics. Then again, maybe their night-kit was better than ours. Maybe they had the equivalent of our Milan missile launcher's MIRA night-sight. The MIRA is passive – it cues on an object's thermal signature – and can see for miles. I passed on my concerns as another set of lights loomed out of the darkness and then another. Behind me, I heard a metallic chorus as the Mk19 and point five-oh heavy support weapons were cocked. Everybody was thinking the same thing: the bastards must have picked up our trail.

Our vehicles were drawn up in a kind of circle seventy-five metres across with the Unimog in our midst. We were permanently stood-to, which meant everybody in the wagons, ready to go at a moment's notice. We were scanning in 360 degrees, although the main concentration of effort was on those lights. In our vehicle, Tom and I sat there with our night optics permanently pinned to one eye. We relayed what we saw to Nick and Jeff in the back. Everyone wore their bin-liners – their helmets – except me. I'd worn mine in training, but had consigned it to a stowage position on the wing-mirror bracket since crossing the border. It was heavy and restricted my vision. I was in no doubt, however, about what might happen next. The first we'd know of it if these people clocked us would be the whistle of salvos as they brought their artillery down on us. These people were gunners. Artillery is what they did best. And we'd killed two of their own and were holding a third.

The lights came closer. And then, quite unexpectedly, they started to weave.

For the next ten minutes, we watched as they crisscrossed the desert. There was no method in their search pattern. It was clear that they were looking for their missing comrades, but equally that they had no idea where to begin searching. At their closest, they must have come to within a couple of kilometres of our position as every so often a shout reached us on the wind. It was unnerving, because it sounded like they were in our midst. We just sat there praying that they didn't extend their search pattern for us. The bottom line, though, was that we were best off staying still. Effectively, there was nothing we could do but sit there, watching them look for us.

We wanted to get the whole exfil operation accomplished as quickly as possible. Graham drafted a signal and handed it to H. As well as containing a synopsis of the 'contact', it also carried our urgent request for a Chinook. The idea was not just to off-load the prisoner and the GAZ, but to use the flight for a replen operation, as well. We were low on fuel and could do with some more water, too. Graham also reminded RHQ to ship us some warm clothing before we all bloody froze to death.

The signal sent, we sat back and waited. Even

though we were only about ten klicks from the contact – and still getting periodically buzzed by Iraqi search parties – we began to feel a little more comfortable. Because we had blokes scanning their heads off, we felt reasonably confident we wouldn't be taken unawares. Gradually, we felt safe enough to break out our flasks and pass round some brews.

As the minutes drifted into hours, though, our frustration grew. We had to believe that RHQ had its reasons for not coming back to us immediately, but when you're staring down the enemy's throat, it's difficult not to lose patience. It was close on three hours before we finally heard the tell-tale crackle that presaged the return signal.

A couple of minutes later Taff jogged over and gave us the news. It was good and bad. The exfil was on, but not until tomorrow night.

The head-sheds gathered at Graham's vehicle. I asked him how RHQ had reacted to the news of the contact, but he was curiously noncommittal. He urged us to turn to the matter in hand: making plans for the helicopter's landing site RV (LSRV).

'Why couldn't they have fucking organized the thing for tonight?' Alec said. 'As it is, we're dangerously exposed, what with that vehicle, the prisoner and the bodies in the back.'

'We should have buried the fuckers,' Tony said, before turning to Graham. 'What was wrong with tonight, Boss?'

Graham shrugged. It seemed as if his brain was vacationing on another planet. 'I don't know,' he said, distantly. 'I guess they had their reasons.'

'So, what are we going to do?' I asked.

Graham turned towards Tony.

'We ought to get to a point that's close to the LSRV tonight – say, five to ten kilometres from it – and put it under observation. If it's clear, we can then confirm the time and the location with RHQ before they send the chopper.'

Everyone agreed. We looked at the map and found a position about seven kilometres short of the LSRV that looked as good as anything in the vicinity for pitching our LUP. I glanced at my watch. It was only about ten-thirty, but we would have to get moving. The designated LUP site was almost forty klicks away and with the area crawling with enemy, we were going to have our work cut out for us, if we were to make the location in time.

The first ten kilometres were agonizingly slow as we inched through the enemy search grids – such as they were – to get to our new LUP. The further south we got, however, the less activity we saw. Eventually, it petered out altogether.

Come five-thirty, we found ourselves on an immense gravel plain with an unrestricted view of the LSRV. We set up our daylight hide and started to go about the thousand and one things that needed to be done before any of us could rest.

It took longer than usual to get squared away owing to the suddenness of our departure from the previous LUP. Equipment had to be unpacked and repacked, so that everything was exactly where we needed it, when we needed it. After the adrenalin rush of the contact, there was not much talking. Everyone went about their tasks in a quiet, methodical way. Particular attention was paid to our weapons. The incident with the GAZ had shown we could go from normality to a full-blown emergency in a matter of moments. This was nothing, of course, we didn't know already, but the reality of it had been breathtaking. All around me, people were stripping their weapons and cleaning them. A jammed gun didn't bear thinking about. Having come about as close as I ever wanted to get to an Iraqi, I recharged each of the magazines for my M16, removing the bullets and loading them again to help ease the spring. Then, I sat down and did the same for my sidearm.

When eventually it was my turn to get my head down, I found it difficult to sleep. An LSRV is a tense time during any operation. A helicopter lays a big noise footprint. The enemy was agitated and close. I wanted to be shot of the prisoner and the vehicle and get back to what we were supposed to be doing, looking for Scuds up north. The missiles were coming down on Israel and Saudi at a steady, though unspectacular, rate. The conjecture in Riyadh was that Saddam was holding the bulk of his Scud arsenal back for the mother of all salvoes, possibly involving chemical warheads.

General Schwarzkopf had promised the Israelis we'd be there when it counted. And where the fuck were we? After a week, we were damned near back where we had started, wet-nursing a lone Iraqi prisoner.

I rolled over, trying to get comfortable on the rock-hard sand.

Christ, if the Israelis only knew, I thought, they'd have launched a full-scale invasion of Western Iraq.

SIX

We set up watch eight kilometres from the LSRV and waited. It was a clear night, with a nigh-full moon and a sky full of stars. Tom, Nick, Jeff and I kept the brews and the chat going as we scanned the horizon, but it was difficult not to let the cold get to us. Ahead, stretched the immense gravel plain that had been earmarked for our rendez-vous with the helicopter. It was bathed in an eery luminescence. I tried to picture the Chinook crew as it prepared to lift off from its remote staging post close to the Iraqi border. In the old days, they'd have called it a bomber's moon. For those whose business it was to fly nocturnal military missions in 1991, however, PNGs and radar had obviated the need for bright nights. Privately, the RAF crew might be cursing us for making them go over the border on a night such as this, as it would only help the Iraqi triple-A batteries. But then, if these guys couldn't do it, nobody could. I'd never come across such a professional bunch of flyers in my life. They were the modern-day equivalent of the Lysander pilots who flew in and out of occupied France during the Second World War. Some people called them bonkers. Maybe they were, but without them, I'd have starved, died of thirst or run out of fuel many times, both here and elsewhere, during my time with the Regiment.

As we'd sat in the wagons, waiting for dark to descend, we'd witnessed one of those spectacular sunsets that you often got in the Middle East. The sun had settled as a big orange-red ball in the western sky, its colour and intensity deepening with every minute of its passage towards the horizon. As it finally slipped from view, a light veil of cloud and the ever-present band of dust-laden air left blood-red ripples in its wake. Even Nick, not one to muse on these things, remarked upon its beauty. Normally, this might have induced a string of piss-taking from Tom, Jeff and me, but none of us said anything. I guess we all felt a certain sense of awe. In days gone by sailors and travellers would have looked upon it as a portent. I dare say, given the tenseness of our situation, some of the more superstitious amongst us may have been given to thinking along the same lines.

With the sun's departure came the onset of another bitter night. The near-freezing temperature was exacerbated by a stiff northerly wind. We were all tired, but the need to stay vigilant was crucial. I decided to pep things up a bit. I began to hum.

'Blimey,' Nick said, from his position behind me, 'what's got into you?'

'I feel great,' I said. 'I've never had such energy. It's the same for you, isn't it, mate?' I added, nudging Tom.

'Yeah,' he replied, not quite sure, I could tell, where all this was headed, but stringing along for the hell of it. 'Never felt more alive in me bloody life. That's right, isn't it, Jeff?'

'Yeah, mate,' Jeff replied from his position in the back, next to Nick. 'You mean, you don't,' he said, prodding the BFG.

'No, I feel completely bolloxed.' Nick scratched his close-cropped head. 'I don't get it. Did I miss out on some grub or something?'

I shook my head. 'It's the sugar,' I said. 'We all take sugar in our brews. You don't. It's that simple, mate. You should put sugar in your tea. Then, you'd be like us.'

'But I hate fucking sweet tea.'

'Well, then, on your own head be it,' Tom said, realizing now that this was part of my campaign to get a uniform brew standard for the crew.

'Yeah,' Jeff added, 'you should take a leaf out of the Maoris' book, mate. They never even dreamed of going into battle without first downing a mug of treacle-sweet Quick Brew.'

'This is a piss-take, isn't it?' the BFG said.

All of us shrugged in a picture of innocence. 'No, mate, it's the truth.'

Nick lapsed into an introspective silence. I looked left and right at the two vehicles beside ours. From the profile of the huddled forms in each, it was obvious that both Taff's and Tony's crews were as cold and pissed-off as we were. Occasionally, we got up to stretch and move around. The cold seemed to home in on my aches and pains, threatening to turn me into a geriatric before the night was out. For the sake of the spoof on Nick, though, I was determined to maintain the illusion I was on top of the bloody world. I was pretty sure that within a few days we'd all be drinking the same tea from our four flasks. It helped cut down on the logistics.

We'd been on watch for more than three hours, keeping our eyes peeled for enemy, when we heard the tell-tale sound of the Chinook coming in.

To my left, I caught a muffled cheer from Frank and Buzz above the rising wok-wok sound of the rotors. Taff's 110 was parked up ten metres to our right, its arc of observation adjusted slightly to enable it to lock into that of another 110 a kilometre away, one of a pair assigned to the north-east corner of the rectangular box that had been set up around the LSRV.

Squinting through the binoculars, I saw a dark shape against the star-bed, but it was a momentary lock. The pilot was flying unbelievably low – so low, in fact, that for an instant I thought it was a vehicle on the skyline. In the run-up to hostilities, the RAF had converted a couple of Chinooks to a special ops configuration, adding all kinds of missile warners and jammers to help the aircraft penetrate hostile territory. In the end, though, the only real safeguard against getting a missile up the rear ramp was to fly low and stay low.

I relocated the Chinook and realized just how low that was. As it drew closer, flying almost directly towards us, the faint glow of its twin exhausts winked in and out as it hugged the gently undulating contours of the land to the south.

But the noise was something else. In the stillness of that cold night, it seemed as if it would wake the dead. The pilots overshot the LSRV to give it the once-over, then pulled a tight turn. As the Chinook settled onto the ground, the noise grew to a crescendo and we cringed in our vehicles.

'For Christ's sake,' I said to Tom, 'I hope these guys are quick.'

Tom took a last drag on a roll-up held between thumb and finger-nail and tossed it disdainfully away. 'Bleeding crabs don't know the meaning of the word,' he replied. 'This is going to seem like forever, mark my words.'

He was right. The RAF, understandably, don't like being on the ground inside enemy territory, so the Chinook crew kept the engines turning and burning all the time. It's not a situation we like either, because if anything happened and the helicopter became damaged or destroyed, the crew would be coming to war with us, which, I guess, is not something your average RAF crewman expects or signs on for, even in the midst of a major conflict.

In the end, the Chinook stayed on the ground, its engines howling like Valkyries, for three-quarters of an hour. There was a lot to unload: a seemingly endless succession of 45 gallon burmoil drums from which our vehicles would be topped up, as well as water containers. There was also the matter of handing over the prisoner and loading the GAZ, which, I knew, would have taken time. But every one of those forty-five minutes felt like an hour.

At long last, there was a rise in the tempo of the Chinook's engines and suddenly it was airborne. We breathed a collective sigh of relief. It couldn't be long now before it was our turn to go to the LSRV and do some refuelling ourselves.

An hour and a half later, though, we were still waiting. 'What the hell's going on?' Nick asked.

No one answered, because no one knew. We had to maintain radio silence. And in the absence of any information, we had to remain patient.

We passed the time with reminiscences about past operations and, inevitably, some of the stitch-ups that tend to go hand-in-glove with them.

'Remind me to get that short-arse, Taff, for that stunt he pulled with the snake,' Tom said. There was a low chorus of approval from the rest of us. It hadn't been so long ago. We were in Oman, training with the Sultan's forces. After a night climb down the side of a steep wadi, we were all sitting around a camp fire, drinking our brews and shooting the shit. We were dimly aware of Taff in the shadows, tinkering around with some climbing kit, or so we thought. None of us paid him any attention.

Presently, the Welsh One came and sat down with us. Unbeknownst to us, he'd tied one end of a thin stretch of twine onto his boot and a brightly coloured bit of 9 mm rope onto the other. In the flickering light of the fire, it was perfect. Suddenly, about fifteen minutes after he'd joined us, Taff leapt to his feet, shouting 'snake' at the top of his voice. As he hared off, we all saw something leaping for us out of the shadows. It was only a foot long, but bright, like most really venomous snakes are. It also moved like shit off a shovel. That was it. We scattered like a pack of worried sheep, each of us heading for something, anything, that would give us a bit of elevation. Buzz and Frank grabbed red-hot embers out of the fire and ran after the thing, waving their firebrands and screaming obscenities at it. It only dawned on us what had happened, when Taff came back, pissing himself with laughter and trailing a sorry piece of rope behind him. He was lucky, Jeff said, not to have Buzz and Frank surgically implant their burning embers up his fundamental orifice.

Somewhere at the back of my frozen brain, this remark struck a chord. Then, I remembered. Within a moment or two, I'd spilled the beans about Taff's medical condition.

''Ere, Taff, mate,' Tom called softly in the direction of the vehicle to our right. 'You ain't taken to crapping out your mouth, have you?'

'Oh, very funny, most amusing,' Taff called back. 'Feel free to take the piss out of my affliction, won't you?'

'No wonder your shit's turned black,' Jeff said. 'That is a nasty sore, mate.'

'Between your face and your arse, you're a sorry sight,' Nick added.

Between our peels of laughter, I heard Taff's threat to get me. I now reflected that informing on the Welsh Wizard might have been a mistake. Between one of Taff's stitch-ups and the Republican Guard, I think I would have taken my chances with the Iraqis any day.

We hadn't settled long back into the routine when a vehicle materialized out of the darkness. At long last, it was our turn to head down to the LSRV. As soon as the other Land Rover took up the position we'd adopted for the best part of the last five hours, we set off and followed a bearing we knew, eight kilometres later, would get us to the place where the chopper had landed.

When we got there, we couldn't believe our eyes.

When we're on ops, we're conditioned to be meticulously tidy. A fag-butt dropped carelessly over the side of a vehicle can give away our presence to a tenacious enemy investigator. So we're careful. The LSRV, however, was a mess. There were burmoils everywhere. People had dumped them as soon as they were emptied. There'd been no attempt at all at rounding them up. I put it to the back of my mind. We'd take care of that later. Right now, the priority was to get refuelled.

We pulled in alongside another vehicle and got to work. Immediately, I realized what it was that had delayed the proceedings. Somebody had fucked up bigtime. Six vehicles to refuel and not so much as a single funnel to carry out the transfer. Tom, Nick, Jeff and I were already struggling to get the petrol into our tanks and Jerry-cans. For every ten gallons that went in, we probably lost another two or three in the sand around our feet. Everything reeked of precious petrol. But when your fingers are frozen to the bone and your skin's so numb you don't even feel the fuel that's slopping all over you anymore, it wasn't surprising. We did the best we could.

I wanted to find out from Graham how the prisoner and vehicle transfer had gone; also if there was any news from RHQ off the chopper I needed to be aware of. I jogged over to a third vehicle I could see in the gloom beyond the second Land Rover. The deal was two vehicles refuelled while the others stayed on stag.

The third vehicle at the LSRV should have been Graham's.

It wasn't.

As I drew close, I blinked. The vehicle *was* Graham's, only Graham wasn't in it. There in the front seat was Roger, our regimental sergeant major. Roger's a big bloke. The last place I'd seen him was in a tent at the FOB, shortly before we set off for the border. At no point in the operation had there been any suggestion that he'd be coming with us. And yet here he was, large as fucking life. I hid my amazement and held out a hand.

'What the hell are you doing here?' I asked.

Roger was cupping a brew with those big hands of his. 'I'll tell you tomorrow,' he replied, shifting slightly uncomfortably. It was unlike Roger to be evasive.

'Bloody hell,' I quipped, 'they're scraping the barrel, aren't they, Rog. I thought you'd retired.'

Roger turned to me. There was little of that customary ee-by-gum humour in his eyes as he said: 'I've come here to sort you foockers out, haven't I?'

As he leaned back, I got my first look at the bloke sitting beside him. I'd been thinking all along it was Graham, but it wasn't. This was another officer, another major, we nicknamed Gazza. Gazza was B Squadron and a 'Rupert' of the first order – no, make that a 'Rodney'. Ruperts are what we call officers. All officers are Ruperts and I guess most of them can't help it; it's just the way they are. Some Ruperts, though, are Rodneys: blokes who transcend the normal boundaries of officerhood and become something else – stuck-up pillocks. That was Gazza.

'Hiya, Boss,' I choked, 'how are you doing?'

'Cammy,' Gazza said, acknowledging me with a finger to the eyebrow. 'I'm just here for a couple of weeks. Kind of in an observer capacity. Pretend I'm not here.'

Easier said than done, I thought. Gazza was a lazy bastard, though, so maybe, if we were lucky he would stay out of the way. But now I'm really curious.

'Where's Graham?' I asked Roger, as nonchalantly as I could.

'Not now, mate,' Roger said.

'What's happened?' I pressed.

Roger cleared his throat, rolling the phlegm on his tongue for a moment before spitting it at my feet. 'I said, we'd talk about it tomorrow.' He held my gaze for a moment, then went back to his brew. The conversation was definitely over.

I jogged back to the vehicle to find a cheery crew. They stank worse than oil-monkeys on an ocean freighter and their language wasn't any better.

'Where the fuck have you been?' Tom said.

'Skiving, mate?' Nick added.

''Ere, Cammy,' Jeff rejoined, 'remember what a fuckin' Jerry-can looks like, mate?'

'You can all fuck off,' I announced cheerily. 'I've got news for you.'

'What?' Tom said, handing me a Jerry-can while he and Nick manhandled another giant burmoil.

'Graham's gone. He must have shipped out in the Chinook.'

They almost dropped the burmoil on my toes.

'Gone? You're sure?' Jeff asked.

I nodded. 'Roger's here. And he's got Gazza with him. They're both over there, sitting in the front of Graham's vehicle. Large as bloody life. Something seriously weird is going down here.'

'I don't know whether to laugh or cry,' Tom said.

A sloshing, gurgling sound emanated from the 110's tank as more fuel poured out onto the ground around its wheels. We were full. It was time to go.

We sent bikes out to the points where the other vehicles were holed up on stag. I hopped in beside the lads and we fired up. On the way out, we pulled in beside Roger's vehicle.

'Rog,' I said, gesturing to the area we were about to depart, 'what do you want done with the burmoils?'

Roger tipped the dregs of his brew on the sand and belched loudly. 'Dig a foockin' hole. Bury 'em, for all I care.'

Laugh or cry, I thought. 'Er, Rog, it'd take a bloody JCB to dig a hole big enough for that lot.'

The RSM shrugged. 'Who foockin' gives a toss, Cammy?' He pointed to a pile of what looked like dead goats on the back of his vehicle. 'Why don't you just help yourselves to some of those and then we all just foock off and leave this place, eh?'

I screwed my eyes up and followed his gaze. Then I went round to the back of the vehicle. The dead goats turned out to be a pile of bedou coats that Phil, the RQSM, must have shipped in on the Chinook. I could have kissed him.

I grabbed an armload of them and took them back to the vehicle. When the oil-monkeys realized what they were, the mood changed appreciably. It was like bloody Christmas.

We left the LSRV a lot warmer than we'd been when we arrived. With our prized coats wrapped tightly around us, we couldn't have given a shit about the state of the place we'd just left behind. I also scarcely gave a thought to the presence of the GAZ that I could now see forming up in the convoy ahead of us. It was good just to get going, away from that place, the rest of the mission before us.

Graham had gone and that was a big gig. It should have given us plenty to talk about as we drove north again looking for an LUP. But instead we passed most of the next three hours in silence, each man left with his own thoughts about the events that had led to our CO's departure and life ahead under our new and alien command structure.

The LUP was a good one; the best, in fact, since we'd arrived in Iraq. The terrain was slightly undulating, something that can bring its own problems. But undulating is better than flat any day of the week, so our mood was bright. Tony was positively ecstatic, which means I got a smile or two out of him. Not that this big, imposing bloke was a miserable bastard. Far from it. He was just consistent, neither up nor down. A genuine stalwart. I wondered, though, how he'd cope with Roger. Graham had been one thing, but Roger was something else. With Graham in charge, we'd subsisted because people like Tony had held the show together. But now Roger and Gazza were here, it would be very different. To be honest, it was impossible to tell what effect their presence would have on the overall chemistry of the crew. Only time would tell.

The one person I felt genuinely sorry for was George. George was Graham's driver and now he was Roger's. Despite being a Para, George was a great guy. He was also our main demolition man. He could blow up anything. But far from being a Buzz or a Frank, George had his sensitive side. He was a family man who always had some building project on the go around his house. He and Tony got on particularly well, partly because they shared a love of motor-bikes. Everyone liked George, though it said a lot for Roger – or, strictly speaking, the reverse – that none of us were prepared to swap places with poor old George. I knew he would need every ounce of his sense of humour to see the rest of this campaign through. Not only did he have Roger riding up front with him, but he had Gazza, the lazy bastard, cadging a ride in the back.

I left Tony to oversee the vehicle preparations while I marched up to the brow of a nearby incline to oversee the site from a distance. As I looked back, the group was a hive of activity as vehicles backed into their allotted slots and people got on with their jobs to make the LUP secure before sun-up. We reckoned the site had been used before, since there was evidence that the depressions we were backing the vehicles into had been scraped out – probably to give a clutch of tanks hull-down positions. If that was so, we were satisfied it had all been done a long time ago and that there was no imminent danger we'd wake up surrounded by Iraqi T-72s. But you never know.

All in all, it felt like a fresh start. Like I said, Graham wasn't a bad bloke. He just wasn't cut out for the kind of operation we'd been assigned. He should never have been given the job. I wondered what would happen to him. In my time with the Regiment, I'd only ever heard of one other bloke being relieved of his command and that had been an officer who'd refused to agree to undertake a suicide mission during the Falklands campaign. The general consensus on that occasion was that the guy had been right, and so his disgrace had been minimal. Graham wasn't likely to have it so easy. Chances were he'd be finished – his career all washed up. It was like being 'branded'. I actually felt sorry for him, but in the end, RHQ had been right. He had to go.

I heard a noise behind me and turned. Roger was advancing up the slope, puffing slightly. 'Hey, Cammy, not so fast, mate.'

I pulled up. Roger offered me a smoke, which was a rarity in itself. I declined. He laughed. 'Not bloody given 'em up, 'ave you?'

I shook my head. 'Just put one out,' I said lamely. I hadn't. The truth was, I wanted to be alone. When you set up an LUP, particularly one in interesting terrain like this, you need to concentrate, not stand around chatting.

Roger clapped a friendly hand on my back. 'So 'ow are you, then?' he asked.

'Fine,' I said, keeping it tight. 'Busy, you know.'

Roger didn't get it. 'What's your verdict, Cammy?' he asked conspiratorially. 'About Graham, I mean. Did he fuck up? Has this whole operation been a waste of space?'

I kept my eyes on the preparations below. 'No,' I replied. 'Not a complete waste of space. I suppose if the boys had a single criticism it's that we've lacked teeth these past few days.'

Roger nodded sagely. 'Aye. Well, there's a new bloody sheriff in town now, lad. Things are going to change around here, you'll see.'

'Good,' I said. The corralling of the vehicles was almost complete. The GAZ was in position next to

Roger's own vehicle. I scanned along the mounds and ridges, wondering where we were going to put our sentries. Within a few minutes this place had to be secure and we weren't there yet.

'Hey,' Roger said, pointing down into the centre of the LUP. 'What are they up to?'

I followed the line his index finger was taking. There, in the midst of all the activity, were Frank and Buzz, busily setting up the 81 mm mortar. They were arguing like a couple of old women, but there was nothing unusual about that. I realized that Roger was talking about the procedure itself. Setting up the mortars was a vital part of our LUP drill. If we were compromised during the course of our day's rest, the mortars – along with our other heavy weapons – would buy us vital respite and, possibly, a means of escape.

'It's the mortar team,' I replied, not quite sure if Roger was taking the piss.

'Mortars? What the foock do you want mortars for?' Roger said, waving his hand dismissively. 'All they're good for is burning the jebel and making your bloody ears ring.'

Just then, Alec appeared.

'Ah, Alec,' Roger said, turning round. 'Perhaps, you'd care to fill me in on what's been going on around here.'

Alec frowned, not quite sure what Roger meant. The RSM had a tendency to voice the last thought that had been running through his head. Somehow, you were expected to pick up the strands. Heaven help you if you didn't.

Alec stood there, looking blank.

'About foockin' Graham,' Roger boomed. 'I want the bloody works, with no censorship. Can I count on you to do that?'

'Yes, of course, Boss,' Alec said, beaming back at him like a faithful dog that's just been bull-whipped by its master and is ready for a bit more. 'What do you want to know?'

Roger clapped a hand between his shoulder blades and they set off down the slope together like Jack and bloody Jill.

At one point, Alec had been quite a good friend, but today he scarcely gave me a glance. He had never been close to Graham, but then Graham was a loser; not the kind of guy that an ambitious sort like Alec would want to be seen to be hanging out with at all. But Roger was different. Roger was the RSM and a man of influence, even if he did have some daft tendencies. Something in Alec's face told me that he saw Roger's sudden arrival as an opportunity.

I watched Roger go, not quite sure I believed what I'd just heard. Suddenly, all those feelings I'd had about fresh starts after Graham began to drain into the desert. It looked like a case of out the frying pan and into the bloody fire.

When I got back to the vehicle, I told the boys.

'What a fucking tool,' Tom said. 'Oh well, ours not to reason why . . .' He looked towards the east. The sun was just starting to poke above the horizon. 'Hey bleeding ho, guess I'll take first stag, while you layabouts get your beauty sleep.' He loped off, his loose-fitting bedou coat slung over his webbing, giving him a curiously freakish appearance.

'The hunchback of Desert Storm,' Nick said, watching him go and shaking his head. He carried on chuckling to himself as he polished his precious Mk19.

Suddenly, H, the signaller, stuck his head under our cam-net. 'Is Roger here?' he asked.

We shook our heads.

H swore. 'RHQ wants to talk to him immediately.'

At that, we sat up. 'What's going down?' Jeff asked.

The signaller shrugged and left us. A few moments later, we saw Roger and Gazza running over from the perimeter to their vehicle. We strained to catch a word or two that might clue us into what RHQ wanted, but we heard nothing. When RHQ wants to talk to the OC immediately, it means only one thing: trouble.

About an hour later, we found out what all the commotion had been about. Roger appeared under our cam-net and joined us for a smoke. I remembered how he had an uncanny knack of knowing when there was a brew on. Sure enough, Nick was doing the honours at the back of the vehicle. 'One lump or two, Rog?' he called out.

Sarcasm is among a whole host of things that don't register on our RSM.

Roger reached out and grabbed one of my Silk Cut. 'Just for your info,' he said, 'we've got a patrol down. Some guys from B Squadron are missing. They haven't been heard of for three days.'

'Shit,' I said, 'I didn't even know B Squadron was playing over here.'

Roger, who would have known exactly what the Regiment was up to inside Saddam's backyard, lowered his voice. 'It was a foot patrol. It had been flown in by Chinook to report on MSR activity. Don't ask me why. If they did encounter a problem, they're probably E&Eing. If they didn't, I'll lay the biggest bloody fine on 'em when they get back for missing their calls.'

'Who are they?' I asked. B Squadron or not, the esprit de corps throughout the Regiment was such that we felt the loss of any member personally.

'It's led by that feller McNab,' Roger said. He trotted out the names of the others and we lapsed into silence. I remembered my encounter with McNab at the FOB. He was a tough, wiry son of a bitch, qualities that might just see him through, I figured, if he was in any kind of trouble.

Roger got up and moved onto the next vehicle to relay the sombre news to another crew. I knew a couple of the other members of the patrol pretty well. I'd taken 'Legs' Lane through selection and Vince

Phillips and I were old mates. Vince used to be A Squadron, so he was well known to quite a few of us.

'I wonder what they were up to?' Jeff asked, after Roger left us.

'Christ only knows,' I said. 'Foot patrol? Jesus.'

'Yeah,' Nick agreed. 'I thought we had it rough. But a least we got bleeding transport.'

'And now the poor sods are on the run,' Jeff said.

'Or dead.' I chucked the dregs of my tea on the ground. 'I'm sorry, but I don't buy that stuff about missing calls. If nothing else, there's always TACBE.' TACBE was a tactical beacon we carried with us for use in emergencies. It was a line-of-sight system, mainly used for communicating with overhead air-craft. As a last-ditch method of transmission it was pretty fail-safe. Which, in itself, was worrying. Why hadn't any of them used it?

'Maybe the ragheads got 'em,' Nick said.

'After that chat from the CO at the cross-brief?' Jeff asked. 'Prepare yourselves mentally for the worst and all that? Bollocks.'

'I, for one,' Nick said gravely, 'am not going to put a bullet in my brain.'

'That's 'cos you'd have to be a fuckin' marksman to find it,' Jeff said in his best Kiwi. 'And anyway, mate, you're a bloody lousy shot.'

'Sodding digger shite.'

'For the last time, diggers are from Australia.'

'What's the bloody difference? You're all convicts, aren't you?'

And so it went on. I figured it was time to get my head down. I drifted off to the gentle refrain of softly traded insults from the vehicle above me.

I was woken about ninety minutes later. Roger had decided to give us all a pep-talk over at his vehicle. I shook the sleep from my brain and stumbled over there with the rest of the lads. The only people who did not attend were the sentries. We wondered what we were about to hear. Roger was hardly the world's greatest orator, but he had all the facts in his head about what had happened these past twenty-four hours. And we were all dead curious to know.

There was a quiet air of expectancy as we assembled by his Land Rover. Roger stood next to the vehicle; Gazza sat in the front passenger seat.

'Doubtless you all know by now that Graham's been sacked and that I've been appointed to stand in his boots and sort you foockers out,' Roger started with characteristic bluntness. 'One thing I do want to make absolutely clear is that the spotlight is not on you guys. As far as RHQ is concerned, this patrol is doing all right. The problem was Graham. But the problem's sorted; and now you've got me instead.'

His eyes found me, Tony and Alec. 'I'll be working closely with the rest of the head-sheds and relying very much on your experience for the rest of the mission. Again, I stress, that RHQ's action was in no way a reflection of how they view your input into this operation.'

Tony and I remained impassive. Alec looked like the cat that had got the cream.

'As for the future,' Roger continued, 'I'm not going to foock about. We've got a bloody job to do here and we're going to do it, right?'

The assembled company rejoined with muttered endorsements like: 'Fucking A, bloody right and you bet your bollocks . . .'

Roger grinned, then nodded with satisfaction. 'Right. You know me. I'm not going to foock about with these raghead bastards. If they get in the bloody way, we foockin' doost'em, right?'

Another chorus of affirmation from the troops, this time delivered with a mock Yorkshire accent, just to show we were on top of things: 'Aye, we foockin' doost'em.'

'There's no change to the overall plan,' Roger said, winding things up. 'From here, we head north and keep heading north until we get to the MSRs. There'll be no more heading south. I think we're all done with that particular move. Questions?'

'Yeah,' somebody shouted from the back. 'What do we do with the GAZ?'

'We blow the foocker to smithereens,' Roger replied, really getting into his stride.

Claps, cheers and wolf-whistles erupted from the crowd.

Roger's chest swelled with pride. He was into a routine now that was three parts George Patton, seven parts Geoffrey Boycott. 'None of your bloody woofter let's dig a hole and bury the bloody thing with stones. We stuff it full of plastic and evaporate the bastard. Next?'

There were no further questions. Everybody got the gist. Roger gave us what we wanted to hear. After a week of pissing about, we were back in business. I think, if he'd asked us to, we'd have saddled up and rode out to storm Saddam's palace, we were so fired up. Like I said, Roger isn't your master tactician, but he's the right bloke to have around if it's action you're looking for.

We were about to break up the party when Gazza got to his feet. I thought we were going to get a bunch of Rodney–Rupert bullshit about the need for strong morale and keeping our chins up, but Gazza delivered a surprisingly sensitive speech, as it turned out, about his role in the proceedings from hereon in. 'In short,' he concluded, 'I'm not coming in as a head-shed, I'm here as a tom; so things can carry on as normal. Don't let my presence interfere with the decision-making process. A couple of weeks from now and I'll be out of here. I'm just along for the ride. So, er, thanks for having me and let's go kick some ass.'

We adjourned back to our vehicle. It was still only mid-afternoon, so we got a brew going and sat down to chew over our prospects under the new regime.

'Well,' Tom said, 'it looks like there really is a new sheriff in town.'

'You changed your tune a bit,' I said.

'What do you mean?'

'Well, I seem to remember you calling our RSM a tool this morning after his wise words about the tactical value of mortars in the desert.'

At that moment, there was rustle of the cam-net and Roger stuck his head in. For a moment, I thought he must have overheard our conversation, but he just beamed broadly and said: 'Who are the smokers on this wagon?'

Tom and I hesitated. Roger's capacity for cadging smokes was legendary.

Roger shrugged. 'Ay oop, makes no bloody difference to me,' he said, chucking three cartons of Silk Cut, B&H and Marlboros into the back of the Land Rover. 'You can sort that lot out between yourselves.'

For a second or two, Tom and I studied each other in silence.

It was me who eventually broke it. 'Like I was saying, great bloke is our Rog. The best. Wouldn't hear a word against him.'

Tom shook his head. 'What a bloody crap-hat tart you are, Cameron.'

I scarcely heard him. I grabbed the Silk Cut and stuffed them into my webbing. Yup, war was hell.

But with tobacco in my pocket, I reckoned I might just see this one through to the end.

Later that afternoon, I went over to see how George was getting on with the GAZ. As someone who'd done a fair amount of demolition work myself, I wanted to see how he was cracking the problem. I also wanted to see how he was coping with Roger.

I caught up with him over by the Iraqi vehicle. It still contained the bodies of the two officers who'd compromised us.

George was surrounded by the tools of his trade. There were explosives everywhere. And where the ground wasn't taken up with plastic slab charges or bar-mines, it was covered with bits of detonator.

George, I was glad to see, had made a little seat for himself out of two slab charges and was smoking away like a chimney. For anybody not familiar with the art of dems, the sight would be a little unnerving. But George knew his stuff. He was in his element. He'd been told to get rid of something and, being the perfectionist he was, he was going to do a good job of it.

'Wotcher,' I said. 'How's it going?'

George grunted as he wrestled with some tape. The cigarette was clamped firmly between his lips. He finally won his battle with the tape reel and came up for air. 'Good, mate,' he replied. 'Nearly there.'

The dems course is three months long and pretty

intensive. Twelve weeks, eight hours a day, it's an unrelenting routine. We learn about Munro Effect, shockwaves, initiation angles and a neat little formula to do with the breadth and thickness of a target that allows us to calculate how many pounds of plastic we need to get rid of it. The GAZ was hardly a bridge or a building, but it still required knowledge and subtlety to dispose of it properly. The course taught us where to place charges on an axle or a chassis to achieve maximum penetration and cut; how distance between each charge is critical to the overall effectiveness of the explosion. As a graduate of this select course, I was familiar with these things. To George, however, who wasn't just a graduate, but an instructor, it was all second nature.

As I walked around the GAZ, I could see that George had decided to leave the manual on the shelf. A bar-mine is a powerful device – enough to put a main battle tank on its back if you know what you're doing. George had placed not one, but two in the rear of the Iraqi vehicle. As if that wasn't enough, I noticed he'd crammed slab charges, which if you break them down into their individual blocks are like two-pound bricks of explosive, into any gap big enough to take them: between the brakes, up into the engine block, behind the dash; you name it, they were everywhere. George was now involved in the intricate task of connecting them all up with det-cord so that they blew in the right sequence. From the various other bits and bobs around his feet, I could see that he intended to do this one on a timer, set to go off, most likely, when we were many miles from this place.

'I see there's no need to ask how you're going to do this one,' I said.

George shook his head. 'Roger wants it vaporized, that's what he's gonna get.'

'Them, too?' I asked, pointing to the two bodies in the back.

George pushed some buttons on one of his timers to check it was working. 'Uh huh,' he replied, without looking up, 'it's all going up in smoke.'

This was not a decision that RHQ would have taken lightly. Mutilation of the dead is not something we derive any pleasure from. But we were behind enemy lines and couldn't afford to take any passengers, dead or alive. One way or another we had to dispose of the evidence of our encounter. The GAZ and its occupants were about to become history.

'Will you promise me something,' I said, taking the bull by the horns.

'Sure. What?'

'Don't let him get to you.'

George stopped what he was doing and looked at me. 'Who?'

'Roger. You know what he can be like.'

George smiled. 'Bah. Don't worry about me. I'll be fine. I survived so far, didn't I?'

'Yeah, but you've got two of them with you, this time.'

As if on cue, at that moment, Gazza turned up. As an observer, a lot of the time he didn't have anything better to do except be a nuisance. He was about to help himself to one of the brews I'd just made for George and myself when his eyes switched to George's makeshift seat and the fag dangling precariously from his lips. He made his excuses and left, his face a lot paler.

'Hasn't got a clue that one, bless 'im,' George said, without once having given him a glance. With a flurry of last-minute finger activity, he seemed to be done. 'There, that should do it. Now, where's that brew?'

'I don't suppose there's any chance this lot won't go off,' I said, handing him his tea.

'Don't worry,' George replied, 'she'll go. I don't want to come back to this place any more than you do.'

We sat there, drinking our brews in silence. On the surface, this was the same old George; the George I'd known for ages. But, at the same time, there was something different about him. George had a great sense of humour, but I'd seen no sign of it out here. I was worried that things were getting on top of him. When your bread-and-butter business is explosives it pays to keep your wits about you. Being that close to Roger and Gazza, though, was enough to get anyone down.

An hour later, with darkness upon us, we moved out. There was a new mood about the crew as we set off. We were heading north with new leadership. It seemed inevitable that we would shortly see action.

Two hours later, the convoy came to a halt and we all looked to the south. I checked my watch. It was coming up to nine o'clock. Behind me, I heard Nick count down the seconds. Just before he reached zero, there was a flash on the horizon. For a second or two, the light blotted out the stars. Then my night vision returned and the constellations above us with it.

We heard nothing but the wind, so we pressed on.

We drove for several hours through the gently rolling dunes, maintaining our standard drill: vehicles in line astern around 100 metres apart, Unimog in the middle, bikes to the front and sides. The boys took it in turns to ride the Cannons and, right now, it was Tom's go. I had a quick scan, but couldn't see him. Jeff and I had PNGs strapped to our faces, but for the moment we weren't using them. It was that bright. Like a visor, PNGs hinged upwards when you didn't need them.

Of all the environments I have worked in, the night sky in the Middle East takes some beating. Perhaps it was the comparative cleanliness of the atmosphere or the lack of light pollution, but on some nights you could gaze up at the heavens and it would seem like you were in space. This was one of those nights. The moon was waning, but still close to full and there were so many stars it was tough picking out the constellations. Tom and Jeff were both extremely competent navigators. My sense of direction wasn't half as developed, so I had to work on it. To help me and Nick along, we used to play a navigation game during our long night moves. It helped to break the monotony, but it had a constructive purpose to it, too. If you can navigate by the moon and the stars, provided you're out on a night with no cloud cover, you'll never get lost. I found myself picking out Orion's Belt, the Plough and the Southern Cross and computing the points of the compass from each.

'All right, smartarse,' I said to Jeff, when I thought I'd got it cracked, 'give me west from Cassiopeia.'

Jeff took a second to acquire the constellation and one more to point out the required bearing. I checked the compass. The bastard was spot-on. What was more, it was almost like it was in-built with him, as natural as pointing out left and right.

'OK . . .' I continued, determined to catch him out at something, 'how about 173 degrees, using . . . Perseus.'

This time, it took him around five seconds. Nick and I measured his answer off our compasses. 'Fuck me,' said the BFG, 'what are you, Patrick Moore's bloody long-lost cousin?'

'Read those compasses and weep, arseholes.'

Nick gave a snort of contempt. It doesn't pay to get him riled. As the Incredible Hulk is inclined to say, you wouldn't like him when he's angry. We didn't like him much when he was nice.

'Congratulations,' I said, 'you are through to the final round. But to win our star prize – ha-bleeding-ha – you have to give me, in no more than ten seconds, 274 degrees, using the . . . moon.'

'And if I don't?'

'My beautiful assistant, Nick, will tear your head off at the fucking roots. Your time starts . . . now.'

While Nick counted him down, which should have been enough to put anyone off, Jeff got cracking. This was the ultimate test, since you had to know whether the moon was waxing or waning, what time it came up over the horizon and what position it was during its nightly orbit.

With two seconds still on the clock, Jeff indicated the bearing.

Nick checked his compass and shook his head. 'That is unnatural,' he said, with not a little wonder in his voice.

'It's the Maori in me,' Jeff said. 'You've either got it or you ain't.'

We carried on chewing the cud about nothing in particular, just trying to keep ourselves alert. Suddenly, I saw the vehicle ahead come to a stop. We pulled up abruptly and waited. I lowered my PNGs, but saw nothing.

Initially, the stoppage did not cause us any concern. I could see the two guys on the vehicle in front back-to-back scanning the area. Behind me, Nick was doing the same with his pocket scope.

Still, we saw nothing. So, we sat back and relaxed a little.

After about ten minutes, and still no sign of us going anywhere, Jeff turned to me and said: 'What're the fuckers doing up front? Have they dozed off or something?'

I put away the cigarette I'd been about to light up. Even before he'd said it, an alarm started going off in the back of my brain. Something wasn't right here at all. Maybe a vehicle had broken down or, worse, the lead 110 had gone over a wadi.

I was just getting down from the vehicle to go check on the score when I heard the distinctive revs of a Cannon coming down the line.

'Something's up,' Nick announced. I saw the bike at the same moment.

It was Taff. He pulled up alongside us. 'There's fucking enemy to our front,' he said breathlessly.

'No, there fucking ain't,' I said. 'We've scanned and seen nothing.'

'Check the skyline,' he replied, then hauled the bike around and headed back to the front of the convoy.

We trained our night optics and scopes in the direction he'd indicated.

For a moment, I saw nothing. Then, I felt the skin crawl on the back of my neck.

There it was, no more than 300 metres away; the

hunkered-down silhouette of a troop carrier. *Jesus*. I blinked behind the cold eye-piece of my PNG and saw another, its outline blurred by a cam-net. A thicket of masts jutted upwards between them. And then, as my eyes became accustomed to the range, I saw men moving around on the brow of an incline beside the vehicles.

A moment later, Tom, on the other Cannon, appeared out of the gloom and came alongside. I lifted the catch and raised my PNGs onto their hinge.

'Cammy, put the fucker back down, mate. You look better with them on.'

I reminded him he was no oil painting himself.

It took a minute for my eyes to readjust to the synthetic image. I squinted hard at the figures moving around on the ridge and saw the tell-tale glow of a cigarette.

It was a second or two before Tom spoke again. Behind the revs of the Cannon, he suddenly sounded very serious. 'This is not good, Cammy. It's a big position.'

I did a 360 and picked up more men and vehicles through the scope. We fixed each position with the GPS and plotted the coordinates.

Despite the cold, I felt a trickle of sweat roll down my back. They were everywhere.

I struggled to clear my thinking. It was bad enough that we were in the thick of the enemy. But what about the position itself? Was it a fully prepared defensive enclave – complete with minefields, wire obstacles and interlocking arcs of fire – or a temporary position, like one of our LUPs? I thought back to the way we'd just stumbled across it and figured it must be the latter. Even so, things didn't look great. The main concentration of activity was up ahead. The Iraqis were on two low escarpments either side of our track. If they started firing at us, then Jeff was the man in the hot seat. The New Zealander was an OK driver, but he wasn't in the same league as Tom or Nick. There was no time to change positions and Jeff knew that. It only took for him to stall or miss a gear-change and we had a major gang-fuck on our hands. I guess he'd clocked that, too. But Jeff was already scanning the terrain ahead with his pocket scope for obstacles.

Nick leaned forward from his position by the Mk19. 'Push forward five metres and angle off hard-left,' he said softly.

Jeff didn't need to be told twice. It was a sound bit of advice and good to see the team pulling together. By moving in this way, the 110 was now end-on to the main threat, its rear grenade launchers pointing towards the closest of the enemy positions. Our Land Rovers had clusters of four grenade launchers at each corner. They were loaded with white-phos primed to detonate in an air burst around 125 metres away. The launchers are all angled and elevated slightly differently, so that when they are initiated – by a set of switches on the dash next to the driver's position – they provide a comprehensive smoke screen behind which you can make good your escape. That was the theory, anyhow.

I left Jeff and Nick on the vehicle and walked ahead to Tony's lead 110. Alec and Roger joined us. We did some fast talking. This was a major obstacle, and we were right in the middle of it. It was made worse by the fact we did not know anything about the enemy's strength, his depth or his weaponry.

Our options were simple. We could either back up, fight our way out or attempt to carry on through. While we were talking, I kept my eye on the ridgeline. As long as we could see the firefly glows of cigarette pulls we knew we were OK. A second or two passed and no sign of one. The tension mounted. Then an Iraqi took another drag. I went back to the meeting.

Roger listened to the rest of the head-sheds. We told him we needed to pass through this area to get to the MSR further to the north. If we turned back, chances were we'd run into another position just like this one somewhere else. We had to get eyes-on that bloody east–west MSR and start looking for Scuds. We'd practised set-pieces many times like this during our training sessions in the UAE. If things turned noisy, the second and third vehicles would break left and right to open up their arcs of fire. As soon as they – we – started firing, the back two 110s would leg it with the mother support craft in tow. While the

Unimog kept going, the two 110s would pull up around a klick from the action and start laying down a fire-base, taking the pressure off us. Then, after we'd broken for it, they'd catch up with the Unimog and head for the ERV – the emergency rendez-vous. Basically, we could put in as many fire-bases and withdrawals as we needed till we'd disengaged from the enemy.

In short, this was a contingency we'd provided for. The decision was unanimous.

'Let's just fucking do it,' Alec said. 'Death or glory.'

He was only half-kidding. The bottom line was: we pressed on.

I legged it back to my vehicle and briefed Jeff and Nick. It was a risk, but one we had to take.

'Let's hope we've made the right call,' Nick said.

'There is no other call,' I said. 'Sorry, mate.'

We edged forward, watching the enemy for the slightest reaction. A raghead so much as farted and we were poised to go nuclear.

Suddenly, there was a flurry of sparks from the ridge. Someone had stubbed his fag out in a hurry. Others followed suit. The scattered embers looked like fireworks on the Fourth of July.

No question; they'd seen us.

We held our breath, but kept moving. There was no reaction from the ridge. The stalemate was on. They were watching us as intently as we were watching them. Trying to be analytical about it, I knew we held one significant advantage: we knew who they were, while they were only wondering about us. But for how long? Still, we kept edging forward.

And then, a niggling worry bubbled into my mind. If this went noisy, what about the blokes on the bikes? If one of them got hit or dropped his machine going over a boulder, the first we'd know about it would be when we stopped at our emergency RV and found him missing.

I called Tom over. 'Keep tight,' I said, cupping my hands close to his ear. He got the drift and stuck to the Land Rover like glue.

Our only hope was to make our location work in our favour. We were triple-figure klicks inside Iraq. As the head-sheds, we opted to put our trust in an Iraqi assumption that we were just another of their units on manoeuvre.

It sounded good, but none of us were that convinced.

We continued to brass it out, moving slowly, bit by bit; stopping, watching their reactions, moving again, stopping.

There comes a point where you question the decisions you've made. I'd crossed that point an age ago, but Jeff voiced it. 'What the fuck are we playing at?' he said, as the major position we had first seen inched past on our right flank.

We all had the uncomfortable feeling we were driving into an ambush. Each of us was waiting for the first shot that would signal the free-for-all.

The terrain started to flatten out. At one point, we heard the hum of a generator and saw a group of AFVs no more than a few dozen metres to our right. We pressed on and saw more vehicles. It was an armoured troop hauled up for the night – and we'd damn near driven right through it.

And then, suddenly, there was nothing but the wind and the purr of our engines in our ears. My night-scope registered nothing but empty desert and the star-strewn canopy above our heads.

After several minutes of this, Nick said: 'If the fuckers ain't burrowed underground, I think we're through.'

I felt the urge for a good roll-up as the reality started to sink in. We'd passed right through the middle of their lines. We'd made it.

Our sitrep to headquarters the following morning would see to it that this position was bombed before the day was out.

SEVEN

After our move through the enemy position, we were pretty keyed up, I guess you could say elated. We'd been lucky, but then we knew we'd also done a fair bit to create our own luck. We were back where we did things best, in the heart of enemy territory.

As for the vehicle team, I could tell we were acclimatizing. Like the rest of the convoy, we'd pretty much come over with a standard uniform. But as we relaxed, little touches of individual style showed through.

Tom's trade-mark were his braces. These looked like they'd come straight out the First World War or some Alf Garnett episode. He wore them over the top of his lightweight jacket and so tight it seemed like they were doing him a permanent injury. Capping this faintly comical appearance was his webbing, which he'd adapted from an old RAF waistcoat. Like me, he'd played around with the existing pockets and added some touches of his own to cater for those little bits of kit that he considered indispensable: spare bullets, maybe, water, food and grenades.

With Nick, it was his dish-dash. When done properly, these can look pretty good, lending to their wearers a touch of real Lawrence of Arabia style. But Nick never quite managed the technique. It looked like someone had parked a load of vehicle swab rags on top of his head – which, in fact, wasn't that far from the truth. By our second week in Iraq, this thing was really beginning to acquire a life of its own. Whenever Nick was short of a bit of cloth – for anything, he said, but I didn't like to inquire too closely – he used his dish-dash. When people started declaring it a health-hazard, he embarked on a different tack. Now, when he needed to check the oil or rub down his weapon, he cut a little piece off his head gear, then used it. The result made him look like a kind of punk version of Obi-Wan Kenobi. If he met a lifelong native of these parts, he wouldn't have had to worry about using his gun. He would've scared the poor bastard shitless.

Jeff was still too new with us to have acquired many peculiarities. I suspect, if push ever came to shove, he'd have kicked off his kit, daubed on a bit of war-paint, and taken on the Iraqis Maori-style.

With me, it was my metal mug. This thing had more character than a whole battalion of Paras. Years of tea-drinking had stained it progressively darker so that now, even after a good washing, the insides had turned black. Tom was convinced it was a serious NBC hazard and would only drink from it if desperate. No one else would touch it with a barge-pole. I loved my mug, because it was so multi-functional. I did everything with it: clean my teeth, shave, use it as a shovel and even drink from it. For some reason, it became the subject of derision throughout the convoy. Some of the boys would refuse to come over to our wagon and socialize if the mug was present. This led to some ugly talk between Tom, Nick and Jeff about what they would do if they ever caught up with it and I wasn't around. It got to the point, almost, where I couldn't trust them alone with it. So, I watched it like a hawk. Gradually, the threats eased off. I think even those that felt threatened by it most came to look on it as something that gave us war-winning potential.

As much as anything else, our move through the enemy position had taught us a new and vital lesson: because of our location, the Iraqis had thought we were part of the home team. They wanted to trust in the belief we were one of their patrols. Anything less, I suppose, would have struck at the foundations of the belief system that Saddam had built up around them – that they were invincible in the face of the soft Western heathens across the border in Saudi Arabia. Somehow, we had to exploit this arrogance; let it work for us. It'd take balls, but we'd seen it work once and there was no reason why we shouldn't let it work for us again.

So much for the theory. At long last, we were approaching our primary objective, the main east–west supply routes along which Saddam was rolling a lot of his logistics, including a good proportion of his Scud arsenal. The MSRs would be where it all came together – or all fell apart. And despite our current high, the more objective among us knew it could go either way.

The hinge-point in our destiny was Rog.

In so many ways Roger was a great bloke. After the disastrous days of the Graham era, indeed, he was a breath of fresh air, the guy who galvanized us back into action and made us believe in ourselves again.

But he had his limitations. The nub of the problem, I guess, was that he wasn't exactly your deep thinker. Not that any of us thought of ourselves as rocket scientists. With Roger, though, the term 'laid-back' soared to new and hitherto unexplored heights. In the old days, his behaviour would have been portrayed as eccentric derring-do, a whiff of the Drake spirit that made the British great, especially in times of crisis. But in a war that was supposed to be running on a split-second schedule, where everything had to come together like clockwork, there wasn't a whole lot of room for blokes who wanted to play bowls while the Republican Guard's T-72s were pouring over the horizon.

Soon after we set up our LUP, we got out the maps and began studying the MSRs that, all being well, we would hit during the next night's move. Our brief, of course, was to report back any Scud-related activity and, if the situation warranted it, to take it out. But we all knew that if a particularly big and juicy convoy came along that had nothing to do with the Scud, we'd still have a crack at it. And, frankly, looking at the map, there was every chance we'd soon be seeing action.

If the charts were right, there was a significant MSR ahead of us. Not the main, east–west routes that bisected the country, those were still a couple of hundred klicks to the north. This was the MSR that Tony and I had been contemplating bare hours before we'd been compromised by the Iraqi artillery crew. It was characterized by a stretch of road that, for some reason, branched off and looped south for a while, before rejoining it a little way downstream.

If we proceeded north on our current bearing, we would hit this looped stretch of road first. So, the head-sheds grouped and pondered our best approach, knowing that the point at which we hit the MSR was critical. If we did need to engage any targets, we'd take them out, withdraw and lie low for a while, then come back and hit the road again somewhere else. But to do this required a lot of careful thought and strategy and detailed coordination with RHQ. The last thing we wanted was to hit a piece of road that was already under observation by another SAS convoy.

With all this in mind, I turned to Roger, who'd

been pacing impatiently around the vehicle, and said: 'Rog, what's your view on this?'

Roger stopped and looked at us. Then he walked over to the bonnet and jabbed an index finger at the map. 'Listen,' he said, 'I don't give a shit where we hit the road. All I care about is that there are things moving on it. And if there are, mark my bloody words, we're gonna foockin' doost'em.'

Tony coughed. 'No, Boss, it's important we hit the road in the right place.'

'Ah, bollocks . . .' Roger began.

Just then, Alec took a step forward. 'Yeah, Tony, what the fuck does it matter where we hit the damn' thing?' And with that the two of them strode off back to Roger's vehicle.

Tony and I looked at each other. Neither of us said anything, but our thoughts were the same. Roger had just got him a right-hand man. If we weren't careful, the head-sheds were going to be split down the middle. And that wouldn't do at all.

The truth was, Roger didn't know what a lat and long was, much less care. This was worrying because following our daily sitrep to RHQ, the convoy coordinators came back to us with about ten minutes' worth of lat and long information, all of which had to be jotted down and plotted onto our maps. Observing this ritual was important, not to say vital, as it gave us the locations of other convoys operating in our area. All of us – bar Roger, but including Alec –

were aware of the need for deconfliction; that is, steering clear of our own side. The history of covert warfare is full of instances of own goals, so called 'blue-on-blue' or 'friendly fire' engagements, and none of us wanted to end up on that particular list of statistics.

Doubly disturbing was the fact that Rog had already shown his disdain for some of the details that could spell the difference between mission success and failure. The previous day he'd grabbed the radio headset off H, given it a cursory listen, and then asked why H was 'listening to this shit'. It had been the very lat and long information that had just been the subject of our head-sheds' discussion. Luckily, H had taken it upon himself to listen in secretly to this data as and when it came over the ether, like a kid tuning a transistor radio under his pillow after lights-out.

Given Roger's predisposition towards a hasty decision, we also agreed that one of us should hang around and listen in whenever 'Sunray' was called to the radio. Sunray was Roger's call-sign. It was fortunate that we did, because no sooner had Rog departed the meeting than the call went out that RHQ was on the line and urgently seeking dialogue with Sunray.

We got the gen later from H, who, true to form, had loitered around the radio on some pretext or other while Roger crouched next to the set and listened for long seconds while the 'urgent' news was relayed to him. Even though the conversation was one-sided, H got the gist of it.

'How many?' Roger had asked, the irritation on his face rapidly replaced by a more sombre expression. A pause, then: 'A Squadron, you're sure?' Another gap. 'On the run? Jesus, what a foockin' mess.' The one-way conversation continued this way for a minute or so, before Roger eventually signed off and H made himself scarce.

A few minutes later, H was at our wagon giving us the news.

From the sound of it, the other A Squadron half-convoy had got itself into a shit-load of trouble. It looked like we had guys dead, others missing. This was worse than the news we'd got about McNab and his lot. We knew these people well. They were friends, good friends. Their wives and their girlfriends knew ours. Their kids played with ours. Worst of all, was not knowing. Our minds went into overdrive as we tried to work out what had happened and who the casualties were, but in the end we knew it was so much useless speculation. So a bunch of us made our way over to Roger's wagon. We had to know or we'd have gone crazy.

At first, he was irritated that we knew anything about it. Then, after we gave him some bullshit about how we'd come by the information, he merely shrugged and gave us the scant details that RHQ had given him. The other half-squadron convoy had been carrying out a recce on a target when they'd got compromised. One vehicle had been completely shot up. The rest of the patrol had been separated in the firefight, vehicles scattered every which-way and blokes presumed to be E&Eing it back to our lines.

Roger swore that he hadn't been given any names. We believed him. From the look on his face, he was as cut up as the rest of us. All he knew was that there were casualties and some were presumed to be serious.

So now the Regiment had another patrol missing. We tried to put it behind us as we moved out that night, but it stuck to us like dog-shit. The night that Fortune had smiled on our patrol it had also decided to crap on our sister convoy, and from a great height. Our elation had long since evaporated, like fuel spirit in the wind. In a way I couldn't explain, I felt guilty, but from the drained looks on the faces of the men around me, I could see I wasn't the only one.

That night, we reached the looped stretch of road south of the MSR that we needed to observe before heading up-country. It was hard-standing, which at least gave it the capacity to handle large volumes of traffic, but so quiet, we knew we could be there a week and still not see a thing. We figured it was this quiet, because it led nowhere except into Saudi. The real movement was going on east–west further to the north. So, we moved on, edging forward under cover of an especially dark night, till we got to the second road.

Here, we saw the odd vehicle, but it, too, seemed exceptionally still, considering we were almost three weeks into the war. So quiet, in fact, that we elected to drive several kilometres up and down it just to see if we could see anything.

It was my turn behind the wheel. Jeff was out on the bike, scouting ahead of us and at the flanks for signs of trouble. We had four bikes altogether and, as long as the terrain was good, we used them as much as possible. Those few times that we didn't was because the ground just got too treacherous. For treacherous, read rocks, which could suddenly materialize in the form of boulder-fields that seemed to go on for ever. When we encountered one of these, the bikes would be lashed to the Unimog and the riders would return to their parent vehicles. With four bods on the wagon, things were tight, but manageable. Nick, for instance, would have had a tough time swinging the Mk19 with Jeff in the back as well, but if needs must, he'd have done it.

Tonight the terrain was good and it was comforting to know that we had four extra pairs of eyes out there. It was agreed that the head-sheds wouldn't ride the Cannons, as it took us out of the decision-loop should an emergency materialize. It can be an isolating experience sitting out there on the saddle for hours at a time. There is a definite knack to riding a bike in the desert at night. Unlike the vehicle drivers, the bike riders tended not to resort to wearing full PNGs. This was because if anything happened and these heavy optics got knocked off the face, especially during a contact, the rider was left effectively blind until his night vision returned. Instead, most resorted to using the smaller hand-held optics we carried. The technique was to stop the bike, scout the ground ahead for obstacles or other trouble spots, then put the device away, drive up to the periphery of the optics' visual range and go through the whole procedure again.

After almost two weeks in the desert, it was weird to be driving up and down a road again. Because there was still plenty of ambient light from the moon, I decided to drive without PNGs. Nick and Tom used their hand-held optics to plot the way ahead, calling out whenever we approached a cautionary feature, such as a bend in the road or a bad pot-hole. On a night like this, the hand-held night-vision devices probably gave them a range of around 300 metres.

Eventually, we turned off the road and carried on moving north across the desert. The road had been unremarkable except for one thing. We'd noted some large raised hatches set back a little way from the edge of the hard-standing surface and regularly spaced about a couple of kilometres apart.

'Strange place for a sewage tunnel,' Tom said, glancing back at one of these objects as the road receded from view behind us.

I shrugged. 'Lot of shit to shift from Baghdad, I expect.'

Tom nodded, apparently satisfied by some hidden wisdom at the core of this nonsense. But he was right. Way out here, in the middle of nowhere, it was a strange place for anything.

To the east, the sky lit up with intermittent flashes. Another Coalition air raid was dishing it out, most probably on the Republican Guard, which we knew to be holed up in that general area. It was a sight that evoked mixed emotions. On the one hand, we were delighted that the enemy was catching it, since it could only help shorten the war – if you happen to get caught on the ground by a squadron or two of B-52s, it tends to focus the mind on important issues like life. On the other, the raids would undoubtedly be stirring up a hornet's nest of activity, fallout from which we might well catch. In this business, it's always good to let sleeping dogs lie.

A few minutes after we turned off the road, the convoy started to slow. We'd only just had a routine stop, so immediately we knew that something was wrong.

'Oh shit,' Nick said, 'not another bloody enemy position.'

I gently eased on the brakes and lifted myself out of the seat to get a bit of height. The three of us remained in silence for several minutes, staring at the ground ahead. After our move through the large Iraqi unit the previous night, my first thought, like Nick, was that we were back amongst the enemy again. Gradually, however, as my eyes became accustomed to the synthetic ether projected by my hand-held scanner, I discerned something I could recognize in the distance. Like the first stars that come out at night, little pin-pricks of light began to form before my eyes.

'No,' I replied, half-turning to the BFG, 'this is altogether different.'

In front of us was an enormous comms site, lit, like so many other installations we had seen in Iraq, like the proverbial Christmas tree. I could tell that it was a communications complex because, as we edged closer, the whole place was wall-to-wall masts, dishes and aerials. The frightening thing was there was no sign of anything on our maps – another feather in the cap for the int community back home.

We heard from one of the outriders that the lead vehicle had crested an incline and almost driven straight into the perimeter. It had been another near-run thing, but since our lives over the past couple of weeks had been nothing but near-run things, we brushed this one off for the time-being. Later, at our next LUP, we'd remind each other of the need to stay vigilant at all times.

We decided to take the vehicles up for a better look. We sat there for fifteen minutes scanning and taking notes. This would be a big one to report in our next sitrep. There was always the chance that RHQ would come back and ask us to take it out, although much more likely that the job would be assigned to aircraft. Either way, they'd need an exact set of coordinates.

We debated whether or not to use our ranging lasers since there's always a possibility that the energy squirt will get picked up by sensors posted around the site or by some abdul in the wrong place who winds up with the red dot on his tunic. It was a short debate. 'Fuck it,' Roger said, 'let's just do it and get the hell out of here. Personally, I'm about ready for beans on bloody toast.'

So, we lased the place bang in the middle and fed the coordinates into our GPS sets. Roger had a point. If you're going to do something, you might as well do it properly. If you don't, some bright spark in a tent in Saudi is just going to get on the horn and tell you to do it all over again.

Daybreak found H on the radio busily reporting everything we'd seen during the night. We told RHQ that the two routes we'd crossed were inactive and unremarkable, unless they were interested in dispatching us on a hands and knees, do-or-die job down a sewage tunnel into central Baghdad. We also told them about the comms centre.

More in hope than anticipation, we asked if they wanted us to do a FAC on the thing. The problem was, to carry out a meaningful bit of forward air controlling – directing bombs onto the target by radio

– we'd have to use our non-secure TACBEs and that was bound to be viewed as a no-no.

We were right. A few hours later, RHQ came back and told us to forget about the comms complex. The flyboys would handle it without any extra help from us. The exact coordinates we'd passed along – accurate, thanks to GPS, to less than a metre – would be handy when they came to priming their smart weapons, however, so we weren't made to feel totally useless.

The transmission ended with an unexpected directive. The raised hatches we'd seen beside the road were not – surprise, surprise – anything to do with Baghdad's sanitation system, but access tunnels to an elaborate fibre-optic military communications network, which, as far as RHQ could tell, linked multiple Scud launch sites around the country to the command structure in the capital. We were to go back to the patch of road where we'd seen them, get into the viaduct that ran beneath them and sever the line; blow the damn thing up, with extreme prejudice. Furthermore, if we ever came across the hatches again, we were to do the exact same thing – evaporate them.

'Blimey,' Alec said at the head-sheds' meeting, 'somebody, somewhere must really hate those things.'

'Optic cables?' Roger snorted when he was given the news, 'they've been in the sun too bloody long back in Saudi. I'll bet we'll get in that viaduct and find ourselves knee-deep in jundie shit.'

But none of us were that bothered. It was something to go and check out. If it turned out the hatches led to some kind of waste pipe or sewer it would present us with a glorious opportunity to take the piss out of Green Slime. If it transpired, on the other hand, they were right, then we had us some serious blowing up to do.

'If Roger's right and it is just shit,' Nick said back at the vehicle, 'at least we can't stink any worse than we do right now.'

The truth was, I hadn't noticed, but he was probably right. The only water most of us used outside of drinking was for our teeth. Some blokes brought razors with them and that was acceptable. But none of us washed. After a while, you don't become aware of your own smell anymore, which is just as well. Considering we were living in dangerously close proximity to one another, the miracle of it was that we didn't notice each other's either. One theory was that we all stank as bad as the next man, so the smell just cancelled itself out. Another was that the layer of sand that covered each of us from head to toe sealed it all in.

It's surprising how used you get to your own stink. After one jungle trip, I got back to Hereford with a set of combats that had been stuck to my body for six weeks. When I opened up the bag that contained them, I almost died from the smell. The overpowering stench of ammonia could have woken a corpse. Yet, at the time, I'd never noticed a thing; and no one else had commented either.

Another one, I suppose, for Arthur C. Clarke's World Of Weird Shit.

Later that afternoon, I went to see George, the dems expert who'd been responsible for reducing the GAZ to fairy-dust. Bits of bomb kit were everywhere. More disturbingly, I could see that he had his mad explosives head on. You can tell this by asking George a mundane question and checking his eyes for a special kind of unfocused stare you get back.

What I got was real rabid dog stuff.

On this occasion, the overall impression you'd walked into a serious health-hazard area was exacerbated by the presence of Buzz. The two of them were in deep discussion about the best way to access the hatches and blow up the viaduct that ran beneath. It was like watching Dr Frankenstein and his crazed assistant preparing to do a bit of brain-surgery.

George wanted to use incendiary charges, which, set off in the right way, would not just fracture the cables and bring down a lot of shit in the process, but melt them so badly they would be beyond repair. He was seriously enjoying himself, humming and whistling as he went along. It was good to see this. Since Roger had appeared, George had really withdrawn into himself. The poor sod wasn't having a good war. First driving for Graham and now Roger. It was enough to drive anyone mad.

The more George fiddled with his little bits of kit, the more Buzz brimmed with irritation. Eventually, the guy whose next favourite pastime was skinning large animals could stand it no longer. Buzz threw his hands up in despair. 'Come on, George, let's just make bloody bombs here, for Christ's sake.'

'My dear Buzz,' George said, adopting a mock Sherlock Holmes demeanour, 'what do you think we're doing?'

'We're fucking tinkering around, that's what. We've got enough explosives to start World War bleeding Three. Let's just fill the viaduct and blow it.'

'Ah, but that would never do,' George replied, still in the manner of the Great Detective. 'You never know when you might need this stuff. It is a very precious commodity. You should show more respect, Buzz.'

Buzz glanced up and saw me standing there. 'Fucking engineer,' he said, looking back over his shoulder at our chief explosives expert. But it was said without rancour. Everybody liked George, who'd come to the Regiment from 9 Squadron, the Royal Engineers, a dedicated unit that's attached to the Paras for special ops. There was no one better at making things disappear in a hurry.

I was genuinely intrigued to know how George was going to do this one. The viaduct was probably five to ten feet below road-level. At that depth, guaranteeing initiation and then gaining proof that the charge had gone off were not as easy as they sounded.

I asked George how he intended to crack the initiation problem.

'Command detonation,' he replied, matter of factly. 'Technically, we could go for timed or on-site, but command is best, I think.'

I nodded. A timed delay was out of the question because once we left the site, we'd have no proof that the explosive had gone off. And RHQ was big on proof for this mission. On-site detonation was also a little bit messy, since it needed three elements – cocking handle, safety fuse and detonator – to work flawlessly on the way to the explosive itself. Command det, on the other hand, involving a transmitter/receiver to set off the detonator, had a number of advantages: it allowed us to carry out an inspection after the explosion and we could quickly rig the transmitter/ receiver to go into action again if the whole thing failed to go bang as advertised.

'Only problem is,' George said distractedly, 'I just remembered we haven't got any incendiary. So, it looks like we're going to have to use HE after all.'

I glanced sidelong at Buzz and watched his lips break into a sick grin.

Just then, a shadow fell across the ground in front of us. The three of us turned around to see Roger silhouetted against the late afternoon sun.

'How's it going?' he asked, his tone clipped.

George flinched, then told him. When it comes to blowing things up, George never uses one word when three will do. I could see Roger bristling with impatience as George went into the intricacies behind the decision he had just reached.

'Listen,' the RSM said finally, 'just put six bloody inches of safety fuse on it and blow the fucker up.'

George and I both looked at each other. I could see him struggling to work out what I'd already clocked. Roger had some dems experience – quite a lot, according to his record – but I knew this wasn't some quirky facet of his northern humour. This was the spirit of Sir Francis Drake battling to bust loose again.

'Er, Rog,' I said, 'six inches of safety is going to give the poor sod who has to go down that manhole precisely twenty seconds to get away.' I had a terrible vision of George or Buzz getting stuck in the access tunnel as the clock ticked down to zero. The force of the explosion would propel what was left of him into low earth orbit.

Roger looked at me, much like a bear sizing up a persistent fly. 'Bollocks,' he said, eventually, 'you get 36 seconds. Everybody knows that.' He looked at George for support.

The explosives expert had gone back to his kit, but still had one ear tuned to the conversation. 'Actually, Rog,' he said, without a trace of reticence, 'we're using a different kind of safety fuse now. That was the old stuff. Cammy's right. Six inches will get you nine seconds.'

A low sound issued from the RSM's throat.

'Listen,' he said, 'I don't give a shit how you do it, just make sure the bloody thing goes bang, right?'

George gave a cheery wave, then transformed the gesture into something a little less friendly as soon as Roger's back was turned. 'Don't worry. It will.'

Roger made a move back toward his vehicle, then stopped. He turned around a second after George had dropped the universally accepted sign language for 'wanker'.

'Oh, and Cammy,' he said, blithely, 'we're having a head-sheds' meeting over at my wagon. See you there in five, right?'

'Got it,' I said.

'Christ,' Buzz said, as soon as Roger was out of earshot, 'left to his own devices, he'd kill himself.'

'Yeah,' George agreed. 'Only trouble is, he'd take us with him.' He turned towards me. 'What's with the head-sheds' meeting?'

'Dunno,' I replied, pulling myself to my feet. 'I'd better go find out.'

I set off back to my wagon to pick up a brew for the meeting. As I left, I could hear Buzz rubbing his hands and George picking up from where he'd left off on his tuneless ditty.

Igor and Dr Frankenstein were starting to salivate again. Meeting or no meeting, I reckoned it was time to put a little distance between me and the explosives.

*

'Change of plan,' Roger said, as I came up under the cam-net. 'As you know, I was all for pressing north tonight. But Tony here has convinced me we should go take a look at this place.' He pointed towards a spot on the map to the east of us. I squinted past the sunlight that dappled the bonnet of his 110.

The map showed a runway at a place called Mudaysis. Our initial intelligence was that there was nothing there worth checking. I glanced at Tony and was greeted by a slightly pained expression. If the mobility man said it needed to be seen, then that was good enough for me. But the look on his face said Roger had taken some convincing.

'What's there?' I asked.

'Search me,' Roger said. 'That's why we're going. To bloody find out.'

'The point is,' Tony chipped in, 'we can't just ignore this place. First, RHQ needs to know about it. Second, if we do just head north and it turns out there's a bloody great garrison there, it could give us problems.'

It all made good sense. 'What about the fibre-optic cables?' I asked.

'We'll need to do them first, so that's going to limit our drive time.' Tony glanced at the map. 'But I think we can splash them, cut east to the airfield, check it out, and still get pretty far north.'

'And what if there is something at Mudaysis?' I asked. Given Green Slime's propensity for quirky intelligence assessments, there could be whole squadrons of MiGs based there; or, like Tony said, a large concentration of troops.

'Then we'll give the place a bloody good dishing,' Roger said.

I looked around for some second opinions.

Alec was the first to catch my gaze. 'I don't see why not,' he said. 'If there are aircraft parked there, we might as well take them out. If it's just a bunch of jundie NAAFI wagons, we'll leave the place alone.'

'Right,' Roger said. 'With the .50s, Mk19s and the Milan, we'll cream 'em. Besides, the MSRs can wait. They're not bloody going anywhere.'

Roger relayed the substance of this conversation to the rest of the boys shortly before we moved out. We spent about twenty minutes deliberating how we were going to do the airfield recce, before heading for our vehicles. We sat there cupping brews or smoking fags until it was dark enough to start our vehicles. Then we hit the road.

It took us a couple of hours to work our way back to the MSR and the strange hatches we'd seen beside it. When we were a klick away, we called the convoy to a halt. Then, after another quick confab, three vehicles – Roger's, Tony's and mine – headed on towards the MSR. The fourth and fifth wagons moved out five kilometres in either direction along the road to give us warning of any approach. We left the mother support craft behind.

We found the hatch we'd first encountered without

difficulty and deployed around it. Roger parked his 110 right up close so he was ready to remove the dems team in a hurry if the need arose. I drew up in the middle of the road and joined the rest of the boys in a serious 360-degree scan of the area. Tony and his crew did the same from the opposite verge.

Buzz and George dropped down onto the hatch. Within a few seconds, they were joined by Roger. The lid came up without a problem. In an instant, all three of them had disappeared underground with the explosives.

It stayed that way for ten minutes while the charges were rigged. All the kit was preassembled, so the whole thing was set up pretty quick. The longest part of the operation was fixing the antenna so that it would receive the signal from the initiator. In the end, to give it a bit of elevation, George tied it to a stick and stuck the lashed up assembly in the sand.

When it was all set, we met up with the other 110s, picked up the Unimog and drove a couple of kilometres back towards the LUP. Having found a piece of terrain with a bit of height, we stopped and George stood up with his box of tricks. There was no ceremony to it; he simply pulled up the transmitter antenna, fed in the codes and hit the button.

The air reverberated with a resounding boom, a sure sign that the team had done its stuff to the letter. We could report back with confidence that the cables had been cut and the culvert collapsed.

From now on, Saddam would have to find another way of initiating Scud launches in this area.

As we started to drive again, Tom began to rap out a tune on the steering wheel. And then the bastard broke into song:

> *I gave a letter to the postman*
> *He put it in his sack*
> *By early next morning*
> *He brought my letter back.*

And then, without warning, the chorus started. Nick and Jeff in full bloody voice, deep baritone: *He wrote upon it.*

Somehow, even I got caught up in it. Before I knew it, I was chucking it out at the top of my voice:

> *Return to sender*
> *Address unknown*
> *No such number*
> *No such zone*
> *We had a quarrel*
> *A lover's spat*
> *I wrote I'm sorry*
> *But those Scuds keep coming back.*

We carried on moving north, rocking and rolling with Elvis across the Syrian Desert, when suddenly Nick sat up in the back. 'For Christ's sake shut up and stop the vehicle,' he shouted. 'Stop the fucking wagon!'

The second chorus died in our throats.

'We've got enemy,' Nick said.

Tom slewed the 110 to a halt and we turned to look for whatever it was the BFG had seen. At first, I noticed nothing, but then I wasn't wearing PNGs like Nick was. I reached into my pocket, grabbed my night-scope and raised it to my eyes. The image intensifier danced over the terrain behind us and flashed past something bright. I brought it back again and this time held it steady.

There, on the MSR we'd just departed, three vehicles driving along, sidelights-on.

'Shit,' Nick said, 'ten minutes earlier and we'd have been stuffed.'

'Yeah,' Jeff agreed. 'Lucky break.'

Tom passed me a smoke as we waited for them to drift out of range. Situated where we were, three kilometres into the desert, we knew we were nice and safe, but none of us wanted to chance a move with enemy careening along a major highway to our rear.

You never quite know if there's some sharp-eyed little bastard in the back of one those vehicles with a set of PNGs watching you, watching them.

Still keeping my eye on the road, I reached out for the cigarette, but never took it. Something on the MSR had grabbed my attention bigtime.

The vehicles had stopped.

I raised the pocket-scope again.

'What's up?' Tom asked. 'B and H not good enough for you anymore?'

'B and H are fine,' I acknowledged distantly. 'Check what's happening on the road.'

He swung round. Everybody did.

'What?' Jeff asked.

'Fucking hell,' Nick said from his stance above the Mk19. 'They've stopped.'

'So what?' Tom said. 'Arabs have to piss, same as us – and you, you monster.'

'They're not taking a leak-break, dickhead,' Nick said. 'They've stopped right by the section of cabling we just blew.'

'Well, maybe there's something within the system that tells them when and where they've got a problem on the network,' Tom retorted.

Maybe he was just playing devil's advocate. If Nick had clocked it, then Tom had for sure. Or maybe he was simply having difficulty absorbing the truth, like I was.

'We only blew the bloody thing a couple of minutes ago,' Jeff said, getting it. 'Their reaction time's too quick for that.'

Just then, Roger rushed up. He was panting as he said: 'Are you getting this?'

'Yes,' I said. 'The bastards must have rigged an alarm on the hatches.'

'Foockin' loocky, eh?' Roger beamed. 'Green Slime think they're so clever, but they didn't know about that, did they?'

'So what's new,' I said. 'You know, Rog, I really

think we ought to get moving. If those guys are half as smart as they seem, they could easily pick up our tracks.'

Roger went quiet for couple of beats. 'Yeah,' he said, thoughtfully, 'you're right. Time to piss off.'

We edged slowly northwards, the guys in the back of the wagons scanning like mad behind us as we built up the distance from the road. Soon, the MSR and the vehicles on it drifted beyond the range of our night optics, but none of us much felt like cheering. Or singing. We'd save 'All Shook Up' for another night.

We still had some way to go before we hit our next objective. We knew there was enemy at Mudaysis; it was the whole reason we were heading there. What none of us were quite so happy about was the prospect of Saddam's finest picking up our trail and catching us with our pants down in the dead hours.

'Keep your eyes peeled,' I called out to Nick in the back.

In answer, we heard the reassuring double clunk of a grenade being pumped into the Mk19's chamber.

Now, I took that cigarette from Tom.

I smoked deeply, safe in the knowledge, at least, that if they did come for us, we'd hear about it first from the Mk19.

We stopped four kilometres short of Mudaysis and took stock. Then, consulting GPS every step of the way, we edged forward till we could see the perimeter.

Watching the place a short distance from the fence, we picked out lights and a number of buildings through our optics.

We spent two hours staring at the place from a variety of locations, but saw nothing to really excite us. This in itself was not conclusive, since it was too dark to make out much more than outline detail. There could have been a thousand planes around the airfield or, equally, a battalion or two of Republican Guards. One thing we did know, however: if the enemy were there in strength, on this particular night they'd decided to tuck up.

Later that day, we told RHQ about the hatches and our suspicions about an alarm system the Iraqis had rigged to them. We also asked for news about the other half of our squadron, but received little back. All that RHQ added to what we already knew, was the fact that Robert, our sergeant major, was among those missing. I thought back to my encounter with this popular man on Penn-y-Fan in the Brecon Beacons. Robert, the man who had grunted in my ear for the entire 30 kilometre hike, was built like a brick kasi and stronger than any ox. All of us remained confident that if anyone could outwit and outrun the Iraqis, he could. There was a rumour going around that he was actually Clark Kent in disguise.

Our sitrep complete, we decided to dispatch a couple of the lads back to Mudaysis on bikes. Given this was a daylight move, there was a not inconsiderable risk attached to it, but in the end we felt we had little choice. We still needed to know whether there was anything of tactical worth at the airfield and we couldn't spare the time to go back there again en masse.

The lucky blokes were Alec and Joe. Joe was a battle-hardened ex-Para, and a good man to have around you with a GPMG, as any number of ex-Falklands vets will testify.

With bikes, you have to move quite slowly during daylight, as speed increases their visual and audio signatures significantly. However, if you do run into enemy and need to lie low for a while, they do have the advantage of being able to drop flat. With a small cam-net over you, you can lie there unnoticed within a few hundred metres of the enemy, then get up and bugger off as soon as the danger recedes. Try doing that with a Land Rover.

While the bikes were out, we all felt nervous. Just in case, we had someone manning a permanent VHF watch. Three, four, five hours drifted by without a squeak. The only signal that did come in was a notification from RHQ that went: 'BE ADVISED THOSE HATCHES ARE ALARMED. AS SOON AS COVER IS LIFTED, ENEMY WILL BE ALERTED.'

Great. Thanks, guys.

To ease the tension, a bunch of us sat around Taff's vehicle playing poker. Dean, who was one of Taff's crew, was the only bloke on the mission to bring a deck of cards. Like Taff, Dean was an ex-Green Jacket and bit of a shorty. The two of them used to hang out a lot together and were always stitching people up. Dean was a boxer and pretty handy with his fists, both in and outside the ring. Despite his size, I wouldn't have messed with him. He was a great guy and switched-on, too. The one thing you didn't rib him about were his tattoos, which resulted, he claimed, from an encounter with a cross-eyed practitioner of the art while he – Dean – was severely under the influence. The unfortunate engravings covered his entire body.

Following a particularly spirited round, Dean chucked down his cards and announced he had to take a dump. After the obligatory chorus of 'man walking with shovel', everything went quiet – too quiet. Moments later, Frank and Buzz appeared brandishing a camera. They asked which direction Dean had gone. We pointed to an area behind Taff's wagon, then watched as they sneaked off in stealth mode. Buzz had that same daft but happy expression on his face that he wore when he was around dead animals. Unable to contain my curiosity, I upped and followed them, being careful to round the corner of the vehicle quietly. What I saw almost beggared belief. There was Dean with his back to us, his pink and white cheeks quivering as he struggled to deliver a package. Behind him, unnoticed, lurked Buzz and Frank. Buzz was clutching his Olympus and trying desperately to line it up on the target and not giggle at the same time. Frank was behind him, pointing and holding his nose, like some demented photographer's assistant, as Buzz silently recorded the birth pangs of Dean's log. Undetected to the end, Frank and Buzz sprinted off, barely able to contain their mirth. Dean then returned to the game of cards, blissfully unaware of what had just transpired.

Only later, did I find out what Buzz and Frank did with this abomination. The next day, each went out and crapped at the same locale, then joined the two packages together to produce an unnaturally long turd. To help the viewer understand the scale of this thing, they laid a shovel alongside it and started snapping. The result of this elaborate ploy, of course, was a sequence of pictures that showed Dean straining for all he was worth, and then the prize log itself: a two foot monster, which if found by the locals, would have led them to conclude that the desert had been invaded by a species of Bigfoot. Since Buzz and Frank were involved, any such supposition wouldn't have been altogether removed from the truth.

The bikes came back in the mid-afternoon. They had seen activity at Mudaysis, but nothing you could hang your helmet on. Although there were no aircraft visible, there were a lot of HASs – hardened aircraft shelters – each capable of holding a fighter or two. We figured, though, that this wasn't our problem, so ended up sending a detailed map of the place back to headquarters and leaving it at that. We knew that if some clever clogs worked out the HASs were Scud bunkers instead, then, like Arnie, we'd be back.

That night, we had a nice little drama when Chris's vehicle suddenly stopped for no good reason. Normally, this would be something we'd take in our stride, but on this occasion, the 110 had decided to conk out thirty metres beyond a road the rest of us were just preparing to cross. Some way back in the queue, we sat there wondering what the bloody hell was going on. There was no sign of any traffic. We were just plonked there, going nowhere.

Eventually, I dismounted and jogged over to the front of the convoy. When I got to Chris's vehicle, there were blokes crawling all over it. Chris was turning the ignition and pumping the accelerator like we had all the demons from hell behind us, until Tony rushed up and told him to cool it. The last thing he needed, on top of the undiagnosed problem, was a flat battery or a flooded carb.

Roger was right behind him. 'Have you checked the petrol?' he asked.

'Of course I bloody have,' Chris said, fighting an urge to chin him.

We tried pushing it, but six people behind a fully laden 110 is nowhere near enough, so we whistled up another wagon and got some chains out. There was no point fucking around. We'd tow the bugger through the night to our next LUP and fix it during daylight.

The worry is, you get a contact with the chains on and two vehicles are stuffed instead of one.

No choice, but to go for it. A bunch of lads got the chains off the back of Tony's vehicle and started to lay them out on the sand. I was suddenly overwhelmed by an image of an Iraqi armoured column steaming at us full tilt along the road; the whole lot of us getting caught there with our pants down.

'Try the foocker again,' Roger boomed, his characteristic impatience by now tinged with something akin to desperation.

Chris swore, but had a go anyway. There was a horrible clunking and whirring sound from the engine, then a cough as something caught. Tony jumped up onto the bonnet and pressed an ear to the metal. Like a doctor listening to the chest of a sick child, his expression registered concern. But at least the bloody thing was working. The chains were gathered up and within a few moments we were ready to move again.

'We get a contact and she's still acting ropey, no sense in messing around,' Tony offered to a still nervous-looking Chris. 'Get everybody out and white-phos the bastard. Somebody'll stop by and pick you up. Promise.'

A white-phosphor grenade on a vehicle brimming with petrol and ammo would do the trick, no question. Any US reconnaissance would think a nuke had gone off.

We moved off again and pressed northwards. We were still a night and a half's drive from the primary east–west MSRs linking Baghdad with Jordan. Despite our fears of a tail, we arrived at our LUP without incident and went to work happy that we'd got through a difficult night OK.

After all the cam-nets were set and our defensive cordon rigged, there was no let-up. Parts of the LUP looked like a pit-stop. After a normal night's move there's always blokes working on the vehicles, checking them for glitches and so forth. But this was different. Under Tony's direction, all the mobility guys were out on Chris's vehicle, working to diagnose the problem. It didn't take them long to find what they were looking for. Chris had a seriously fucked transmission system.

Thank God for those mobility jocks. Most of us can change a battery when we need to, but rigging a new gearbox is something else. Joe and his mate Ned simply rolled up their sleeves and swapped the damned thing there and then. Within a couple of hours Chris's vehicle was as good as new.

It was in the afternoon that H took another urgent call from RHQ requesting immediate dialogue with Sunray.

Roger wasn't stupid. After the last time, he took this one on his own, telling H he didn't need him around for the next couple of minutes.

Without our eavesdropping system in place, we

wondered what the hell was going on. Those two minutes seemed to last forever.

Eventually, Roger re-emerged. This time, there wasn't any hanging around. He called everyone in. Within a couple of minutes we were gathered by his vehicle. I tried to read his expression, but couldn't, so I gave up. Good or bad, in a minute we'd know anyway.

'I just got the news from RHQ,' he said. 'One of the D Squadron half-convoys has been compromised. Details are scarce, but apparently they were caught on the hop in their LUP. Some of them got hit, some got away. Beyond that, we don't know shit. All attempts to raise them have failed.'

That would have been enough for one day, but we could tell there was more.

'I'm not sure how best to tell you this,' he began again, then paused to look down at his hands. 'They've heard from the other half of the squadron. Two of the guys who were missing have been picked up and are back in Saudi. They're OK, although I don't know who they are 'cos RHQ wouldn't say.'

That was to be expected. For security reasons, names were rarely given over the air. We waited. Rog still wasn't done.

'The bad news is about Robert,' he said. 'He's now listed missing, presumed dead. Apparently, he caught a shit-load of 7.62 during the contact. A couple of blokes managed to carry him for a while, but in the end they had to dump him. Knowing Robert, he probably made them. I'm sorry. Like everyone, I thought he was bloody bullet-proof. What a bastard, eh?'

When he was done, we sloped back to our vehicles. No one said very much. Everyone had their own memories of the sar'n't major. If the reports were true, he would be greatly missed.

Aside from the personal aspect of it all, the SAS was in a bloody mess. We'd started off as Norman Schwarzkopf's Great White Hope; the guys who'd promised to eliminate the Scud threat. At the beginning of the war, four convoys and a foot-patrol had slipped across the border into Iraq. Three weeks later, one of those convoys was scattered to the four winds and two foot-patrols were fucked. To put it another way, more than thirty per cent of the Regiment's strength was on the run. The theme-park had turned into a slaughter-house. How much longer could it go on?

'We'd better pull something from the sodding bag or we're going home,' Nick said, dejectedly. 'Jesus, we're supposed to be the best. If we can't hack it, what happens when the bloody green army goes in? It'll be a bloody massacre.'

Green army is what we call regular troops.

No one answered, because nobody had anything to say. In a way, Nick was right. The green army fought to a different set of rules and weren't our concern. If they did half as well as the flyboys when it came to their turn, they'd do all right. But *we* had to do something and fast – and not just for the honour of the Regiment. The Scuds were still flying and, as far as we knew, we'd done bloody little to stop them. For a bad moment, as we sat alone under the vastness of the desert sky, it seemed that the outcome of the war with Iraq was still anyone's guess. What was worse was the strangest feeling that we were the ones who could still shape the direction it would take.

EIGHT

The following morning, after an uneventful but difficult night move through a boulder field, Roger called us to a head-sheds' meeting at his vehicle. Tony, Alec and I arrived with our brews and gathered around the map he'd spread over the bonnet.

'Well, lads, this is it,' the RSM announced, rubbing his hands together and looking at each of us in turn, 'we're 200 klicks in and staring at our objective for the first time.'

For some reason, Roger had decided this morning to assume the character of a jolly school teacher. I wondered how long it would last. 'All the other roads we've crossed so far have been nothing but blood vessels.'

'Er, what's that, Rog?' Tony asked.

'Blood vessels,' Roger said. 'You know, things in your body that carry –'

'Blood?' I asked.

'Yeah, blood,' Roger said, sharply.

Tony scratched his head. 'Boss, what's this blood stuff got to do with Scuds?'

'Nothing,' Roger shot back, looking to Alec for support. 'If you lot would foockin' shut your bloody mouths for a moment, you might learn something.'

Alec stood there, glaring at Tony and me. Alec was worse than a teacher's pet when it came to Roger. Ever since the RSM had arrived, he'd been mounting a whispering campaign against Tony, the bloke, as it turned out, who'd pretty much held the whole convoy together during the Graham era. Watching him curry favour in this way made me feel sick. When the opportunity arose, I resolved to say something about it. But not here, not now. Today, we had operational issues on our minds.

'The road we're heading for tonight is a big bugger,' Roger continued. 'None of your poxy dirt-track stuff like we've encountered so far. This is like . . .' He paused, searching for some way out, but he knew he was cornered.

'An artery?' I ventured.

Roger stopped and studied me. 'Tony,' he asked, at length, 'what are the issues here?'

Tony took a step forward and the atmosphere changed. 'We've got three roads,' he said with business-like enthusiasm. He pointed at the cluster of routes ahead of us, 'two going east–west and one north–south. The north–south one I don't think we need worry about. We know they're not moving much towards the Saudi border. The main issue with the east–west routes is the accuracy of our maps.'

He traced a finger along the southernmost of the two roads. The rest of us peered and noticed that the line was dotted.

'This one is supposedly under construction still,' Tony continued, 'but the map itself is three or four years old, so what we can expect is anybody's guess.'

'Give us a foockin' clue,' Roger said.

'Well, apart from the fact that the road may or may not be paved, we could run into all kinds of shit – construction sites, worker camps, JCB parks, you name it.'

'If there's trucks and diggers and stuff,' Alec said, 'how do we know if they're military or not?'

'Alec, if you can't recognize a bloody Scud convoy by now, you never will,' Roger said, witheringly.

Alec flushed to the roots of his hair and fell silent. He had a point, though. None of us wanted to open fire on a civvy-manned dumper truck believing it was an APC or a tank.

Roger motioned for Tony to continue.

'In the absence of any intel from Green Slime,' Tony said, 'this is what I think we may find. The dotted road is probably built by now. The other one may well be redundant. I suggest, therefore, for tonight's move we concentrate on the new road, devote all our energies to cracking that problem, before we even think about the other one.'

We measured the distance between us and the dotted line. It was about thirty kilometres from the LUP as the crow flew. A piece of piss on an average night. But I confess to feeling a cold rush of excitement through my veins. This would be no average night. We were poised on the doorstep of our objective. After all the ups and downs, we had made it. It was time to go knock, knock, knocking on Saddam's door.

'When we get eyes-on the road,' Tony went on, 'our best bet is to split. Most of us, I reckon, should stay and watch the MSR for signs of life. But a smaller recce unit ought to go looking for a suitable LUP that's close by. If we're going to stay watching this MSR for a while, we don't want to spend half the night commuting if we don't have to.'

'Good idea,' Roger said, whipping the map off the bonnet and throwing it into his vehicle. 'Well, gents, that's that then.' He looked at his watch and, clutching his stomach, announced he was going to go get some grub.

The rest of us filed out and went our separate ways back to our wagons. I told Jeff, Tom and Nick the news. After the knocks of the past few days, the look of anticipation on their faces was good to see. We sat around drinking tea and shooting the shit for the next hour or so about what we might expect when we got to the MSR; whether the road really was finished or still under construction; how much men and matériel the Iraqis might be shifting on it. Last, but not least, we wondered if, finally, we might be about to meet our old enemy, the Scud, face to face.

The remainder of the morning passed slowly. We took it in turns to get our heads down and go on stag. Soon after lunch I crawled into my maggot and closed my eyes. It took me a while to drift off to sleep. I kept thinking about the rest of our squadron and the boys from the D half-convoy. Maybe now it was our turn to get even.

In my dream, I was back home, asleep on the settee, aware that Jamie was by my side, desperately trying to tug me awake.

Suddenly, my eyes were open and I was staring, not into the face of my younger son, but the ugly mug of Tom.

'What is it?' I asked. People aren't pissing about when they shake you awake. Any trace of tiredness had purged itself from my body in an instant. There was a look of concern on Tom's face, but no excitement, no fear, at least.

'Roger,' Tom said. 'He's called a meeting. He wants to see us all. Now. The whole bloody convoy. Wakey, wakey. It's show time.'

'Shit,' I said, struggling out of the sleeping bag. 'This had better be good.'

'I doubt it,' Tom replied. 'There's all kinds of rumours going around. Something came over the radio about an hour ago. Roger spent the best part of twenty minutes on the horn and hasn't given us any clues since. Most of the boys are resigned to the fact we're about to get more bad news.'

I rolled up my maggot, stuffed it into my Bergen and stowed the ensemble in the wagon. Yeah, I thought, bloody little in the way of good news had come over the air from Saudi these past three weeks.

As I walked over to Roger's wagon, I resigned myself to some bad incoming. Maybe we were about to get the gen on more regimental casualties. Maybe it was the worst kind of confirmation on Robert, the sar'n't major. Maybe RHQ, or some higher authority, had finally said 'enough' and was calling us home.

The look on the faces on the rest of the blokes as we gathered around Roger's wagon said they were thinking much the same thing.

Everyone except the sentries assembled and waited. Rog, who'd been mixing himself a brew round the back of the wagon, suddenly took centre-stage. There was no need to get our attention. You could have heard a mouse fart.

'As you probably know, we just got an urgent flash from RHQ,' he started. 'Something has come up. A target. A big one. And they want us to take it down.' His face broke into a grin. 'This is it, lads. We just won the foockin' pools. And about bloody time.'

A mixture of relief and shock swept through the group. It took us a moment to believe what we had just heard.

Roger held his horses for a second or two to allow the news to sink in. Then he pressed on. 'It's a communications site about 40 to 50 kilometres to the north of here. Just beyond the second MSR. According to RHQ, it's a major link in the chain of command between Saddam and his Scuds. Without it, he's going to be hard-pressed to launch anything in this area. So, we've got to hit it – and hit it hard.'

The target was called Victor Two. Beyond that, and what he already told us, Roger claimed to know little else. This did not stop a flurry of questions from the rest of us – about enemy strength, what we might expect in the way of defences, when we were going in, etc, etc.

'The job's got to be done tomorrow night. RHQ said there was no compromise on that. I guess they must have their reasons. We know this is a very important target. As for the rest, we're just going to have to be patient for a few more hours. I'll know more later in the day when they send details. That's it.'

There was an appreciable air of excitement as we got up to leave. Just then, Roger called Tony and me over. Thinking it was a head-sheds' meeting, Alec picked up the vibe and wandered over, too. But Roger waved him aside.

'Congratulations,' Roger said to me and Tony, a smile on his lips, 'you've got the recce.'

Tony and I looked at each other. Over his shoulder, I caught Alec's expression. Not surprisingly, he looked a little pissed off. I'd no idea why Roger chose me to accompany Tony, whose place on the recce was assured by virtue of his mobility skills. I guess that's just the way it goes sometimes.

'When?' I asked.

'Tonight. As soon as it's dark. I know I don't have to tell you how foockin' important this is. And I know, too, I can rely on you not to indulge in any bloody heroics. All you have to do is locate the target, report on it, then find us a way in and a way out. One other thing. Don't get foockin' caught. 'Cos whatever happens, tomorrow night, the rest of us are going in. And if you lot stir the place up, it's going to make life very interesting.'

'Touched by your concern, Rog,' I said.

Roger clapped me on the back. 'Well, good foockin' loock. I'll see you before you head out.'

For the next hour, Tony and I huddled over a map on the bonnet of his vehicle working out how we were going to do this one. We had to cross one, maybe two big roads, then get to the target, spend as long as it took on-site to get the information we needed, before coming all the way back again. It was going to be a hard night.

We were helped by a constant stream of advice and

brews from Buzz, Frank, Alec and a bunch of other guys, who'd gathered around us to see what all the fun was about. After fifteen minutes, we were joined by Tom who'd been sent by Nick and Jeff to find out what was going on. They'd only heard they were on the recce when somebody had passed by and told them what lucky bastards they were. I wanted to give them the gen, but I needed to concentrate on the routing more. Tom kept pressing me for news. I felt like a parent on a long journey bombarded by questions from his kids about when they were going to get there. Eventually, I had to tell him to go back to the vehicle and wait. They'd all know soon enough.

There were two big issues associated with the route. The first was the road we had to cross. Whether it was hard-standing or still under construction, we needed to check it for activity. The second was a building next to the road. It was marked on the map as being about where we needed to cross. The building would provide a useful reference point on the route to the target, but we needed to know more about it: like if it was a toll-gate or a works-site, for example, or something else altogether.

The recce was designed to achieve three things. First, it had to plot us a bomb-proof route through to the target. Second, it had to confirm the exact location of the target and that the target was what the int people thought it was. And third, we had to get as much information as we could on it without getting compromised.

Crossing the roads would be especially interesting, and with Roger's words about not getting caught still ringing in my ears, I knew we had to get it right. If for any reason Tony and I got separated, we agreed to RV close to the mysterious building. From there, provided everything went OK, it was only a short distance to Victor Two.

When I finally got back to my wagon, the boys were frothing at the mouth for news.

'Well,' Nick asked, 'what's the score?'

I chucked the map onto the passenger seat on my way towards the back of the vehicle. 'Fuck all till I've had a smoke,' I said. I'd been on it for an hour and a half and needed some space. I wandered off a little way and sucked on a Silk Cut, wishing it had been something closer to a Capstan Full Strength. A few minutes later, I drifted back to the wagon again. The boys had already spread a map on the ground. There was a full mug of tea waiting there, too; a roll-up beside it.

'Cheers,' I said.

'Wrong time of the month?' Nick asked, giving me a horrendous smile.

'Yeah,' I said, laughing, 'and since when were you bloody Claire Rayner?'

We spent the next hour or so going over the plans: the route we'd take, the crossing of the roads and what we might expect when we carried out the close target recce. We weren't sure whether we going to do the CTR in the vehicles or on foot. Ideally, we needed to look at the target from 360 degrees, but if it was as big as Roger said, that might prove difficult. CTRs are difficult things to do properly. They take time and a lot of concentration. On this occasion, time was something we had precious little of. In an ideal world, we'd have asked RHQ for a 24-hour extension and hung around the following day, keeping eyes-on. The reason we couldn't was nothing to do with the enemy. Our main fear was that RHQ would change its mind and call the whole thing off; send in the bombers instead. If we were going to see action, we needed to press on and get everything in place quickly. Shit or bust, we had to do this thing in a night.

We spent the rest of the afternoon squaring away our weapons and optics and making sure we had enough ammunition. There's a science to the way you pack a vehicle, since everything must be where you want it when you need it. The balance can easily be ruined by stowing even the smallest thing improperly. Since we were heading into the teeth of the enemy, we now had a lot of extra kit on board and it took time and effort to maintain this equilibrium.

Eventually, night began to descend and we readied ourselves for the off. There's a temptation to succumb to your impatience and say: fuck it, we go now. But we just had to wind in our necks. Moving early might so easily get us spotted. And then, the Iraqis wouldn't just have us, the recce party, but the LUP site as well.

In case either party did encounter any problems, we'd earmarked a place roughly equidistant between the target and the LUP where we could all meet up again. In the event we were compromised, we'd make for this point and wait there for the others; if they were, Roger would dispatch someone to this emergency R V who would guide us to wherever they had established their new LUP. There was always the possibility, of course, that we might lose our vehicles at the target area and have to go on the run. That being the case, Roger, Tony and I agreed that the ERV should be manned only for the first night and half the second. If we hadn't made it by tomorrow midnight, we were on our own.

As we sat in our vehicles, waiting for the light to seep into the horizon, the rest of the LUP decamped. If there was a drama, they'd need to be ready to go in an instant. For them, it would be a night of watching and waiting. Even though we were headed for unknown territory, I knew where I'd rather be.

A couple of figures appeared out of the darkness – Roger and Alec, coming to pay their last respects.

Roger cut the BS and came straight to the point. 'Remember, whatever you do, don't get foockin' compromised.'

'Charmed, I'm sure,' Nick said, fortunately too low for Roger to hear.

As Roger moved off to talk to Tony, Alec offered some more constructive advice. 'Don't worry, Cammy. Anything happens, we'll be at the ERV. Good luck, guys. Have a good one.'

And with that, we were on our way.

Things started to look iffy when we were barely two hours into the journey.

We'd been bearing down steadily on the first MSR for a while, our eyes darting between the horizon and our GPS sets at shorter and shorter intervals. Between them, the map and GPS said we should have been within visual range of the road ages ago. Now we were on top of the damn thing and there was no sign of it.

If I was concerned, Tony was even more so, since navigation was meant to be second nature to him. It didn't help that for the last 200 metres, as we edged closer to the very spot where the road was supposed to be, we'd hit a field of ridges that made the wagons pitch and roll like trawlers on a high sea.

Reading the GPS sets was almost impossible under such conditions, so we had to stop a lot and this merely added to our growing sense of frustration.

If we couldn't find a bloody road – even if it was meant to be under construction – then what hope did we have of finding our target?

A few dozen metres after our last stop, Tony and I pulled up and compared notes for the umpteenth time. Tony's GPS was a few hundred metres out of alignment, but that should not have been catastrophic. We still should have been able to see something.

In the end, it was an innocent remark from Buzz that gave the game away. A good man on a bike, he was crouched beside Tony's wagon assessing the terrain for its rideability. 'Shit,' he said, while Tony and I were gazing up at the stars, silently cursing the Pentagon's GPS satellite constellation, 'I'm glad I'm not driving a bike over these ruts.'

Tony and I looked at each other. Then, we ran over to where Buzz was still squatting. We examined the ground by his feet. 'What?' he asked. 'What did I do?'

'You're a bloody genius,' I said.

Around the vehicles, other patches of terrain told the same story. What we were standing on – what we'd previously mistaken for troughs and ridges – was no accident of nature. The ground was littered with ruts – there were hundreds of tyre-tracks, all on top of, or crisscrossing, each other. We'd been on the MSR for the last 200 metres and not even known it. Who said the damned thing had to be paved? Finished or not, this was it. Tony and I allowed ourselves a chuckle. There was nothing much wrong with our nav-equipment or our maths. We could proceed towards the target, safe in the knowledge we were on the right track.

Ten kilometres further north, we hit the next road.

The first thing that struck us was the strip lighting.

It lit the damned thing for as far as the eye could see. There were three lanes in each direction, crash barriers in the middle and storm drains down the side.

'For Christ's sake,' Nick said. 'That's not a road. It's a sodding autobahn.'

I looked across at Tom who was behind the wheel, expecting to see the grim expressions on our faces reflected in his. But he was smiling.

'What's the score?' I asked him, slightly annoyed at his indifference.

His response, at least, was honest. 'Hey, Cammy, no one said this was going to be easy.'

We pulled the two vehicles up side by side. I moved over to Tony's 110 where Frank and Buzz were both busy scanning the area with their night-scopes.

'How the fuck are we going to crack this one, Tony?' I asked.

It was quite a piece of engineering, made all the more incongruous by the desert backdrop. From where we were, it shimmered like the Las Vegas Strip.

'Don't these ragheads know there's a war on?' Frank said from behind his scope.

I couldn't help thinking that a little more effort might be required on our side to seriously screw the workings of the Iraqi national grid. I made a mental note to send a signal to that effect back to headquarters. These guys obviously had power to burn.

We sat there and watched it for a little while, but

didn't see a single vehicle. It was like it was completely dead.

A garage was situated close by. It was the building we'd identified on our maps in the planning stage. We'd hit it smack-on. God bless the Global Positioning System, I thought, overcoming my prejudices of the previous hour. It appeared to be deserted. We got back in the vehicles and moved forward another hundred metres, then pulled up and took another look.

There was still no sign of movement, so I sent Frank and Nick out on foot. We'd picked up nothing on the thermal imagers, but we needed to be sure there weren't any Iraqis hunkered down inside.

We watched them move forward. They were the perfect team. Frank equalled Nick in size and build, but scored slightly higher on the beauty stakes. We covered them until they disappeared round the side of the garage complex.

'Christ, imagine being woken up by those two,' Tom said softly to my left. 'Your worst fuckin' nightmare.'

After Frank and Nick had given the place the once-over, Nick came out and gave us the thumbs-up.

We drove over, pulled onto the forecourt and parked in the shadows beside one of the buildings.

Frank and Nick met us as we parked up.

Buzz, Tony's driver, asked: 'Anyone seen the gents? I'm crying for a dump.'

Nick was already sniffing around the pumps. He

told us he could give both vehicles a good deal on the leaded if we hung around while he did a bit of GBH on the pump-locks.

'Nah,' Frank said. 'Let's find somewhere they do coupons.'

We took a closer look at the road. There was no doubt it was a major obstacle. The drainage ditches were two to three feet wide and a couple of feet deep. The crash barriers in the central reservation were bolted into position. Furthermore, there was a chain-link fence fifteen feet high on either side to prevent goats and other animals from straying on to the road. It stretched away into infinity with no visible break.

On the way back, the fence wouldn't be a problem as we could literally blow our way through it. Sixty-six millimetre on the chain-link and a couple of big charges on the central reservation and it was history. The problem was the way in. We needed to stay covert until the attack went noisy. As things stood, there was just no way we could get the convoy across this piece of road without waking up half the scattered population of Western Iraq.

Time was getting on. Somehow we had to cross the road, survey the target and get back across the motorway to the LUP before first light. In the end, we realized we had no choice. The only option open to us was to drive down the road in the full glare of the lights and hope we could find a crossing point somewhere else. It was a risk, but the alternative was worse. When the night was over, we had to have plotted a fool-proof route to the target and back. We wouldn't get another chance. The mission was on for the following night, whatever.

We got back into the vehicles and coaxed them out onto the motorway. With the lights beating down on us, we drove for one kilometre, then another, craning our necks for any sign of a break. Nothing. Half the Republican Guard could have been holed up on the other side of those lights watching our progress as we drove like idiots on parade along that deserted highway and we wouldn't have been the wiser. I felt as vulnerable and exposed as I'd ever been.

I passed a lit roll-up to Tom and tried to enjoy a smoke myself as the motorway lights shot by above us.

'This feels fucking weird,' he said.

'Yup, mine, too,' I replied, looking at the reed-thin abortion of a cigarette I'd taken from his tin. 'Here, try a tailor-made one.'

He looked at me and forced a smile. 'Fucking crap-hat.'

We kept going. Ten kilometres clicked by on the dash. Then another five.

Several times I considered turning back to the petrol station and checking the road in the other direction. Then, suddenly, after fifteen minutes of this madness, we saw what we were looking for: a break in the central reservation and no fencing either side. The drainage ditches were still there but we quickly filled some sandbags and drove off the road and into the sanctuary of darkness. We plotted the position on GPS, picked up the bags and pressed north.

Within another fifteen minutes we caught our first glimpse of the target. We stopped a couple of kilometres short of it and surveyed the area. There were a lot of lights dotting the desert in front of us. It reminded me for some reason of a small town near Hereford called Ross-on-Wye. It was certainly big enough.

Scanning through the night scopes, we could make out the main communications mast, plus a rash of dishes and antennas. We double-checked the GPS. There was no doubt about it. We had the right place.

'It's huge,' Frank said.

If it wasn't for the fact that the interesting parts were in an underground bunker I would have seriously suggested a different plan of attack: bringing in aircraft with laser-guided munitions. Tony and Frank thought this was a realistic option. It still wouldn't have been a picnic for us: we'd have been close to ground-zero squirting our laser designators at the target for the bombs to home on.

I'd taught CTR a number of years earlier and knew precisely what we were meant to do. There's an acronym we use – SLAMMAE – which describes the whole procedure: strength, location, arms, method, morale, aids and equipment. Ideally, we needed to know all these things about the target before we withdrew. In addition, we were supposed to draw up interim attack plans, plotting such things as routes into the target, the position our fire-control groups should take up, potential obstacles, etc, etc. The more you glean from the recce, the easier it is during the attack itself. That's what they say, at least.

I knew that we were faced with a big problem here. It was already two-thirty in the morning and, like good vampires, we had to be back at the LUP before sun-up. If we hung around and did a thorough CTR on Victor Two, we were never going to make it. On the other hand, we could see that the target was enormous and needed to be thoroughly checked out before we went steaming in there.

Decision time. What the fuck do we do?

Tony and I agreed we should move a little bit closer, then make up our minds. We inched forward till we were about a klick away from the main antenna mast and then held another confab. Our vehicles were so close I didn't need to get out of the passenger seat. I simply leant over and whispered: 'Maybe we should request to stay on target a little longer. What do you think?'

Tony thought about that a moment, then shook his head. 'No. Let's do it by the book. They wanted us back by the end of the night, whatever. Christ knows we ought to stick around this place a little longer, but if we do it might jeopardize the mission. I don't want to be the guy who's responsible for that.'

Me neither. So, ever so quietly, we withdrew, until the lights of Victor Two receded and we were back in the open desert, heading for the motorway again.

'You know,' Tom said, passing me a smoke, 'if we'd done that on your CTR course, you'd have failed us, wouldn't you, you bastard?'

'Probably,' I said, still troubled by the decision we'd just taken. 'We just didn't have the time tonight to do anything else. I guess that's war for you.'

'So, what happens tomorrow?'

'We're going to be busy,' I replied. Under normal circumstances, we'd do a 'confirmatory recce' on the night of an attack, just to make sure that all the things we'd found out on the CTR were still valid. Our confirmatory recce, however, would be like starting from scratch.

'But the place is big, man,' Jeff said, latching onto my next thought.

'It's fucking huge, you mean,' Nick said.

There was a moment's silence as we all reflected on the night's work, then Nick piped up: 'Please, sir, can I go sick tomorrow? I'm afraid I'm not feeling very well.'

'You've been sick for years, mate,' Tom said. 'Dr Tom says, fuck off.'

I filled a large cup of coffee from the flask and

passed brews to the three of them. I asked Tom what he thought of the target.

'Difficult one. We could do with the whole bloody regiment on this.'

Yeah, I agreed, but we weren't going to get it. We were all the help we had.

NINE

We made it back to the LUP just as the sun was inching above the horizon. Our return trip had been done at breakneck speed, each of us conscious of the race against the light. We were lucky in that we encountered no sign of the enemy.

Cam-nets were being thrown onto the vehicles as we swept back into the encampment. We got our vehicles linked into the others' arcs of fire, put our own cam-nets up and then got to work.

First up was a head-sheds' meeting. Tony and I wandered over to Roger's vehicle, where we not only found Alec, but Gazza as well. To be fair to him, Gazza had done pretty much as he'd promised to do when he came in with Roger on the Chinook resup. For the most part, he'd left us to get on with things the way we'd trained to deal with them.

Perhaps it was precisely because he'd kept to himself that I was a little surprised to see him now. Gazza had spent most of his war with the convoy eating and sleeping. I don't once remember him doing any night-driving, nor putting in any graft on his vehicle at any of the LUPs. No wonder George, who did all the driving and all the grafting on that vehicle, was having such a miserable war. Whenever I found myself thinking about Gazza, I got angry. Today, I didn't have the time or the energy to waste on the man. The way things were looking, this was the day that would shape the rest of our lives. For some, it would probably mean a body-bag. Gazza ranked low on my list of things to worry about.

Tony and I gave them the low-down on the recce. Despite our inability to get any hard intel on the target itself, Roger, Gazza and Alec were pleased with the way things had gone. We'd found a way across the roads, we'd plotted a route into the target and we'd confirmed that Victor Two was both where and what RHQ said it was. And, I pointed out to Roger with a grin, we hadn't got foockin' caught.

Over the course of the next hour, we went over what we knew and what we didn't.

The most glaring omission in our preparations was the lack of any real information on the target itself. In the period since we'd first been apprised of the mission, we'd got little extra from RHQ on what we might expect inside Victor Two. If they had any more info on the place, now was the time to hand it over.

Roger and Gazza disappeared to file a sitrep to the

FOB and to request more data on the target as a matter of urgency. Tony and I, meanwhile, sloped off back to our vehicles for some hot food and drink.

After noshing, Jeff, Nick, Tom and I took it in turns to go on stag, while the rest of us got some sleep. After the exertions of the night, we were tired. Despite a mounting feeling of excitement, I was able to get my head down for around four hours.

By midday, I was up and about again. I spent the next hour sniffing around the other vehicles for information. Roger had been in purdah most of the morning, huddled over the radio, exchanging information with RHQ.

Because I'd been out of the picture for a while, I wanted to be sure I hadn't missed anything. It mattered, somehow, that our wagon got a good slice of the pie. I didn't want to be relegated to guarding kit or manning a radio. I couldn't really explain this need to see action. Any sensible human being would have run a mile in the opposite direction.

I supposed that it boiled down to a couple of things: this is what I'd always signed on with the SAS to do; and how could I hang back when others were in the firing line? If there was going to be action, I knew I had to be in the thick of it. Anything less, and I might as well have hung up my boots and gone into hairdressing.

My forage for information was, for the most part, fruitless. If people knew anything, they were keeping it to themselves, most probably for the same reasons that I was hunting down the gen in the first place. Nobody wanted to be left behind. The blokes knew that this was it. The big one. Everybody was out for the best slice of that pie.

In the event, I didn't have to wait long. At two o'clock, Roger called me over to his vehicle. More intel had come down from RHQ on the target, he said. I got out my pad and started scratching notes.

When my brain caught up with what my ears were receiving, the writing suddenly ground to a halt.

It was, I imagined, like hacking into a classified data-base and suddenly getting into the holy-of-holies. Roger was spouting information about the target I couldn't believe we knew. And it kept getting better.

First off: details of the target perimeter. The outer layer was a fence around ten feet high, most probably chain-link. Next, after around 10–15 metres, we'd encounter a low wall. This was standard intel stuff, but it still never failed to impress me.

Then, we were into the compound itself. Next to the mast, which we'd seen clearly on the CTR, was a building. We were to aim for a door on its southern side. Once inside, we'd find two flights of stairs going down, then a long corridor with multiple rooms leading off it. We were to access the second door on the left and blow the switching gear contained within it. Destroy it completely.

I looked up from my notes. 'How the fuck do they know this stuff, Rog?'

He shrugged. 'I don't know and I don't ask.'

But I could tell even Roger, a man who'd allowed many of life's finer points to pass him by, was asking himself the same questions.

'All we have to concern ourselves with is annihilating that equipment,' he said, after some thought.

'What the fuck does switching gear look like?' I asked. 'I'm not even sure I know what it is?'

'It doesn't much foockin' matter what it bloody looks like, or what it is,' Roger replied, testily. 'We'll blow the foockin' lot. No bloody messin'.'

That took care of that one, I thought.

After all the false hopes and let-downs of the past three weeks, I couldn't allow myself to believe that this was finally it. I asked Roger whether he thought we were going to do it.

'No question,' he said. 'I just got the "confirm" signal. Short of Saddam choockin' in the foockin' towel, there's no going back.'

Far from showing signs of war-weariness, Saddam had recently upped the stakes by launching an attack on the Saudi coastal town of Khafji. From what we'd gleaned on the World Service, it had taken some fierce fighting to recapture it. The likelihood of the Iraqis calling it a day by sundown had to be remote.

'Have you given any thought to what I'm going to be doing on this one, Rog?'

'You're fire support group with Tony. It's a plum job, Cammy. We'll be relying on you to keep the ragheads off our back.'

Roger must have seen the momentary flash of disappointment in my eyes. I'd wanted to be a part of the dems team; one of the crew that went down into the bowels of the bunker itself.

'You and Tony had a fair crack of the whip with the recce,' he said. 'I'm doing this strictly on a rota basis.'

'Sure,' I acknowledged, 'no problem.'

Roger's usual breeziness evaporated for a moment. 'It's going to be quite a work-out tonight, mate. We're all going to have plenty to do. You're not going to be disappointed, I guarantee you.'

'So, when do we get the details?'

He looked at his watch. 'O Group's in about two minutes. You might as well stick around and grab yourself the best seat in the house.'

I caught up with Tom, Nick and Jeff for a few brief moments as they made their way over to Roger's vehicle. Irrespective of what they were about to hear, they pressed me for news. I told them we were FSG and that we were going to have our work cut out for us. Privately, to Tom, I added: 'You're not going to believe what you're about to hear. In fact, mate, you are going to cream your knickers over this.'

He glanced at me suspiciously. 'Is this some kind of crap-hat wind-up?'

'No, mate,' I said, shaking my head, 'this is the real fucking McCoy.'

That wiped the smile off his face.

We gathered around a model of the target that Roger had got a number of the lads to put together on the other side of the vehicle. It showed, with the aid of rocks and pebbles and lines in the sand, the route we'd be taking in, the MSRs and the target itself. When everyone was there, Roger ran over the basic outline, covering much of the ground he'd been over earlier with me.

Then, he took questions on the target: how many personnel we could expect, the height of the perimeter wall, whether it was patrolled by guards and so on. Some he could field, others he couldn't. There were estimated to be thirty men on-site. The wall was approximately five feet high. As for guards, it was impossible to tell, since the CTR hadn't gone in close enough to get that kind of detail.

'We're gonna drive there the same as the recce-ers did last night,' Roger said, washing up the initial Q & A session. 'We'll do a quick recce, get the remaining answers we need and then do it.'

There was a murmur of appreciation from the floor.

Next, Roger went over the plan in detail, paying particular attention to what each group was expected to do. There were three groups in total. The dems party, or assault group, would go in on foot. This was to consist of Roger, George, Alec, Buzz, Frank and Gazza. Its duties were simple: get into the building and destroy the communications switching gear that lay inside.

Glances of appreciation and thumbs-ups were exchanged between the blokes who'd been selected for this particular job.

'We'll cut the fence and move forward to the wall. If we can't get over it, we'll blow it, but the priority is to stay covert as long as possible,' Roger said. 'Ideally, I'd like for the assault group to get to the door of the building before things have gone noisy. If the door's open, well and good. If it's locked, we'll blow the foocker.'

'Who goes inside?' George, the chief dems man, asked.

'You, me, Buzz and Alec,' Roger replied. 'You and Buzz will place the charges, while Alec and I do corridor clearance. Now, listen, I know there's some confusion around here as to what this bloody switching gear looks like. Basically, I don't foockin' care. We place the charges on anything that looks like a foockin' computer or a radio and we'll grenade all the other rooms off the corridor, just in case. All clear?'

The rest of the assault team nodded.

'We'll use percussion-cap timers on this one,' Roger continued, ''cos at least then we'll bloody know the job'll get done.'

More nods of assent. The percussion cap triggered a length of fuse that would burn for three minutes before detonating the explosives. Once the fuse started running, nothing short of human intervention or an act of God would stop the thing from blowing. Under Roger's plan, there would be no Iraqis left alive down there to intervene. As for God, I had to trust in the belief that He wanted to see the Scud threat eradicated as much as we did.

'What about covering fire on the way in and out?' Scouse asked. Scouse was a quietish sort of bloke who manned the point five-oh on Chris's vehicle. He was a nice enough guy and capable in his work, but not someone I tended to hang out with much. His work on the heavy machine-gun would be vital to the success of the mission.

'Cut to the next part of the programme,' Roger said.

The dems team would be accompanied almost all the way to the target by the close fire support group, or CFSG. The CFSG consisted of blokes from two vehicles: Keith's and Taff's. The wagons themselves would be brought as close as they could to the main target area – ideally, to within 300 metres. Then, the CFSG would go in the rest of the way on foot, stopping around 100 metres short of the switch-gear building to provide covering fire for the dems team. Bringing the vehicles in so close was risky, Roger agreed, but ultimately necessary: when the shit hit the fan, both the assault group and the CFSG would need to exfil in a hurry.

As for the Fire Support Group, our party consisted of three vehicles: Chris's, Tony's and mine. Our job was to find suitable positions overlooking the target and to provide covering fire for the dems and CFSG teams. As soon as things went noisy, it would be up to us to neutralize any and all interference with our support weapons, the Mk19, the point 50 and the Milan.

So, that was the master plan and, as they went, not a bad one. The only pisser was the fact that our vehicle only had room for three bodies. Somebody had to go onto another vehicle and that bloke was Jeff. It had been decided he'd join Tony's team for the duration of the Victor Two operation. I'm not superstitious, but it didn't feel right breaking up the team. I tried to put it to the back of my mind and hoped Jeff had, too.

There was no doubt that Victor Two would be a tough nut to crack, but looking at the faces around me, I didn't see anyone complaining. We'd asked for something like this and got it. There were thirty of us against thirty Iraqis holed up inside an important strategic target. You couldn't ask for much fairer than that. I felt the adrenalin starting to pump. It was time to go make amends.

We were just about to file out, when there was a reedy cough from someone at the front. Recognizing it as a plea for attention, I looked up and saw Gazza elbowing his way into a little bit of space next to the model.

I nudged Tom. 'Allo, allo,' I whispered, 'what's all this then?'

Tom shrugged. 'Search me. Never saw him before in me life. Who is he?'

I suppressed a smile as Gazza cleared his throat again.

'As you know,' he began, 'I'm really just an observer here, but I'm sure Roger won't mind my adding a little bit to what he's just said.'

I glanced at Rog and saw him bristle. This was as new to him as it was to us. And from the look on his face, not entirely welcome. I wondered what was coming.

'I know we're all going to have our work cut out for us tonight, but even so, it's important that we all remember one thing when we go in there, guns blazing,' Gazza continued. 'The chances are there will be civilians in and around the target area – technicians and engineers and so forth. In the heat of the moment it'll be tough to tell these guys apart, but I'm going to ask you to try. This isn't their war, it's Saddam's and the military's. There's been a lot of shit in the media back home about collateral damage and civilian casualties. When this thing is over, it's important for the Regiment not to be tarnished with the same brush. So, think before you shoot. I don't want to see any civilian casualties tonight, is that clear?'

I felt a surge of anger rise in my throat. I guess everyone else felt something similar, because there was an uncomfortable pause while Gazza just stood there, staring at us while we stared back at him. None of us had any time for this jumped-up officer psych bullshit. Then, thankfully, Roger stepped in. He looked as serious as I'd ever seen him.

'All right lads, listen up. We've got to hit this target and hit it hard. RHQ has laid it on the line. Saddam's Scuds are still in business. He's firing 'em at Saudi and he's firing 'em at Israel. After all the foockin' bombs that the crabs and the Yank air force have dropped, those missiles are still flyin'. It might look like we've got this war all foockin' sewn up, but we ain't. You know that. I know that. If Sarin-tipped rockets start falling on Tel Aviv or Jerusalem, we might as well all go home, because the Israelis are gonna swarm into this desert like flies on shit. And then, there won't be any bloody Coalition anymore and that raghead bastard will have won. Just like that.' Roger paused, looking at each of us in turn. 'Tonight is our chance to make sure that never happens. So, let's give Victor Two a foockin' doostin', eh?'

Then, he dismissed us.

Roger had given us a lot to chew on, but it was Gazza who most pre-occupied us when we were safely back at our vehicle.

'What the hell was all that about?' Jeff asked. 'All that crap about civvies and collateral damage.'

'I have no idea,' I replied. 'The guy stays out the way for the best part of ten days, then comes up with that shit. Wow.'

'Ten days of pent-up bullshit is a lot to get off your chest in one go,' Nick said, dispensing tea into our mugs.

'Do you get bullshit off your chest?' Tom asked.

'Fuck off. You know what I mean.'

'That was a typical bloody Rupert speech,' Jeff said. 'They're always trying to justify their existence. That's what that was all about. The guy wanted to make his mark before do-or-die time.'

'Yeah, but why bang on about civilians?' I said.

'What do you mean?' Tom asked.

'I mean, when I walk into a room and three guys are pointing a gun at me, the last thing I need is a debate in my head about whether one of them is a civvie or not.'

'Yeah, I see what you mean,' Tom said, nodding his head. 'It sows the seeds of doubt.'

'Hey, don't let it get to you,' Nick beamed, handing round the brews. 'We're a team. We'll kick ass tonight.'

I stared back at that big bloody grin and felt glad that this giant of a bloke was on our side. 'Right,' I said. 'We're a team.'

I looked at Jeff, but he remained impassive. 'Keep your head down tonight,' I said, attempting to keep it light.

'Yeah,' he replied, staring into his brew and nodding sagely, 'Tony's got a shit-awful driver.' Then he looked up and grinned evilly. 'Nearly as bad as you, Tom.'

'Fucking Kiwi-shite-fruit.'

We sat down, the four of us with our backs to the vehicle, sipping our brews while the sun bathed our faces. In a minute or two, the preparations would start in earnest.

It took me a while to purge Gazza's speech from my mind. That should have been the end of it. But unbeknownst to us, his words would return to haunt us before the night was out.

The last few hours of the afternoon saw us checking and rechecking our wagons prior to the signal to move out. There was a lot to do. All non-essential kit and stores were removed from the fighting vehicles and stowed on the Unimog. This included all our spare water, fuel, rations and ammo. What came and went was decided by democratic process. Nick, Tom, Jeff and I debated the combat value of each little item before giving it the thumbs-up or thumbs-down.

Some pieces of kit were removed, regardless; like our Stinger surface-to-air missiles. If any of us did get captured, the Yanks wouldn't have thanked us for letting them fall into the wrong hands.

We also removed our Bergens and shoved them on the Unimog. In their place, we packed our much lighter and more streamlined E&E Bergens. For a fugitive, these contained such essentials as a respirator, a couple of bag-rations, an extra water bottle, a hand-held Magellan GPS set and NBC trousers. The latter weren't so much for the event of a stray anthrax bomb, as surviving the extreme cold.

At the bottom of my own E&E Bergen I packed my little short-wave radio set. This was very much a personal choice. It's not just that I'm a news junkie. When you're three hundred miles from anywhere it's nice to know the little things that matter; like the war's gone nuclear or it's over.

Once we'd got rid of the items we didn't need, we repacked what was left. This had become a familiar ritual since crossing into enemy territory, but today there was attitude behind the lads' efforts.

We also made sure we broke out some extra ammunition for the support weapons. In our case, this was a couple of additional boxes for the Mk19. On the other wagons, the point 50s were already tooled up with a 200-round box of ammo, another next to it with the seals off, ready to clip right on. The same applied to all our GPMGs.

The guys with the Milan had shoved a missile up the tube already with several back-ups within grabbing distance.

As time passed, the 110s looked less like fighting vehicles and more like battleships, with weapons and ordnance bristling from every nook and cranny of their body-shells. The Unimog, meanwhile, grew like a jubilee bonfire. When we were done at our vehicle, I wandered over to take a look at it.

I came round the back and found George tinkering with the end of a long bit of wire coiling down from the tailgate.

He looked up and shielded his eyes against the setting sun. 'Hi, Cammy. How's it going, mate?'

'We're done,' I said. 'How about you?'

'Pretty much.' He nodded to the fully-laden mother support craft looming above him. 'What do you think?'

I squatted down next to him and studied his handiwork. Because the target was a big one, we had no men spare to guard the Unimog. We knew that nothing we could do would hide this bulging monster adequately, so we reached a rapid decision: we'd rig it with all our remaining explosives so that if the Iraqis did find it while we were gone and decided to go joyriding, it'd be the last thing they ever did.

'Nice,' I said, patting the bar-mine to which he was putting the finishing touches. 'And the other stuff, the charges for the target?'

'All squared away.'

I noticed he was unusually tight-lipped. 'What do you think, George? About tonight, I mean.'

He looked at me. 'Piece of piss, Cam.' He grinned, but then something in his eyes died. 'You've seen the place, mate. You tell me.'

Against my better judgement, I conjured up an image of the dems team shooting their way down the stairs of the bunker, shit flying all around them. This was more akin to CT work, the anti-terrorist building-clearance duties with which we were charged back home. Taking down a place that's full of hostages and bad guys is one thing, but killing the enemy, concentrating on not getting killed yourself and trying to do your dems job at the same time, is another. As the guy who made and placed the charges, George would be in the thick of it.

'No worries,' I said, getting up to leave. 'Just watch yourself down there.'

I wandered back to our vehicle to find the guys checking their personal weapons and Nick lovingly oiling and re-oiling his Mk19. It was a sight I'd seen a dozen times since arriving in Iraq as Saddam's uninvited guest. So why did it look so different?

No talking. There was none of the usual chit-chat. It took me a second or two, but that was it.

Nick glanced up and saw me. 'What's happening?'

'Nothing,' I said. 'It's quiet, too quiet.'

He smirked. 'Sounds like it's time for a brew. I'll get one going.'

Ten minutes later, sitting with the lads beside the vehicle, I tried to relax, but the conversation kept on drifting back to the attack. The arrangements were all in place; each man knew what he had to do. But there were still any number of things that could go wrong. I reassured Tom and Nick that the recce had been done by crap-hats and that this shortened the odds of there being any serious cock-ups.

'Cammy, are you talking about the same crap-hats that took us on an excursion down a fucking Iraqi autobahn?' Tom said.

Now, I'm worried.

We spent the next hour or so squaring away the vehicles prior to the removal of the nets. Then, the four of us sat down and checked our E&E Bergens. The composition of these is pretty much down to the individual. With me, it was essential stuff, like a compass, my little short-wave radio (in case things went chemical or nuclear), my baccy-tin survival kit, food, water and fags. When we were satisfied, we flung our main Bergens in the Unimog and hung our smaller E&E bags on our 110. Finally, we sat around in a circle and debated where we would head for if the shit hit the fan.

'Well, Saudi, of course,' Nick said. 'It's closest.'

'Nah,' Tom said, 'it's got to be Syria.'

'What about Jordan?' Jeff asked.

We thought it was about time we checked a map.

In truth, there wasn't much in it. We were about equidistant between the three. We did some more thinking, then got down to brass tacks.

'Well, I thought Saudi was shit,' Tom said. 'No booze, no birds and no bloody discos.'

We agreed. Saudi was out.

'What about Syria?' I asked.

'Have you ever seen Syria on *Wish You Were Here*?' Tom said.

Good point. We shook our heads.

So, that left Jordan. Even though it was vaguely allied with Saddam, none of us had ever been there and the beaches were meant to be quite nice.

Jordan it was.

When the banter died, I still felt the need to do something and decided to make everyone a stew – a little delicacy I call 'gunk'. I was digging some bag rations and tins of meat out of our food box at the rear of the vehicle, when Tom came round to the front of the vehicle. He got out a route map, pondered it a moment, then called me over.

We got into some details about the route and the impending attack – stuff I thought we'd got taped. But he had his baccy tin with him and some spare fags all rolled up and so we talked and smoked and went over the salient points all over again. After a while, I tried to get back to my stew, but then Jeff came over, a couple of brews in each hand. I made my excuses, but he, too, hit me with a barrage of questions and I felt compelled to stay, listen up and answer his points one by one.

An hour of this passed. Then, Nick came over and announced with a broad grin on his stupid face that grub was ready.

'If this is going to be our last supper,' he said,

spooning out chunks of meat, 'the last thing any of us wants to remember is that unrecognizable shit you cook, Cammy.'

After feigning some hurt pride, I got them to agree, that when it was all over, the next dinner was on me.

After the scoff, each of us spent some time alone. Some found it in them to catch some rest before we moved out; others, like me, checked and re-checked their personal kit. I went through my E&E Bergen again, ensuring it had all the things I needed if we had to go on the run. Then, I lay down beside the vehicle and allowed myself a few moments' reflection.

There was no doubt we had a hard work-out ahead of us. Thirty of us against a well-defended target. The odds said some of us wouldn't be coming back, but that was the way of it. Come what may, I knew we'd give the pricks a pasting.

I recalled Harry Taylor's final words as I set off down the Himalayas. In the dozens of mock contingencies we'd planned to while away the hours as I'd been champing at the bit to get back, we'd never envisaged anything like this. As bad as the risks were, I knew Harry would have given his eye-teeth to have come with us.

I thought of Jade and the kids back in Hereford. I hadn't written or received anything since leaving for the Gulf – none of us had. I didn't even have a photograph. I had crossed into Iraq – we all had – devoid of personal details that could be used against us if we were taken.

There were no loose ends. If anything happened to me, Jade and the kids would be all right. Most times before an operation, there's too much on your mind to think about the people you've left behind. But that night, under a cold Iraqi sky, I felt the need to tell her something.

I sat down and wrote a last note on the back of a signal transmission fax-pad, telling her where I was and why I was writing. I didn't really know what else to say.

Looking around for inspiration, I'd seen some of the other guys doing the same thing: sitting alone or walking a short way out into the desert to kick a little sand and square away those last stray items in your mind before it's too late.

I taped the letter to the inside flap of my Bergen and left it with the other things that had been cached on the Unimog. Maybe somebody would find it if things didn't work out, maybe they wouldn't. Either way, I felt better.

We moved out just before dark, our 110 and Tony's mobility vehicle at the front. The plan was to get on target by midnight to give us enough time for a quick, final recce before things went ballistic in the dead hours between one and three.

TEN

The crossing of the motorway passed without incident, so we pushed north, maintaining the standard drill for an approach to target: vehicles in line astern, stopping, scouting the ground ahead with our night scopes and thermal imagers, moving on, stopping again.

As we approached the target area, the sky grew brighter. This was something I hadn't noticed the previous night. There'd been plenty of light around the motorway, and lights had dotted the desert like fireflies when we finally got eyes-on. But this brightness was something else, or so I thought. I remarked on it to the others, but they didn't see anything new or remarkable about it. So, I put it to the back of my mind and concentrated on the things that were happening to us now, in real-time.

Closing in on the wire perimeter, we found a dirt-track not shown on our maps. We stopped. It seemed

Taff's vehicle. Attached to the roll bar is the Milan missile system, an anti-tank weapon. Fixed to this is the MIRA, a detachable thermal heat image sight. A very good bit of kit.

At the LUP preparing for the Victor Two attack. All non-essential stores were loaded onto the Unimog. This was then booby-trapped with explosives. So if the enemy find it and mess with it in any way, Bang...

The author rigging up a bar mine to attach to the bonnet of the 110. This was to prevent weaponry falling into the hands of the enemy if we ever had to ditch the vehicles. Last one out fires the fuse and blows up the wagon. The downside was that it meant driving around with a huge landmine staring you in the face.

Moving off for the Victor Two attack. Each vehicle tries to stay in the same tracks as the one it's following to minimize the trail that's left.

Recovering kit from the Unimog after the attack on Victor Two.

Taken straight after the attack on Victor Two. The author getting some sleep after a hard night's work. Note that the M16 with spare grenades is still close to hand.

The squadron resupply. The four-ton trucks are in line astern down the right. We'd drive along the line picking up the stores from each truck.

Eating a delight that Tom threw together at the squadron resupply. The rule is whoever has the biggest spoon wins. Note the bottle of rum on the Land Rover tail-gate. It provided a welcome change if used in tea.

Endex. This was the whole convoy after we'd passed back over the border into Saudi.

The red, white and blue became standard at LUPs towards the end of the patrol in order to ward off over-zealous Coalition fighter pilots.

The author shaking hands with General Schwarzkopf after the patrol was over.

My vehicle just before crossing the border back into Saudi. Nick's standing at the back, Jeff's next to him, Tom's driving and

When cigarettes were low we had to resort to rolling tobacco. In the hessian-covered box at the front of the picture is a Stinger ground to air missile system.

An LUP near the end of the patrol. The LUP in the background shows just how effective the camouflage was. The maggots [sleeping bags] aren't hanging out to dry, they're airing. Remember that by this point they'd been lived in without a decent clean for about two months.

to lead in the direction we wanted to go. Tony dismounted and spent some time checking the track while Frankie and Buzz scanned the area with their optics.

The night was dead still. There wasn't a breath of wind. Occasionally, in the distance, a dog barked. Desert dogs hunt in packs around pockets of habitation, so I wasn't unduly alarmed. But the thought crossed my mind that there might have been guard dogs in and around the target itself, and we'd missed them.

I shook my head and got out the vehicle, telling myself to deal in facts, not idle speculation. I walked over to Tony's 110. Roger and Alec came, too.

Moving on tracks, either on foot or vehicle, is not a decision we take lightly. The results can be fatal. Ambush is a constant danger. We concluded on this occasion, however, that because of where we were – somewhere the enemy would never expect us – it was a risk worth taking. Taking the track was easier on the vehicles and made a lot less noise.

So far, so good.

We ducked down low, just in case some sharp-eyed Iraqi was out here, perusing the skyline.

'OK,' Roger whispered. 'Close recce time.' He looked at Tony and Alec. 'We'll go in there and see what we can see. We'll take George, Gazza and Frank with us.'

'How long?' I asked.

'I don't know. Minimum thirty minutes. Maybe as

long as an hour. We'll find a suitable RV up the track. Somewhere you lot can wait while we're gone. If you hear shots, that's the signal. Go, go, go. If you lot get compromised, take out the threat and drive straight onto the target. Do the foockin' business.'

We split up and returned to our vehicles. Then, I heard a familiar refrain through the darkness: 'Enemy? No bloody problem. We'll foockin' doost 'em.'

Shit. And it had all been going so well.

About 300 metres from the target perimeter, we pulled off the track and stopped. The recce crew assembled in the darkness and went forward on foot. We watched them until they disappeared from view behind the undulating terrain.

By now, the adrenalin was really starting to pump. One way or another, we were committed. If anything were to happen now, we'd go straight into our immediate action, all guns blazing, shit or bust.

None of us hoped it would come to that.

While the recce team was out, the remainder of us waited. Our five vehicles were off the track, parked side-by-side, engines off. Most of the lads were sitting stock-still in their vehicles. In the distance, there was more yapping from the desert dogs. We pricked up our ears and listened, but the baying quickly died and we settled down again.

We passed the next ten minutes without saying a word. Because we were all edgy, it was enough just to sit there, tuning into the sounds around us: the creak of a vehicle, pings and taps from our cooling engines, the faint crackle of a jet passing high overhead.

After fifteen minutes and no sign of any rumble at the target, we forced ourselves to relax. Nick, Tom and I started chatting quietly. About football, fast cars, birds, beer. Anything to relieve the tension.

And then, we heard engines. A vehicle was on the move somewhere between us and the target. And it was coming closer.

I heard someone rasp: 'Stand-by. Stand-by.'

Behind me, Nick swore and went into action. I heard a sound – *kerklunk* as he disengaged the cocking lever and swivelled the Mk19 through 180 degrees.

Damn. It looked like this thing was going down.

The vehicle came round a bend in the track fifty metres away. It was a bus, heading for us full-tilt, running lights-on. For a moment, everybody froze. There was no time to scoot and hide. The damned thing was almost on top of us.

Our 110s were pulled up by the side of the track. Some of us were in the vehicles, some of us standing around them. As the bus drew nearer, we could see people on board – about twenty all told, almost certainly soldiers from the target area.

Our senses were so finely tuned, we went into automatic mode. We covered our weapons, but not obviously so. I kept mine held loosely under my shamag. Twenty-four pairs of eyes locked onto the bus.

My finger instinctively tightened on the trigger.

Wait, wait, wait.

For a brief second, I felt raw fear. I knew we had the situation covered, but it didn't stop a cold ball from lodging in my stomach and playing havoc with Nick's stew.

I saw the Iraqis' expressions as the bus thundered by. It took me a moment to realize that, for the moment, the danger was over.

I looked at Tom and neither of us said a word. I took a roll-up from his baccy tin. We both took a few good drags.

'Fucking hell, that was close,' he said, eventually.

Nick was hunched over his position at the back of the vehicle. I could see his head throbbing as only Nick's head does when he's ready to go off.

I got up and walked over to the other Land Rovers. Everyone was beginning to come down.

Taff said: 'They think we're fucking Arabs, let's be a little more convincing.' He already had his bonnet up and a couple of the lads were bent over the engine.

Collectively, we all forced ourselves to present a more relaxed picture. We smoked, we chatted, we waited.

The respite was short-lived. A moment later, a bloody great JCB lumbered around the bend.

'This place is getting like Clapham fucking Junction,' Tom said.

'I can live with this,' Nick said, grinding his teeth, 'providing the fucker doesn't stop.'

It didn't.

As it ploughed past, some of us actually managed to wave.

Several more vehicles went past us. None of the occupants seemed to give us so much as a second glance, but somewhere in the back of my head an alarm bell started ringing. For a handful of men, there was a lot of activity around here.

I didn't know how much longer we could maintain this charade. We'd already stuck around too long. It was time to get going. I looked at my watch. It was now over an hour since the recce-ers had gone. Where the bloody hell were they? Had something gone wrong? Worst-case scenario, had the whole damned lot of them been captured?

Thank Christ, a few moments later, they reappeared.

Roger picked me out of the crowd. 'Head-sheds' moment,' he said, his voice a hoarse, low whisper.

The four of us gathered in a circle. 'What's up?' I asked. 'What's happened?'

'Change of foockin' plan,' Roger said. 'The place has been foockin' bombed.'

'What?'

'You heard. The target has been visited by the Royal

bloody Air Force. Or, more probably, the foockin' Yanks.'

It took me a second to get a handle on what Rog was saying. I didn't know if he was accusing us of having botched the recce or if he was telling us the job was done and we could all go home.

'It must have happened between last night and now,' Tony said, quickly filling in the gaps. 'Parts of the fence and perimeter wall are down and the main building has been damaged.'

'So, much for fucking intelligence,' remarked Alec.

'Green Slime,' I said, 'you never can trust 'em.'

'Yeah,' Tony added, 'so let's hope they got no more bloody surprises for us.'

I turned to Roger. 'What's the bottom line?'

'The building's taken a good pasting. There's rubble and shit everywhere. We'd never even find the door, let alone get in. But whoever did this, didn't do a very good job. The mast and its array of dishes are still up and working.'

That explained the light and the vehicles we'd encountered. More than likely the buses had carried in the repair teams. They must have worked around the clock under banks of arc-lights to get the place running again.

So, the mast had to go.

Had Victor Two been a wounded animal, blowing it up would be like severing its head. We couldn't take any chances. We had to make sure.

Roger quickly went over how the new scenario would affect the demolition teams. On the face of it, their task had been made easier, since they no longer had to fight their way into the bunker. All our explosives would be concentrated on the communications mast instead. Roger reported a number of vehicles in and around the target area, but we reckoned there weren't enough to present any problems.

When Roger finished, I rushed back to the lads and briefed them. At the end of it, I felt troubled. Something was wrong. Something was missing. At first, I couldn't put my finger on it. Then I got it.

As we drove past Roger's vehicle I stopped and yelled: 'Hey, Roger, do we fuckin' dust 'em or what?'

'No,' he replied, managing a laugh, 'we shake their foockin' hands.'

A last nod, a moment's eye contact with the other lads and we split up and moved out.

The three vehicles in my section, the fire support group, headed north and east to a position where we could provide our covering fire. The plan called for the two others, the vehicles with the dems and assault teams on board, to move out in four minutes and stick to our far right.

We edged forward as stealthily as possible. As soon as we left the track and began cutting east, we became aware of a large berm to our left. Sticking to the ground below it would keep us off the skyline, so we inched into its shadow and stayed there for as long as possible.

Our eyes darted between the berm and the target to our right. There was no one on the berm and the target seemed quiet. Visually quiet, at least. It was impossible to hear anything above the low grind of the Land Rover's engine.

Eventually, we left the lee of the berm behind, crossed a small mound field and pulled up at our allotted position. We switched off our engines and took stock.

The three Land Rovers were positioned in line abreast and five metres apart, each angled differently to cover the threats to our front and side. Chris's vehicle, the one with the Milan missile launcher, was on the right, with my Mk19 wagon in the middle and Tony's point 50 to the left.

The ground between us and Victor Two, now no more than 300 metres away, was flat and open. We could make out the mast and an enemy vehicle in front of it. Behind the vehicle, at the base of the mast, was the building that had taken the hit from our bombers. It lay in ruins.

To our front, barely 200 metres away, was a group of brick buildings. I didn't like the look of them, but figured it was too late to do much about it. If there were soldiers inside, we'd deal with them when we had to.

Moving right of the target was another enemy

vehicle and, a little way beyond it, a small building. I could see that it was close to the point where the two close-fire support group vehicles were about to deploy.

We settled down and waited. The CFSG wagons would now be on their way. We scanned like crazy, but couldn't see them. I hoped this meant they were still behind the berm. In the distance, we could hear those dogs barking again. Otherwise, the desert was vast, starlit and silent.

To my right, Tom rubbed his hands. Behind me, I heard the crack of Nick's knuckles as he flexed his fingers ready for action.

'How are you doing?' I asked Tom.

'OK,' he replied, tautly. 'You?'

I grunted and raised the optics again. Now I could see the two CFSG wagons. I squinted for some better resolution. There was a momentary flurry as the dems team and the assault group off-loaded, then only stillness as the two CFSG wagons, like us, settled down and waited.

I scanned forward, trying to get a glimpse of our blokes as they crossed the open ground in front of the target, but saw nothing. The imagers were OK for picking up vehicles, but lacked the power to identify soldiers moving stealthily at the extremity of the system's range.

It was then that I realized that the enemy vehicle on the far right would have a clear view of our guys as they crossed the ground in front of the mast. I knew the assault team would have clocked this, but hoped that the vehicle was empty all the same. It would make life simpler for everyone, the enemy included.

Beyond the enemy vehicle and the tower, lights twinkled in the compound that had reminded me the previous night of Ross-on-Wye. I could see now that this was a big encampment, full of tents. Being around 500 metres from the mast area, though, I hoped that it was distant enough not to get drawn into any firefight until we were either gone or ready to depart.

I stopped scanning. There was nothing more we could do, but wait.

The seconds ticked into minutes.

We strained for sound, but heard nothing.

I looked at my watch. The time was moving at an unreal pace. We had been here barely fifteen minutes. It could have been an hour.

I was just allowing myself to indulge in the hope that the dems team had placed its charges and was moving off target, when there was a volley of three shots followed moments later by a vicious burst of machine-gun fire from the direction of the mast.

I only learned what had happened later, of course, but events on the other side of the target area had rapidly assumed their course soon after the assault group was dropped off by the two vehicles in the CFSG.

With the target clearly in sight, Roger, George, Alec, Buzz, Frank and Gazza slipped away from the Land Rovers and stole towards the mast. They hadn't got far when they realized they had problems.

One of the buildings tagged by the close recce-ers was now clearly identifiable as a guardhouse. There were also two prepared bunker positions no one had clocked nearby. Worst of all, the righthand of the two vehicles in front of the mast was occupied. This they could tell from a quick scan with a thermal-imager, which now registered at least two bodies inside.

They held a hurried confab. If the dems team was to stand any chance of planting its explosives success-fully, it'd need time. The best way of creating time, the group agreed, was to keep the operation from going noisy for as long as possible.

Contrary to some portrayals in the movies, we don't have a silenced wonder-weapon that can take out a dozen bad guys with nothing more rousing than a corresponding number of coughs.

The assault group knew that, unless the Iraqis in the truck were asleep, there was fuck-all chance of getting the dems team past it.

They realized they had no choice but to get the drop on the men inside, preferably without firing a shot.

While the dems team crawled for the mast, Frank and Gazza veered off towards the vehicle. Frank –

big, experienced and ugly – led the way, with Gazza close behind. They ran across the open ground in front of the mast, stopping every so often to crouch and listen. They reached the blind side of the vehicle, paused a moment to catch their breath, then pressed their ears to the canvas awning.

Nothing. All quiet.

Frank then gestured to Gazza to keep the back of the vehicle covered while he checked the cabin.

He moved silently down the side to the passenger door. The cabin was too high to see in. Holding his 16 in his right hand, he reached up with his left, grabbed the handle and pulled the door open.

Frank jumped up onto the running board and poked his gun into the side of the soldier behind the wheel. A pair of eyes stared back at him, wide with surprise and terror. Frank put his finger up to his lips.

He had a split second in which to study his captive. The Iraqi was a kid; no more than eighteen or nineteen years old. He was alone. Frank pressed his fingers to his lips and gave him an extra prod with the barrel of his rifle just to remind him that resistance was useless.

But the kid was either brave or stupid – or, more than likely, he panicked. His hand leapt for the rifle on the seat beside him.

Frank had no choice. He shot him three times.

Silence descended on the desert for a few brief

moments. Then Gazza stepped onto the tailgate and emptied an entire magazine into the back.

Victor Two had gone noisy and then some.

'That's woke the fuckers up,' Tom said, after the second burst of firing stopped. He jumped up onto the back of the wagon, ready to feed the voracious appetite of the Mk19 grenade launcher.

There'd been discipline in the first rattle of shots, none in the second. So, we all presumed battle had been joined. Our eyes strained desperately for signs of a reaction from the Iraqis, but despite the breakout of an apparent gun-battle in front of the mast, another period of silence followed.

In the distance, the desert dogs started barking again. The sound drifted up from the tented encampment. It was just a matter of seconds now before this thing went ballistic. We held our breath and our fire.

Still, nothing happened. Then, suddenly, there was movement: men running, around the buildings to our front, range 200 metres.

'Tom, Nick,' I shouted.

'Got 'em,' Nick replied with unnerving calm. The silence was split by an explosion from the muzzle of the Mk19.

Kerboom.

I opened up with some rapid, short bursts on the GPMG, aware now of the juddering and pitching of our vehicle as Tom and Nick began pouring grenades onto the buildings. Nick was giving it everything. Tom was checking the belt-feed, ready with a fresh box of ammo the moment it was needed. Every couple of seconds, he'd lean out and loose off a few well-aimed rounds of his 16.

All this was going on a foot above my head.

The noise was unbelievable. *Boom, boom, boom*, as grenades leapt from the Mk19 at 300 rounds a minute; the sharp, staccato rattle of the .50 on Tony's vehicle to my left. I thought my drums would explode.

My initial burst with the GPMG had dropped the soldiers by the buildings. I could see bodies in the flashes of explosions from the Mk19 and sparks from the ricochets of .50 rounds, as the bullets pinged off the walls.

I stopped firing and did a quick scan with my night scope. I could see more Iraqis crouched and weaving to our front.

Flashes from their weapons bloomed across my vision. I dropped the scope and started up with the GPMG again. Then the .50 began hammering at them.

We were making good progress, when suddenly everything went very quiet to my left. For a second, I couldn't work out what had happened. Then, over the chatter of my own weapon, I heard a shout that chilled my blood.

'Stoppage!'

And again. *Stoppage.* It was Scouse on the .50.

I snatched a glance over my left shoulder. Where moments earlier this mother of all machine guns had been spitting flame and going like a kango-hammer, it was now silent. The .50 was the most temperamental bitch of a weapon I had ever come across. We had lost a good chunk of our fire-power and it showed.

Bullets rained down on us from the Iraqis to our front.

Just when I thought it couldn't get any worse, a series of loud explosions tore up the ground in front of us, barely twenty metres away.

'Tom, where the fuck is that coming from?' I yelled. It seemed to be heading in from behind.

I swung round and saw flashes from the top of the berm we'd navigated beside on our way into the target. At first, I thought it was our guys firing at us. The berm had been clean as a whistle; not a sign of any enemy on it as we'd travelled in.

And then it dawned on me. Nobody *on* it. But maybe a whole regiment on the other side.

Tom and Nick must have got the message by telepathy or maybe they worked it out for themselves. Nick swung the Mk19 and started to put a box of 200 rounds into the general area.

As they did so, the thought started going through my head: this is *impossible*. There are supposed to be no more than thirty Iraqis here. Yet, it seemed like we'd tripped over a Republican Guard reunion.

The respite triggered by Nick's salvo on the berm

was brief. After a couple of seconds, fire started coming down from the top of it again. Bullets punched through and whined their way off the skin of the vehicle. I let rip with a quick burst on my 16, then swung back to the GPMG and let the fuckers in front of us have some more.

The bastards were everywhere. The ground ahead of us crawled with advancing enemy as the Iraqis took maximum advantage of the stoppage on the .50. My GPMG was scarcely making a dent.

I knew then it was going to be a bad day at the office.

If we were having it bad, then so was the dems team. Roger, George, Alec and Buzz were crawling towards the mast when first Frank's and then Gazza's gunfire rattled across the compound. Their immediate reaction was to hug the ground and stay low.

Each member of the team was strapped from head to toe with explosives. The dets were in and the fuses attached. The dems team was, in effect, a four-man walking bomb primed and ready to blow.

'Shit,' Buzz managed behind gritted teeth. 'If a bullet finds any of us, they won't even find our fuckin' socks.'

At that moment, the skyline reverberated with a burst of fire from a Mk19 grenade launcher. Suddenly, bullets started to fly everywhere.

Propelled by a chorus of oaths and expletives, the dems team rose as one and crossed the remaining seventy-five metres to the mast at Olympic speed. George and Buzz slid under the girders like a couple of baseball players going for home runs and started to pull the HE off their bodies.

Roger and Alec took up station behind them, their 16s ready for any counter-attacking assault. Stray bullets ricocheted off the tower above, the hits cracking against the darkness like flint-strikes. Other rounds tore into the ground by the base of the tower. Otherwise, it was nice and quiet; their presence there apparently unnoticed.

While Roger and Alec kept up a commentary on what was happening around them, George and Buzz got to work, attaching charges to each of the legs of the mast. It took them a couple of minutes to do the business, then George yelled they were done.

'Go,' Rog shouted back. 'Light the foockin' candle and let's get out of here.'

George fired the initiator and the fuse started to burn. He and Buzz gave Roger a quick thumbs-up. The group of them then readied themselves for the dash across the compound to the two CFSG vehicles that would remove them off-target. The hope was that Frankie and Gazza were already there.

At that moment, the ground around them erupted under a hail of bullets from the berm.

'Jesus Christ,' Buzz shouted, as they dived for cover behind the concrete and steel base of the mast. 'Where the hell did that lot come from?'

'I don't know,' George said, 'but we've got less than ten minutes before *this* lot blows and takes us fucking with it.'

Roger poked a toe out from behind the steel girder and nearly had his foot removed by gunfire.

The four of them exchanged meaningful glances. Nobody needed to say a word. Behind them, oblivious to the drama, the four fuses merrily continued burning.

In a momentary lull between the volleys that rained down from the berm, Buzz glanced towards the heavens and said: 'Scottie, if you're up there, mate, this would be a great time to energise.'

I checked left and saw Jeff frantically trying to help Scouse sort out the stoppage on the point 50. Tony and I were doing our best to cover for them with heavy bursts from our GPMGs, but the fuckers kept coming for us like something out of *Night of the Living Dead*.

Above and behind me, Nick was having to alternate his fire between the bastards on the berm and the enemy to our front. On top of that, we were getting incoming from various other parts of the compound. If I'd had time to think about it, I'd have crapped me a river, but fear was a luxury we didn't have time for. If we'd ducked for a moment, they'd have been on us.

In short, they were everywhere.

Nick's last barrage to the front seemed to relieve some of the pressure from that quarter. A string of explosions and most of the Iraqis went to ground. I could still see the odd muzzle flash, so I let rip with a good long burst on the GPMG, tracer one in five, hoping that the sight of phosphor-tipped bullets would make those that hadn't already got their heads down think hard about how badly they wanted that posthumous medal.

Depressingly, it was apparent that most of them did.

But then, we got a much-needed break.

After what passed as a lifetime, the .50 suddenly sprang back into action. Scouse and Jeff started firing like men possessed to make up for lost time. The Iraqis to our front now had point 50 and 7.62 from our GPMGs raining down on them at the same time. Every ten seconds or so, we got some extra help from Nick and the Mk19.

Just when it seemed we were beginning to make a bit of an impression, a series of resounding cracks burst through the air above us, as a freightload of something that looked suspiciously like triple-A whipped past our heads.

'Where the fuck is that lot coming from?' I shouted.

'Looks like somewhere beyond tent-city,' Nick roared back.

He swung the big grenade launcher around, ready to give this new threat a few bursts, when the tracer dipped and veered to the right. A string of it ploughed straight into Chris's 110.

The three of us could only look on in horror as anti-aircraft shells smacked into the Milan mount, pinging off it every which way. H and Chris, who'd been in the back, firing at the berm behind us, seemed to explode out of the vehicle.

For a moment, I didn't know what to do. I wanted to help, but any diminution in our fire-power would allow the enemy to overrun us. In any case, I wasn't sure I'd find anything left of them. I'd never seen a man hit by 57 mm, but I was damn sure it wouldn't be a pretty sight.

And then, suddenly, as if by a miracle, they both bobbed up on the other side of their vehicle and started firing again.

My feeling of gratitude was very temporary. Fire from the front. More from behind. Triple-A coming for us in depth. The battle was descending into chaos. Every one of our weapon systems was pouring fire in different directions and it still wasn't enough.

I glanced back and shouted to Tom: 'How's your E&E kit, mate?'

He knew what I was saying. Before the night was out, chances were those of us who were still alive would be spread to the four winds, legging it for Syria or Jordan or Christ knows where.

I got a response I didn't expect. 'Cammy, was that a crap-hat I saw with the .50?'

Fuck it, I thought. Does this guy ever let up?

If we were going to get through this, we needed to

think about withdrawing off-target – now. The longer we stuck around, the greater the chance of their reserve units being pulled in and seizing control.

The trouble was, we had no word from the demolition party to say they were off-target. Each vehicle had a comms set, but H, hunched low in Chris's vehicle with a radio strapped to his back, was now on the job full-time, desperately trying to raise the dems team.

I yelled to him: 'H, how's it coming?'

He looked up and shook his head.

I did some fast thinking. Our fire from this position had pretty much served its purpose. The Iraqis had us fully ranged. If we stayed here any longer, we'd all be dead meat. The salvo of triple-A that had ripped through Chris's vehicle served as a wake-up call for us to boogie.

At that moment, a burst of well-aimed fire from the CFSG wagons ripped across the top of the berm, providing some welcome respite. I shouted across to Tony and Chris that now was the time to move. We agreed to withdraw about a hundred metres, doing something in the process that the Iraqis on the berm might not expect: advance towards them, all guns blazing.

We positioned our three vehicles to the side of the main concentration of troops along the berm. The track we'd driven along into the target area was now just a short distance away. All we were missing was the order to get the fuck out of here.

While Tom rushed over to help H try to establish comms with the dems team, the rest of us poured up the mound to join battle with the enemy.

As we tore over the crest, we saw why Victor Two had become such a serious health hazard.

Below us, in a long trench stretching way off to our left, was a fucking great nest of trucks parked nose to bumper.

Those Iraqis that weren't along the berm, exchanging fire with us round for round from a few dozen metres away, were in the parking lot from hell pouring bullets at us like there was no tomorrow.

In case I'd missed something, I snatched a glance across the compound towards the mast, but it was still there, large as life.

For the first time, I couldn't help thinking we might have bitten off more than we could chew.

Unbeknownst to us, the dems team had been off-target for several minutes. Following the burst of fire from the CFSG vehicles, the incoming that had pinned the assault team behind the mast suddenly dropped.

Roger, George, Alec and Buzz saw their chance and went for it.

The change in their fortunes was short-lived. Just about every Iraqi not on the berm saw their break and began pouring fire on them as they ran, hopped, dived and crawled across the compound.

George took two bullets through his trouser legs.

Like the others, he was so focused on reaching the two CFSG vehicles that he never felt a thing. Against all the odds, the four of them made it without a scratch.

Frank and Gazza were already there. Roger did a quick head-count, swore, and did another. The second tally told the same story.

Two people were missing.

It was then that somebody remembered Dean and Taff.

Both of them had gone forward to take some pressure off the assault team. And now they were nowhere to be seen.

'Maybe they've legged it back to the RV,' Gazza offered. The RV was the place by the side of the track where we'd encountered the bus and the JCB.

Roger looked at his watch and swore again. A bullet ricocheted off the roll-bar by his head and whined off into space. The two vehicles responded with a 360 degree burst of rapid automatic fire.

'Fuck it,' Roger said, 'if we don't go now we're never going to get out of here. They must be at the RV.' To those around him it sounded more like a plea than anything else. He slapped the side of the wagon. 'Let's foockin' go!'

Before the clutch could engage, there was a shout from the back. Dean and Taff were sprinting towards them out of the darkness. Somebody had spotted them just in time. Hands reached out and hauled them on board.

'What the fuck happened to you?' Buzz yelled, as the Land Rover headed away at top speed pursued by the second vehicle.

'Oh, nothing much,' Taff said breathlessly. 'Some bloody raghead jumped me, didn't he? Luckily, I K O'd him in the first round.'

Taff and Dean had been making their way past some vehicles when a door opened and Taff suddenly found himself wrestling with an Iraqi. Dean, who'd been in front, ran on, unaware of the drama. In the scuffle, Taff lost his rifle, but after a desperate couple of seconds, managed to twist the Iraqi off his back and punch him so hard that the bloke went down and never got up. Dean, who'd realized something was wrong and had come back for him, saw the closing seconds of the fight. Taff picked up his rifle and the two of them ran on, just in time to catch the last bus. It had been a damn' near-run thing.

The two 110s headed for the RV. They were attracting fire like flies to a piece of shit. Everyone hoped that they'd come down the track and see us there, waiting for them, but life ain't like that and we were nowhere to be seen. In fact, we were most probably still on our way back from our forward position at that time, between firefights.

Either way, in the confusion of their withdrawal off-target, the CFSG vehicles got split. One lot dismounted at the RV and did a quick recce for us; the other hared straight for the ERV – the emergency rendezvous point – which was about a klick and a half beyond the perimeter. They were joined a moment later by the other vehicle, which had decided that we, too, had to be at the ERV.

It was there that they sat and waited, listening to the sounds of gunfire and explosion as the battle continued to rage at Victor Two.

'For foock's sake,' Roger barked, 'try and raise the fire-support group on the radio.'

Signallers from both vehicles fired up their sets and started working the frequencies, but all they got back was a wall of static.

On top of the berm, the firefight continued. We were flat on our bellies giving them everything we had from our M16s and 203 grenade-launchers. We didn't waste time dismantling and manhandling vehicle-support weapons up the mound. Small arms and grenades had to do. Half the fire-support group – Jeff, Nick, Tom, Chris, Scouse and me – were spread out along the top of the mound firing at anything that moved. It was like Armageddon and Doomsday rolled into one.

Nick had ripped off his shamag and was pouring bullets into the trench. In the flash of a grenade explosion I caught sight of the back of his head. It looked like a pressure cooker set to blow.

It was starting to get fucking hairy. Tom and Jeff fired bursts of double-taps at a position that had started to lob HE grenades at us. You could hear bits of shrapnel zinging through the air past our heads, interspersed with shouts of 'changing mag!' and the occasional 'stoppage!' from the lads as they worked their 16s.

Explosive rounds were now being pumped into the Iraqi vehicles below. I could see grenades going off, ricochet sparks everywhere.

All around us was the crack, thump and whine of small arms hitting the mound to our sides and front. Every so often, it was accompanied by an Anglo-Saxon oath as a near miss forced one of the lads to duck.

Below us, windscreens were shattering and tyres bursting, but, thank God, there were no fires, no explosions, as I suddenly noticed a bowser in the line of vehicles.

I passed word down the line. 'Watch that fucker. If that's fuel and she blows, we'll all go up with it.'

Things were going badly wrong. The dems team was now major over-time on target and we were dangerously exposed.

I sprinted back to where the vehicles were and found Tony. We rapidly considered our options. These were to fuck off to the RV, stay here and go out in a blaze of glory, or shoot our way into the target area and extract the dems team ourselves.

We decided to give them a couple more minutes. If we'd still heard nothing, we'd have no choice but to go in and get them.

Boom, boom, boom.

More firing from the rear of the battle area. It was our old friend the triple-A gun and it was getting closer again. Rounds streaked over our heads.

Scouse and Chris legged it down to the vehicles. Scouse jumped into the 110, swung the .50 in the general direction of the enemy emplacement and fired a good, long burst. Chris kept going, catapulted himself into the next Land Rover along and lined up the Milan.

There was a blinding flash as the missile left the tube. For a moment, I thought the damage the mounting had sustained had caused it to misfire. But the Milan shot off with a whoosh, wobbled as it climbed, then steadied as Chris brought it under control and steered it towards the target.

I never did see whether it struck the triple-A emplacement because over the noise of everything else, we'd all heard a crackle of static.

Tony and I shot a glance at H and saw him give a thumbs-up.

Thank Christ. The dems team.

H yelled: 'Got 'em. They're off-target.'

Tony and I yelled to the other lads with one voice: 'Bug-out time. Let's fucking *move*!'

We both knew this was going to be a bitch. The lads still on the berm descended one at a time, while the rest of us increased our rate of fire. The last men down poured as many bullets and grenades as they could into the trench.

I waited for the call from Tony. The three vehicles were fired up and ready to roll. Tony yelled, 'ready', and I shouted to the rest of the lads: 'Go! Let's fucking go!'

Tom was already behind the wheel of our 110. I said I'd heard he was a crap driver, and turned to check on Nick. No sooner were we all aboard than the first Iraqis began pouring over the top of the mound. Nick fired a last burst at them, giving us a couple of seconds respite as the Land Rover struggled to build up speed. Then, the bullets were back, winging over our heads, thumping into the sand either side of us and punching through the vehicle's skin.

'Fucking hell,' I shouted.

Tom drove like a man possessed. None of us could fire back, we were being shaken so badly. Putting distance between us and the enemy was now our only hope.

I shouted back over at Nick to see if he was OK. His position was by far the hairiest. He could see everything – the flashes, the gunfire, the tracer; he was literally staring into the gun-barrels of the enemy. Me and Tom, we could only hear it, thank Christ, but that was enough.

Suddenly, up ahead, we saw something.

'Jesus Christ,' Tom yelled, 'they're sending bikes out after us.'

Sure enough, as we bounced across the desert, I

could just make out the silhouette of a bloke on a motor-bike coming for us head-on.

There was a flurry of activity as we readied ourselves for another firefight. Then somebody noticed that the bloke on the bike looked curiously like Joe.

We held our fire. It *was* Joe.

The two parties converged. Joe did a quick tally on us, then swung round to get back on track for the ERV. It turned out that he'd gone after us on his own initiative when all attempts to raise us on the horn had failed. Soon after he drove off, however, Roger's signallers managed to get through. A brave bloke is Joe. He deserves every gong he's got.

As we closed on the ERV, Nick was still being tossed around like a rag doll. He required all his strength just to hang on. 'Tom, what fucking wanker gave you a driving test?' he cried.

We pulled up at the ERV in a screech of brakes. Tony and I checked over the fire-support group. I could scarcely believe it. Everyone present and correct. People had stopped bullets in their Bergens – some even had bullet holes through their clothes – but we had sustained no serious casualties. It was incredible.

We legged it over to Roger and the rest of the convoy and heard more good news. The dems team had made it back, too – again, pretty much without a scratch.

I felt like shouting at full volume, but we weren't safe yet.

I ran back to my vehicle and jumped in beside Tom. We set off at full tilt, aware of the need to cross the motorway before the enemy deployed along it to cut off our retreat.

We collected some stuff we'd cached on our final move in to the target and pushed quickly south, desperate for the desert to swallow us up once more.

It was as the night enveloped us again that we saw a series of explosions rip across the horizon behind us. One, two, three ... We waited for a fourth, but it never came. We were too damned exhausted to care much. The mast was history and we were on our way home, mission accomplished, all hands accounted for.

We made it back to the LUP practically on first light. Having defused the bombs on the Unimog, we set about settling back in. It didn't take long. We'd been so many days at this LUP now, it had practically become our home.

While Roger and the signallers got on the blower to RHQ, those of us who weren't on stag started doing the rounds. People moved from wagon to wagon, shooting the shit and getting the news. Everyone was on a high.

Gradually, the details of the battle emerged: Aaron's determination to take out a fuel bowser with a 66 mm anti-tank round, Roger leaving his weapon behind ...

I walked over to Taff's vehicle just as the Welsh

One was finishing the story of his hand-to-hand fight with the Iraqi.

'What happened?' I asked Dean, who was sitting back against the Land Rover and smiling.

'I had to save his arse, that's what happened.'

'Do I smell scandal?' I smirked, delighted at the prospect of something to wind Taff up about for a year or two. 'Tell me all the gory details.'

Taff overheard us. He held up his hands from where he was holding court and said: 'Hang on! Hang on! Don't listen to that tosser, Cammy. I'll give you the real story.'

He started to tell me like it was, but kept getting interrupted by Dean.

'Christ, Cammy, you should have heard him, mate. It was pitiful. All I could hear was this voice. It was like a baby's, going over and over –' and then he broke into a dreadful, childish wail – 'Dean! Dean! Heeelp! Heeelp!'

Everyone burst out laughing. But, then, everyone knew the truth. Taff was such a proficient boxer he hadn't hurt the Iraqi any more than he needed to. A sharp punch to the chin and the Arab had gone down for the count. He'd be waking up about now, alive to tell the tale to his wife and kids one day. Not a lot of people would've gone out of their way to do what Taff had done. The Iraqi had been a lucky man.

I left Taff's wagon as the conversation turned to the matter of the detonations. I walked over to Tony's wagon, where another group had gathered, including George.

'Shit, George,' I said, 'you ought to go over to Taff's vehicle and fast, mate. You're getting a right bloody slagging over there about your dets.'

George's eyes widened. 'Excuse me,' he said, lifting a trouser leg and wiggling his fingers around inside the holes made by two bullets, 'I risked life and limb to destroy that bloody mast and they're having a go at me?'

I sucked my teeth, ''Fraid so, mate.' I nodded at the holes in his combats. 'What are those things, anyway?'

Frank, who was standing nearby, belched on a mouthful of tea, winked at me and said: 'He snagged himself on a bit of barbed wire, but is telling anyone who'll listen they were made by bullets. It's sad, really.'

'That's not fucking true,' George said, starting to get really wound up.

'So what did happen?' I asked. 'About the dets, I mean? Did you put four bombs on the target?'

'Yes,' George replied.

'How many went off?' I probed.

'Er, three.'

'Well, then,' I beamed, 'that was a fuck-up.'

'Mine went off,' George said resolutely, 'it was Buzz's that didn't.'

Buzz, who'd been shooting the shit over on the

other side of the group, pricked his ears up and turned around. 'What am I being accused of here?'

'Old George reckons you didn't fire the grip-switch on your bomb, mate,' I said. The grip-switch fires the safety fuse that leads to the detonator and the bomb itself.

'That's not bloody true,' Buzz boomed. 'Mine went off.'

Frank snorted. 'Touchy, isn't he?' He dug George in the ribs and jabbed a thumb at Buzz. 'Yeah, I'll bet that was where the fuck-up was.'

'Now, listen you,' Buzz said, squaring up to Frank. 'At least, I didn't empty an entire magazine into the back of a truck. Does the word covert mean anything to you, Frankie Boy?'

Now it was Frank's turn to be defensive. 'Now hang on,' he said, putting his tea down on the 110's bonnet. 'That wasn't me. It was that stupid tosser who checked the wagon out with me.'

'You mean, Gazza?' I said.

'Right,' Frank said, nodding vigorously. 'And after that tender little speech he made about us making sure every shot counted. Christ only knows what – or who – was in the back of that thing.'

Just then, the man himself loomed out of the shadows.

'What's up?' I asked. I noticed he was carrying a clipboard under his arm.

'Body counts,' he replied, digging a pen out of a

breast pocket and doing his best to look officious. 'I need a tally. How many enemy do you reckon you took out?' He looked at each of us in turn.

I thought I'd heard everything, but this took the biscuit. Whose idea was this? And what was it supposed to achieve? Were we meant to daub little matchstick men on our wagons just to show how macho we were?

'Boss,' I said, wearily, 'I haven't got a fucking clue.'

Gazza was about to open his mouth, but thought better of it and wandered off. That, thank God, was the last we heard of it.

I finally made it back to our wagon and got down to the business of sorting things out. Nick was oiling the Mk19. Tom and Jeff were cleaning their weapons, too. The air was thick with banter and repartee.

'I don't know what you're cleaning that thing for,' Tom said, glancing back at Nick, 'you couldn't have fired off more than a few rounds.'

'What are you having a go at me for?' the BFG replied, switching his gaze to Jeff. 'It was his bloody weapon that jammed. And after all that instruction we got from Paddy, as well.'

I remembered our 'music lesson' from the weapons' specialist before we crossed over the border; a sup-posed A–Z on how to prevent a .50 machine-gun from seizing up on you in the field. I guess it only went to prove that some of these things are all fine and dandy in theory, but when it comes to action, they translate very differently.

As other tales of heroism and lunacy emerged, the camp echoed to the sound of laughter and cheers. It took many hours for the story of the night's deeds to work its way out.

Some of it was less amusing. The boys from the Close Fire Support Group, for example, said they were unsure when people first appeared on the berm whether they were soldiers or civilians. Recalling Gazza's speech, they'd held their fire for vital seconds. In time, the mood began to swing. We started to probe and ask questions about some of the bigger issues that had conspired against us.

Why, for instance, had we not been told that Victor Two had been bombed between the recce and the mission itself? And how was it that the intelligence community had so grossly underestimated the strength of the enemy on the ground? All of us knew the difficulties of enemy-threat assessment. But to be out by 1000 per cent seemed a tad extreme.

By the early afternoon, confirmation started to come in from RHQ that Victor Two was no longer in operation. Reconnaissance had shown that the place was in a complete mess. On top of it all, the mast was down and no signals were emanating from the facility anymore. We'd done everything we'd been asked to do.

George, I noticed, allowed himself a smile.

After dark, we pressed north to take a look at the MSR, but after the excitement of the night before, the whole thing was a bit of an anti-climax. After six hours of seeing nothing, we pulled back to a new LUP site.

In the course of the night, concern had started to grow about the state of our supplies, especially in the ammo and water departments. Our ordnance stocks were now down to less than fifty per cent and our water reserves were reduced to under a quarter. Fuel state wasn't much better, being approximately one third our regular provision.

In the LUP, saner heads began to mutter thanks that we hadn't encountered enemy on the MSR. If we'd had to fight, the chances were we'd be clean out of everything by now.

It was becoming rapidly clear that we needed a major resup, something more than a Chinook alone could handle. Fortunately for us, RHQ had already started to turn its attention to this problem.

Its solution wasn't just innovative or bold. It would go down in the annals of the Regiment as a complete classic.

ELEVEN

Forty-eight hours after the attack, RHQ decided to solve our fuel problem with another Chinook replen. In the meantime, they promised, they would work on a solution to the wider resupply problems that faced us. We gave them a grid for a patch of turf that we knew and promptly got word back that the flight would be on that night.

Shortly after the call came in, Roger summoned Alec, Tony and me to a head-sheds' meeting. I pretty much knew what was coming because we'd aired the issue the previous day. Now that we were well integrated into our surroundings, we found that we were spending less and less time on the bikes. But that gave us a problem in turn. Because we were one vehicle down, there was a physical lack of space within the convoy. Somebody had to go.

'We've got to lose two blokes,' Roger announced briskly. 'Sort it out between yourselves.'

At first, we reckoned we should lose one each from Air and Mountain troops, but looking at the candidates this proved impossible. Everyone from those two units was either involved in some vital task, such as manning the Milan, or was a highly proficient driver. In the end, we decided it was the guys with the least experience in the Regiment who should go.

I reached this conclusion with reluctance because of its impact on our vehicle crew. But there was logic in the call and, when push came to shove, I knew that it was the only one that was justifiable.

The grapevine was already ripe when I got back to the wagon. Three pairs of eyes watched me expectantly.

'Jeff,' I said, 'I'm fucking sorry, mate.'

He threw his hat on the ground. 'For fuck's sake! You mean, that's it? Endex?'

Jeff had done service in the New Zealand SAS before coming to Stirling Lines. He was a damn' good soldier. But, deep down, he knew why we had come to the decision we had and that it was irreversible.

'If there's any way of getting you back, we will,' I said lamely. I meant it, though.

Jeff said nothing. He wandered off a little way to be alone. Presently, he was joined by H, the other guy to get his marching orders. Within a few minutes, though, Jeff was back, his mood changed. He was back to his old self, keen to get on with the things that had to be done. That's why people like him are in the SAS. They pick themselves up and move on. I'd have had him back any day of the week.

That night, we formed up on a big gravel plain about twenty kilometres from the LUP, adopting the same formula as the earlier Chinook replen flight. Jeff drove with us to our picket station, then dismounted, ready to jump into Roger's vehicle to go down to the LSRV, which was about two klicks distant. He shook hands with the three of us, gave our rubber rat a clip round the head for good measure, and saddled up. Half an hour later, we heard the Chinook come in. It stayed on the ground for ten minutes – long enough to get the fuel off and the boys on – and then took off and flew south, its flight profile worked out, no doubt, to avoid key Iraqi air defence sites.

An hour later, we were down at the LSRV fuelling up from the burmoils it had left on the ground. We bitched and cracked jokes about being one pair of hands short for this thankless task, but it did not feel right and we drove back to the LUP in silence.

It was no longer the same team, but we figured we had a job to do still; so we just got on with it.

Later that day, two and a half days after Victor Two, we received a bizarre request from RHQ: proceed south to an area called Wadi Tubal and find an RV that was big enough to accommodate all four convoys safely. They'd elected to resupply the lot of us in one go.

Roger's reaction summed up our own: 'How the

foockin' 'eck are we supposed to hide four convoys, when we've had enough damned trouble hiding our bloody own?'

As soon as it was dark, we made our move. Wadi Tubal was a large wadi system about thirty kilometres from our start-point. We hit its northern extremity without any problems and started looking.

Five hours later we found it: a wadi within the overall wadi complex about 800 metres long and 150 wide. Its sides were steep, but not vertical. All in all, it was a good defensive position – vital if we were going to have the Regiment's entire combat strength in Iraq holed up within it for a day or two. But what really sold it was the fact you could be just a few metres away from those cliffs and not even know it was there.

In our book that's about as perfect an LUP as you get.

As soon as it was daylight, we fired a signal back to RHQ. We sent them the grid location along with a request for the time and direction we might expect the other convoys to arrive. With so many vehicles converging on one location at once we had the potential here for a 'blue on blue' engagement of frightening proportions. We had to get it right or we'd all be slotting each other.

Within an hour we got an answer: 'EXPECT CONVOYS ANY TIME FROM MIDNIGHT TONIGHT TO 0400 THE FOLLOWING MORNING.'

In return, we passed on our method for guiding the others in. We gave RHQ the lat and long of an RV a few kilometres from the wadi where a couple of our vehicles would stand picket duty all night. Once we'd verified the approaching convoy was kosher, one of our vehicles would escort it in.

The night passed slowly as we waited for them to arrive. The two Land Rovers on picket were Alec's and Taff's. The rest of us sat around the wadi killing time.

Two topics dominated the conversation: the state the other convoys would be in, along with the sort of action they might have seen; and the degree to which someone, somewhere had cocked up over this resupply operation.

To get to the point where all four convoys needed topping up at the same time smacked of poor planning. We also had no idea how they intended to get fresh supplies to us. Clearly, a Chinook flight – or even several – was out of the question; we were just too many. Which pretty much left a C-130 resup mission.

That so, the most obvious delivery method would be an air-drop, although we couldn't be sure RHQ hadn't got something else up its sleeve – like landing the Hercules nearby and having us replen directly off the back of the aircraft.

Though we were right in one respect – RHQ had indeed got something else up its sleeve – the plan didn't involve a C-130. It would be a while before we found out how they were going to pull it off and, in retrospect, I'm glad I didn't know then, because it verged on the insane.

It was nerve-wracking enough just waiting for the other convoys to come in.

The first one arrived an hour and a half before first light. It was one of the D Squadron mobs. We were just about to give up on there being any others that night, when the second, the other half of our own squadron, showed up.

Twenty minutes later and daybreak was upon us. The other D Squadron convoy had missed its window of opportunity. We wouldn't see those lads for another twelve hours, when darkness fell again. In the absence of any word from them or RHQ, we hoped they were out there lying low and not detained at the pleasure of Saddam's interrogators.

Our impatience to get together and shoot the shit with the other half of the squadron was palpable, but we just had to sit and wait while they got themselves ready. So, it was several hours before we finally got to find out about the engagement that had led to the death of our sergeant major, Robert.

Having been guided in by Taff, the other A Squadron lads were handed over to us and shown their position in the wadi. The idea was to give each half-squadron convoy its own patch, its own space.

The layout of the wadi itself helped. Every few hundred metres, the sides were punctuated by small ravines where flood tributaries had etched their way into the main body of the river bed. The two D Squadron units were situated opposite each other at the eastern end, with us and the other A Squadron half-convoy roughly in the middle. The supplies, when they arrived, would be laid out at the western end. When everything was in place, we'd all line up and help ourselves to food, fuel, water and ammo like punters in a self-service canteen.

One thing the British Army loves is its logistics.

We showed the other A Squadron lads to their ravine, which was just across the way from us. We told them where the sentries were and pointed out the bug-out route in case we were compromised. Lastly, we gave them the coordinates of the ERV – the emergency rendez-vous – and then just left them to get on with it: setting up their own sentries, linking their arcs of fire in with ours and generally squaring things away. The one thing we didn't need to do was throw any cam-nets over the vehicles. For camouflage we simply relied on the topography.

By about eight o'clock they were ready. Several of us made our way over. The first guy I ran into was Shug, the bloke we'd stitched up back at Hereford by putting Stilton Polyfilla behind his radiator. We sat down with our brews and he told me the story of their contact.

Robert had been tasked with leading a two-vehicle recce of a big radar and communications site. His vehicle acted as probe, the other as fire-base. They managed to infiltrate the perimeter, no problem. For a while, everything seemed to be going well. But then they started to encounter concrete defensive obstacles and a lot of barbed wire – warning signs that maybe they were getting a little too far in than was good for them. They were scanning like crazy and picking up a lot of other shit, too, like trench-positions, but these were empty, or so they thought.

They kept going until they were a stone's throw from the facility. Suddenly, a bunch of Iraqis stood up in a trench behind them and let them have it with guns, grenades, everything. They must have been lying low because Robert's crew never registered a thing on their thermal night-sights.

His driver knew there was no hope of escape to their front. The whole area was littered with uncharted trench lines, not to mention defensive positions. So, he threw the 110 into reverse, electing to do a 'hot-extraction' the way they'd come.

'It was crazy, of course, but I guess he didn't have any choice,' Shug said thoughtfully.

'What happened?'

'For a while he did OK, weaving in and out of trenches, still in reverse and going like shit off a shovel. But then, I guess, their luck ran out. They got hit by a packet-load of incoming and Robert took several rounds in the legs. The driver became disorientated and took a wrong turn. They shot over a berm at about thirty miles an hour into a hole that had probably been dug for a tank. The 110 ploughed straight into the far wall and Robert got catapulted out. The other two blokes were very badly knocked about, but somehow they managed to crawl free of the wreckage. They picked Robert up and carried out a fighting withdrawal, each of them taking it in turns to carry the sarn't major and fire back at the ragheads.'

That really got my admiration. Robert was a big bloke; he probably weighed in at fourteen or fifteen stone. Yet these guys had managed to carry him and give the enemy something to chew on at the same time.

'They got about a couple of hundred metres from the Land Rover and found some cover, a small mound,' Shug continued. 'Robert was pretty delirious at this point and bleeding badly. His legs and hips were shattered. The enemy was moving forward and giving them a shit load of grief.'

'Where was the other vehicle?' I asked.

'Still at the RV. They never moved. You know why?'

I shook my head. 'They never plotted an ERV before they went into the target. Poor bastards had to sit there and listen to the contact going down and pray that the guys on foot could make it to them. Trouble was, the enemy was pushing them further and further away. In the end, they had to make a decision.'

'Who?'

'Brad and Sharky, the two lads that were carrying Robert. They lugged him as far as they could, but they were being harried by the enemy all the way. Going on like that was impossible. One of them offered to shoot him.' Shug paused to take a pull of his tea. 'You know Robert, Cammy. He wasn't having any of it. He ordered them to leave him a weapon and get the hell out of there. The poor sod had had it anyway. He just wanted to take a few of them out before he died. That was the last anyone ever saw of him.'

Brad and Sharky spent the rest of the night dodging the enemy and a further two days and nights on the run. They finally managed to use a TACBE to establish comms with a Coalition fighter flying high overhead. The pilot relayed the news to Saudi and RHQ was duly informed. They were picked up by the rest of the half-squadron, which was talked onto them by radio from RHQ.

Hearing this story, my heart filled with mixed emotions: grief for the sarn't major, anger at the needlessness of it, admiration for the way these individuals had conducted themselves once the die had been cast.

Mistakes happen in war. But once this operation was done and dusted, we had a bagful to learn from. I knew that the Regiment would absorb these lessons and emerge stronger from them. That it had in the past was one of the things that had helped make it the best fighting force in the world.

Shug did have one good piece of news. One of the Bravo Two Zero patrol members had shown up in Syria after a remarkable piece of E&Eing that had taken him most of the way across Western Iraq. The fate of the other seven members was unknown. The fact that one of them had escaped was, on the one hand, encouraging. The others might not be far behind. Experience, however, said that it didn't bode well. In the meantime, we continued to hope.

As I said goodbye to Shug and wandered back to my vehicle, I had no way of knowing that this was to be our last meeting. The master-joker – a guy who knew how to take a good joke, himself – was killed in a shoot-out a few days later.

Shortly after lunch, when we'd exhausted the chit-chat with the other half of the Squadron, Roger called Alec, Tony and me to a head-sheds' meeting. Word had just come down from RHQ. They wanted us to get back up north and re-establish eyes-on with the MSR. Somebody had just woken up to the fact that, with all the convoys moving south to Wadi Tubal, we didn't have anyone maintaining a watch on Saddam's supply routes.

When I told the boys, they were incredulous. 'What the fuck?' Nick said. 'We've just come down from up north.'

'I know,' I acknowledged. 'It's a strange call, no mistake.'

'What doubly pisses me off,' Tom said, 'is that we left the MSR to do a job down here and now we're being sent back again before we've finished it.' He was talking about the fact there was still another half-squadron out there, waiting to come in.

'Do we have enough fuel to get back up north?' Nick asked. 'It must be a 160-klick round-trip to the MSR.'

'It is and we don't.' I turned to him and smiled. 'We're just going to have to go on the scrounge.'

Fifteen minutes later, our fuel gauges read full again. Nick didn't even have to call on his considerable powers of persuasion, as the D Squadron boys were extremely helpful. They gave us all the fuel and water we needed, no questions asked. I think they had some sympathy for us. We expected to be out in the field again for two or three days. As soon as the resup arrived, we'd be called back down to Wadi Tubal.

We moved out at 1530 in the full glare of the afternoon sun. The only time we'd rolled in daylight before had been following our contact with the Iraqi artillery patrol. The one thing that justified this daylight move was the fact that we knew the terrain. But it was a strange feeling, and not a little unnerving.

After leaving the wadi complex, we maintained a good steady pace until we hit a wide gravel plain. Our wagon was third in line, 200 metres behind the one in front and a similar distance from the one behind. Spacing between vehicles usually quadruples during daylight moves, unless you hit bad visibility.

Because we were so exposed, we slowed to a crawl to keep our visual signature to a minimum. Haring across this huge, flat expanse of nothingness would have kicked up a trail of shit the enemy could have seen for miles. So we dropped our speed and kept it down, stopping every 500 metres or so to do our GPS checks.

It was on one of these pull-ups that the lead vehicle, Tony's, clocked something protruding from the sand a short distance off the convoy's righthand side. We spotted it, too, and got the optics onto it. It looked like a piece of an aircraft. A little further on, we saw another object. This was clearly a fin of some kind – either from an aircraft or a missile. Either way, it didn't seem anything to get too excited about, so we pressed on.

Then, we noticed something else; on the horizon, dead ahead. A scan showed it was a house. After a quick confab, we decided to check it out, but cautiously.

It turned out to be a derelict farm-building; part of some corral, erected by the bedou, no doubt, to provide shelter for their livestock. We dismounted to give the place the once-over. It was, thankfully, quite deserted.

Suddenly, there was a yell from one of the blokes

who'd wandered a little way into the desert to examine a pile of stones we'd seen from the building. A group of us rushed over. Behind the stones, which turned out to be the top of a well, was a pile of dead goats. Christ knows how long they'd been there, but the stink was unbelievable.

We were still trying to work out what had happened, when somebody found another piece of the wreckage we'd encountered earlier. This time, there was no mistaking it. It was part of the fuel tank of a missile; a large one. Most probably, a Scud.

Jesus Christ.

It hit most of us in the same instant. A noise started going off in my head that sounded like the shrieking violins that accompany Norman Bates's shower attack in *Psycho*.

And then, it changed, still in my head, into a series of high-pitched whistle-blasts I knew all too well: Chemical attack.

We ran back to our vehicles, each of us scrabbling for our gas masks. It seemed to take me an eternity to get mine on. All the while, my mind was tumbling: Saddam had used Scuds to gas the Iranians in the 1980–88 war. We'd stumbled into some kind of test range. If this was sarin or some other such nerve-agent, we were all dead. Any second now and the first guy would start frothing at the mouth . . .

I flung myself down next to our vehicle. We carry detection paper with us that tells us if we've been exposed to chemical or biological agents. Standard practice is to stick the stuff onto strategic parts of our vehicles. We happened to have one on the wheel-arch.

I located it, scraped the shit off and held my breath. I expected to find it had changed colour or, worse almost, to watch it turning blue before my eyes.

It was the same shade of grey.

I blinked. It was still grey.

Thank Christ.

My own observation was confirmed by others. We were all right; shaken, but OK. There was no evidence of toxins. The area was clear.

I exhaled and started to breathe again.

None of us hung around to do any amateur forensics, so to this day I still don't know what killed the goats.

We left that place reminded that the conflict could still play out in a variety of unpleasant ways. I noticed, too, that I wasn't the only one who'd dug my NBC noddy-suit out of the back of the wagon and placed it in a more accessible location, just in case there was a next time and it turned out to be for real.

Soon after dark, when our Magellan GPS sets told us we were still some way from the MSR, the convoy ground to a sudden halt. We sat there scanning like crazy till we saw a figure loom out of the darkness in front of us.

It was Roger.

'Have you got your radio handy?' he panted.

'Yeah,' I said. 'What's going down?'

'No time to explain. Just get it set up. I'll be back in five minutes.' And with that, he disappeared.

'Fuck,' Tom said, 'sounds urgent.'

'Right,' I agreed. 'We'd better get cracking.'

We dragged out the 319 frequency-hopping radio and set her up. The whole procedure is pretty intricate, not least because, due to a bunch of physics I really don't understand, you need four times as much antenna length at night as you do in the daytime. Thirty metres of the stuff snaked out from the vehicle by the time we'd finished. We waited for Roger to come back.

Ten minutes later, he showed up again. The radio was tuned and ready. A dull static sound crackled across the silence.

Roger glanced at the set, then looked at me. 'What the foock's that?' he asked, pointing.

'Er, that's the radio, Rog.'

'I foockin' know it's a radio, smartarse. What's it doing out here?'

I scratched my head and looked at the others, not quite sure if I wasn't the one who was going bananas here. 'You asked us to set it up. Not ten minutes ago.'

There was a momentary pause, then Roger said: 'Not *that* radio, you wankers. I meant that little short-wave jobbie you keep in your Bergen, Cammy.' He tapped his watch. 'It's time for the results. On the World Service.'

I was so gobsmacked, I just stared at him.

'You're obviously not a Leeds supporter, Cammy. I can see it's no bloody good trying to explain to you.' He clucked irritably and stomped off in the direction of another vehicle.

A second or two of stunned silence followed. Then, Tom said: 'What a nobber. I thought we had some kind of flash message inbound.'

'Me, too,' I said, making my way out to the end of the antenna.

'I'm all for a good joke,' Nick volunteered, 'but what if we'd had a contact?'

'Hereford, nil . . . Baghdad, 30,' Tom said.

We packed the kit up. Five minutes later, we were on our way again. We reached the MSR at almost nine p.m.

Things were uneventful on the Baghdad Highway that night, so we withdrew to an LUP some distance from the road and sat out the day, fully expecting to have to go back again as soon as darkness fell for another night of thumb-twiddling. Fortunately, we were saved from a complete night of boredom by the intervention of RHQ, which told us late in the afternoon to get ourselves back to Wadi Tubal after half a night eyes-on.

The resup convoy had arrived. It was time to go stock up.

'Say again,' Tom said, when I relayed the news. His eyes narrowed in disbelief. 'Did you say *convoy*?'

'Right,' I nodded. 'No Chinooks, no airdrop. Turns out they drove a bunch of vehicles all the way in from Saudi.'

Nick whistled. 'And I thought we were the only crazy mothers around here.'

'Sorry to disappoint you, mate,' I replied, 'but we're in good company.'

Because we already knew the place, there was no need for anyone to meet us outside the wadi and guide us in. After several hours' hard journeying from the MSR, we drove straight into the dry river valley, took a hard left and pulled up in front of the resupply RV. Our mouths dropped. Even after the tip-off that RHQ had elected to do the replen with a convoy insertion, we expected to see Land Rovers and Unimogs, not four-ton trucks.

In the sketchy light of the pre-dawn we could see about fifteen big four-tonners at the far end of the wadi. Crates, burmoils, Jerry-cans and all kinds of other shit littered the ground around them.

'Fuck me,' I said, 'the last time I saw this much mess was at Greenham bloody Common.' In the good old days of the Cold War, long before Ronnie and Gorbie started to patch things up, we'd stood the occasional guard-duty over US cruise missiles based at RAF Greenham Common in Berkshire. The crap around the peace-camp there was definitely reminiscent of what we now saw before us.

Mess, of course, is anathema to us because of the signature it leaves. Unlike regular LUPs, however, this time it didn't seem to matter quite so much. There was no point trying to pretend we weren't in Wadi Tubal. If the Iraqis came for us, we had the place pretty well protected. We'd just have to fight our way out. Somehow, with the entire Gulf combat strength of the Regiment here, it was a prospect I almost relished.

After our initial surprise, we soon came down to earth again. There were priorities to attend to: ourselves, for a bloody start.

Tom pulled the wagon into the slot we'd nabbed for ourselves before our mission to Dead Goat City. In the half-light, I could make out a figure sat square in the middle of it.

'Bloody hell,' I said, turning to Tom, 'some bastard's nicked our spot.'

I jumped down from my seat and raced over to where the bloke was sat on his Bergen. I fully expected to find some chippy sod from D Squadron there, but instead I found myself staring into the fresh-faced features of Jeff.

'What the –' I started. 'What the hell are you doing here?'

'Wotcher, mate,' he said, cheerily. 'I figured you bastards would probably end up dead if I didn't get back here pronto. So, here I am. I managed to wangle myself a place on the resup convoy.'

'But what about the vehicle?' I said, pointing to our 110. We still only had room for three. That part hadn't changed, nor would it.

'Gazza's getting pulled out. I guess his time's up. He'll be going back to Saudi on the resup convoy. I guess that means I'm on Roger's wagon for the duration.'

I pulled a face, but Jeff was philosophical. 'Hell,' he said, 'at least I've got George for company.'

Just then, Nick and Tom showed up. 'Good R&R, mate?' Tom said.

'When the going gets tough, the old Kiwis fuck off,' Nick added. He grinned and extended a giant hand. 'Good to have you back, mate.'

We were together again.

'Right,' I told the lads, as we followed the rest of the half-squadron into our gully, 'let's get squared away quick and grab some of this lot before there's nothing left.' As the last unit to arrive at the wadi, we'd found ourselves right at the back of the queue; something that struck us as peculiarly unfair after we'd found the bloody place. Looking at the three other half-squadron convoys, it was clear they'd filled their boots. I just hoped there was some left for us.

Soon after sun-up, the head-sheds were called over to a meeting at Roger's vehicle. There, we saw a couple of familiar faces: Phil, our RQMS, and Dave, the guy we'd met at the fort prior to our infil across the border. Phil, it transpired, had organized the truck convoy into Iraq, while Dave had commanded it. Knowing both of them, I didn't doubt they had quite a story to tell. I promised I'd catch up with them later to hear how they'd done it.

They began by explaining how the resup would pan out. Five trucks were positioned in the middle of the wadi, each containing a particular commodity. There was one for water, another for fuel, a third for clothes, a fourth for stores and a fifth for ammunition. Our convoy would be called forward a vehicle at a time and allowed to proceed down the line helping ourselves to the things we needed.

In addition, Phil explained, he'd brought with him from Saudi a whole team of specialists who could help us sort out our equipment. There were vehicle engineers from the REME, signals technicians for our comms kit, weapons experts from the Small Arms School; you name it, they were here.

Phil offered me a smoke and I accepted it gratefully. I'd long since run out of my ready-mades and the roll-ups were getting decidedly thin.

'By the way,' Dave said, 'we've brought some spare B Squadron lads with us, too. They'll be standing watch and manning the defensive positions so you lot can get your heads down and catch up on some gonk. Don't say we don't look after you.'

'Any chance you could dig us a bloody swimming pool, then,' Tony said.

Dave laughed. 'Fuck off. This isn't Club bloody Med, you know.'

'Christ, you could have fooled me,' I said. 'Nice one, mate.'

'All part of the service.' Dave looked at his watch. 'See you in about forty minutes, then.'

We were just trooping out, when Phil stopped me. From behind his back he produced several cartons of cigarettes. Bless him. He'd recalled my plea during our short conversation before we departed the FOB.

'There's more where this came from,' Phil said.

'Cheers, mate. I owe you.'

The regimental quarter-master sergeant shook his head. 'No you don't, old son,' he said, giving it plenty of cockney, 'compliments of HMG. So, keep up the good fucking work and don't smoke 'em all at once.'

I got back to the wagon and tossed a pack of Marlboros Tom's way. It was just as well I came back with something as they'd been hard at work while I was gone 'degungeing' the vehicle.

Degungeing entails the removal of all the rubbish that accrues during an op and disposing of it in a way that will not arouse the enemy's suspicions. Stuff that can be burnt, like paper and old teabags, goes straight into an incinerator; durable items – the links from our ammo belts, for instance, and old food tins – get bagged up and, where possible, removed altogether. On this occasion, it had been decreed that the stuff that couldn't be burned would be shipped out in the four-tonners.

When you're in your 'degunged' state you're particularly vulnerable. On the good side, you are clear of all the crap you've amassed over the past few weeks; the downer is, you're minus your most basic kit, weapons included. In essence, everything has to be removed and then repacked alongside the new provisions so it's where you want it when you need it in a hurry.

Consequently, when we got our signal to get in line for the replen, we didn't hang around. At the stores vehicle we were delighted to see that, in addition to the usual tinned and powdered food, Phil and his team had brought a lot of fresh produce in with them. We left crammed to the gunwales with chickens, steaks and assorted vegetables; ingredients that would all disappear into a succession of stews and curries over the coming days. There was even a bottle of rum to wash it down with – another nice touch. Next up, the clothes wagon. Here, we were issued with new socks, arctic vests, duvets, new combat fatigues, extra webbing and brand-spanking-new Bergens. After the bullet-holes some of these backpacks had collected at Victor Two, this was no bad thing. At the ammunition truck we not only picked up bullets and grenades, but batteries for our torches and GPS sets, extra magazines and even new M16s and 203s if ours were looking a bit knackered or bashed about.

Finally, after stop-offs at the water and fuel wagons, we were done.

Then came the hard work. Back at the gully, we repacked and didn't stop until the vehicle was ship-shape. Lunchtime came and went without so much as a culinary whiff. By mid-afternoon, the vehicle was ready and we were starving. Tom prepared the food, while the rest of us sipped rum aperitifs. After an hour or so, an exotic-looking stew appeared. I'm no gourmet, but even I had to confess it was delicious. To complete an already absurdly civilized picture, we even invited the blokes from the next wagon along to partake of our tea.

In the afternoon, the socializing began in earnest. Blokes from D Squadron came over to us and we drifted over to them. Word of Graham and Victor Two had already filtered across the network and they wanted to know all the gory details. For the rest of the day and well into the night we shot shit like it had never been shot. They listened aghast to our early problems, nodded sagely at the decision to ship Graham home and pulled our legs something rotten over our claims about the odds we faced at Victor Two. We expected nothing less, of course. But after all was said and done, there was no dispute that this had emerged as the biggest and most decisive special forces' engagement of the war – so far.

That's not to say they hadn't had their own successes – and disappointments. One of the D Squadron convoys had caught a complete Scud convoy on the ground, just as the rocket was being prepared for launch. A quick signal home and in no time a bunch of American fighter-bombers appeared. The D lads vectored the aircraft onto the target and carried out the necessary laser designation for their smart bombs. The target was splashed from several direct hits, the Scud itself vaporizing into a billion pieces as its liquid fuel ignited in a violent, incandescent explosion.

Like us, one of the D Squadron units had been badly compromised.

They'd been sitting in their LUP, quietly minding their own business, when the Iraqis suddenly showed up in force. In the enemy's first wave attack, two Land Rovers got destroyed. A third became separated from the rest of the party as it fought its way out of the encirclement. In the chaos and confusion, some of the lads had to escape on foot. In one outstanding piece of bravery, one bloke carried his badly wounded E&E partner for 15 km. The injuries were sustained from a bullet that had passed right through his chest, just missing his vertebrae and vital organs. They managed to escape by hijacking a car and haring it to the Saudi border. In the process, they'd even found the decency to pay the Iraqi whose car they'd nicked with as much escape gold as they'd had on them.

In the aftermath of this episode, the D Squadron

half-convoy managed to piece together what had led to this compromise. It turned out they'd positioned the LUP less than half a kilometre from another LUP used by a different unit the previous night. Big mistake. In all probability, the Iraqis had come across the first LUP and decided to stick around to see if the SAS 'terrorists' would come back. They didn't, of course, but the Iraqis got lucky with the second group instead. Setting up the ambush thereafter should have been a piece of piss, but fortunately for the Regiment, the ragheads let it go off half-cocked. Even so, it had cost us dear. I thought our compromise had been bad, but it made me think how lucky we'd been.

Each half-squadron convoy had its own nightmare story to tell. For the other D Squadron unit it had been the time when they found themselves targeted by a couple of patrolling US fighters. Without warning, the two aircraft loosed off a salvo of AGM-65D Maverick missiles at their LUP. The AGM-65D is a heat-homer and, by the book, the vehicles inside the LUP – their thermal signatures hotter than the surrounding desert – should have been blitzed. By a stroke of good fortune, however, the Mavericks exploded between the vehicles, causing damage, but nothing terminal. Out of respect for our American cousins' at times wayward identification procedures, we'd since taken to laying out Union Jacks whenever we stopped. I noticed a bevy of them around us now.

The chat continued after dark. We wondered how

things would shape up from here. The Coalition air forces were still pummelling Iraq, but most speculators believed it could only be a matter of days, if not hours, before the ground offensive began. So, how would we fit into this picture? We'd pretty much defeated the Scud. That much was clear from some of the signals that had been coming in over the past twenty-four hours. Did that mean we'd be sent home? Or did it mean we'd be dispatched up north again for more of the same?

We started to dream up outrageous scenarios. Maybe, since we were all gathered together, they'd send us out on a regimental work out – the lot of us, *en masse* – against some really fat juicy target. Like a dam or an underground nuclear facility or something. Or maybe they'd pitch two half-squadron convoys against something slightly less ambitious, but no less exciting, such as an airfield or a barracks. There were those who were convinced this was in the offing. Others begged to differ. I was caught somewhere in the middle, hoping for action, but nagged by a sudden and inexplicable onset of foreboding.

Something at the back of my mind – some small voice – had me disturbed; as if my whole equilibrium was off-kilter. I tried to put my finger on it, but I couldn't.

Eventually, the chat died and we all drifted back to our wagons. It was weird, heading off to grab some kip under the stars, but thanks to the detail of sentries

– drawn from a mob of blokes provisionally entitled E Squadron – that Dave had brought in with him, a night of proper sleep lay ahead. I settled down in my maggot, eager for my thoughts to slide into oblivion. But sleep wouldn't come. My mind kept tumbling with thoughts of the war – what had passed and what might still be.

Slowly, I came to understand the cause of my disquiet.

We were strategic troops. The SAS had been brought into being to wreak havoc on the enemy's lines of supply. Every shot was meant to count. And, whenever we'd been used in accordance with those principles, pretty much every shot had.

It was when we were misused that things tended to go wrong.

Around the time I joined the Regiment, a story had been doing the rounds at Stirling Lines, which made the blood of every one of us boil. It concerned an alleged remark made by a senior officer in the British special forces' hierarchy during the Falklands War. Soon after the landings that signalled the beginning of the British land offensive to recapture the islands from the Argentinians, the Parachute Regiment took a great many casualties in their spectacularly brave assault on Goose Green, a tough Argentinian stronghold. Overnight, they became heroes; and the name of Colonel 'H' Jones, who'd led the assault and died in the process, passed into legend.

According to people who said they knew, the SAS,

who'd been covertly harrying the enemy for some weeks behind their lines as well as passing on vital reconnaissance information, were told they 'needed to be seen to be taking casualties' to elevate the Regiment's profile back in London. Less than a week earlier, a Sea King helicopter transferring troops between two warships had struck a seabird and crashed into the South Atlantic. Nineteen soldiers from D Squadron who'd been on board had drowned as a result.

Seen to be taking casualties. Sometimes, there's no bloody pleasing some people.

Whether or not the remark was totally true, I could see it coming back to haunt us now. The Gulf War had entered a critical, yet curious phase. Together with the air forces of the Coalition, we'd pretty much taken the Scud out of the loop. In essence, we'd all but completed the job we'd been assigned to do. But with the land war brewing, there was a lot to be done on the broader front. Saddam was still in Kuwait and showed no sign of moving. My concern was that someone in London or Riyadh was going to wake up one morning and tell RHQ that the SAS needed to justify its existence if it wanted to stay in Iraq. And with that kind of pressure on it, I reckoned it wasn't beyond the bounds of possibility that the guys safe in Saudi might just be tempted into some kind of 'mission impossible' – something to go down in the regimental annals for all time. Fine, I figured, if the target was worthwhile – if it was strategic. Not so fine, if it turned out to be a poxy irrelevance – a place where we could be 'seen to be taking casualties' for some arcane political purpose in Whitehall.

As I lay back on the sand with the heavens spread above me, I finally put my finger on what had been troubling me.

In one significant respect, we were no different from any other foot-soldiers. We might have been the British Army's elite, but if push came to shove, we were expendable. Cannon-fodder. Like any grunt in time of war.

It was an unsettling realization.

Just as I rolled over in a determined effort to go to sleep, the sky erupted with a deafening roar as a flight of jets shot over our position. Everyone roused themselves and tensed, but the bombs that would have struck us had the planes been Iraqi never came. There were a number of muttered curses from those around me, then only silence split by the occasional snore as everyone lapsed back into sleep.

As I lay back on the sand, a fine, almost imperceptible mist settled on my face. For a moment, I was gripped by fear – the same dread feeling that had dawned on us beside the pile of dead goats.

This time, however, I rationalized it and kept quiet, rolling over to check the piece of NBC paper that I'd kept on me since the incident at the well. In the beam of my penlight, I could see that it was clear.

For me, this curious, inexplicable incident served two purposes. It summed up how much we'd all grown up since that first nervy night when we slipped across the border. More importantly, however, there and then, it helped to clear my mind.

As a result, within a few moments, I was asleep.

I awoke the next morning well after first light and got up feeling refreshed, my Duracells fully recharged. Soon after the first brew of the day, we got to work on clearing up the wadi. As Phil was in charge of this operation it gave me a chance to find out the background to the decision to drive the convoy into Iraq.

The moment RHQ realized the severity of the replen situation, it reached a tough decision: since airlift would not solve the problem, the only alternative was to drive the much-needed matériel to the Regiment in Iraq. When General Schwarzkopf was told, he was surprised, apparently, but supportive: 'Let me know how you're going to do this and I'll divert all the air and land assets I can spare to make it happen,' he'd told our planners in Riyadh.

The day the convoy left, the weather turned shitty and Schwarzkopf was forced to report that fighter cover would not be available till it cleared. RHQ said bollocks to that and just drove, hell for leather. The Regiment had an appointment to keep and it wasn't waiting for anyone. When Schwarzkopf found out he was incredulous: 'Whaddyamean "they just drove in"?' he told the poor messenger who'd delivered this piece of news. The information was repeated. 'Goddamn, those Brits have balls,' Schwarzkopf muttered. 'Give 'em all the help they need.'

Dave's technique for crossing enemy territory was simple: nobody stopped for anything; they were to keep going, no matter what. With no escort, the four-tonners couldn't afford to get into a firefight. Unless, of course, it was real close, in which case, they'd just have to pull up and think again. 'Boss, what do you call "real close"?' one of the drivers had asked him. 'Something that breaks your windscreen,' Dave replied. 'Now let's all saddle up and fuck off.'

For twenty-four hours they'd driven hard, pushing on, on, on to Wadi Tubal. They didn't have any PNGs, so the whole drive was done in daylight. They met two obstructions along the way, both of which were dispatched by air-delivered laser-guided munitions vectored to their targets by hand-held LTDs. I asked Dave if he was worried about the return journey. He was remarkably philosophical about it. They'd shot their way in and they'd shoot their way out again. These guys really were larger than life.

Soon after I got back to our vehicle, word came down that Roger wanted all senior ranks to gather for a talk later in the afternoon in an area away from the resupply wagons.

'It can't be haircuts,' Nick said, preening himself in the reflection of his goggles.

'Or our beards,' Tom added, scratching the growth on his chin. 'We're at fucking war.'

'Maybe you're not allowed into theme parks with stubble,' Nick said. 'They think you're a bender or something.'

'Who knows?' I chipped in. A talk with the RSM was serious. Something was in the wind.

'Do you think this could be it?' Tom said, later. 'The big one.'

'Maybe,' I nodded. 'Let's just hope it's a worthwhile target.'

Later that afternoon, I grouped with the senior NCOs from A and D squadron. While we waited for Roger to open the meeting, you could taste the excitement in the narrow gully where we'd all gathered. No question about it, this had to be the regimental work-out half of us had anticipated.

It was then that I glanced over my shoulder and saw Phil. I was still trying to work out why the Regimental Quarter Master Sergeant – our food-king – was at a planning conference that had all the makings of a war-party pow-wow when Roger stood on a boulder and the meeting kicked off.

It took a few minutes before we got the gist of what was happening here. It was a case of our ears working fine, but our sodding brains not believing the inbound message.

'Fuck,' I heard Tony say behind me. 'It can't be.'

I turned around. 'It is.'

One hundred kilometres inside Iraq, Britain's biggest war since Korea going on around us, and the warrant officers and sergeants of the Special Air Service had been called to a mess meeting.

It was serious business. Definitely no laughing matter. Top of the agenda was the forthcoming summer ball, followed by an outstanding mess account and the weighty matter of whether or not the sergeant's mess could afford a new suite and some nice blue curtains.

The motions were discussed, passed and the minutes recorded in a notebook so they could be transferred back to Hereford.

On my return to the vehicle, I stopped cursing and burst out laughing.

'What is it?' Nick asked.

I tried to get the words out, but the tears kept rolling down my face.

Nick, Tom and Jeff stared at me like I'd flipped. They must have been thinking: Poor old sod. A month behind the lines and he's gone, a headcase.

Eventually, I managed to tell them about the meeting in the gully.

Their reaction was pretty much the same as mine. Disbelief. Anger. Laughter. Hysteria. It took us most of the rest of the afternoon to stop crapping ourselves.

Later, I managed to see this side-show in its true

light. Who cared if it was British bureaucracy at its worst? It showed that even in the enemy's backyard, we were in control. Totally relaxed. Life went on and nothing was going to interfere with it.

The SAS had some new curtains to choose. Saddam could go swivel.

D Squadron moved out later that afternoon, back to their old stamping ground along the MSR. Soon after they'd departed, Dave and Phil noticed Russ and Brett were missing. Both were part of the spare B Squadron contingent who'd joined the resup convoy to help out.

After a thorough search of the camp and the surrounding area, we reached the inevitable conclusion: they'd gone along for the ride as 'hostages' of D Squadron.

RHQ took an extremely dim view of this. At the first opportunity, a message winged its way to the miscreants: enjoy the next five days, fellers, but you're on the first Chinook replen flight out. Anyone not on board could expect some swift justice.

Both A Squadron half-convoys hung around for one more night. The following day, we received our orders and headed out, leaving Phil and Dave and the rest of their mob to clear up the wadi before they, too, shipped back to Saudi.

They didn't want to hang around. Rumour had it the Coalition land offensive was imminent. It was bad enough having to fend off the Iraqis. The last thing

Dave needed, however, was to run into the psyched-up might of the US Marine Corps as it steamed across the border full-tilt towards Baghdad.

Even Dave had reservations about who would come out the victor.

Me, I was in no fucking doubt.

TWELVE

After Wadi Tubal, we headed back to our old friend the main east–west MSR. Our brief was to look for – and, if necessary, destroy – any Scuds that might have slipped through the net. Traffic was light, but we kept our eyes peeled anyway. You knew at the back of your mind that Saddam was bonkers enough to try something desperate; and that included dispatching a full-up Scud convoy down the Baghdad–Jordan highway to the rocket-launching grounds that dotted this area.

Two nights later, and not a whiff of anything remotely resembling a Scud, we realized they weren't coming; not here, at any rate. But with no sign of any fresh directive from RHQ, we could see ourselves ending the war here. After the fever-pitch excitement of the previous week, the danger now was slow death by boredom.

And then, on the afternoon of the second day, I found myself summoned to Roger's wagon.

'Christ,' Tom said, rousing himself from his sleeping bag, 'remember to take your cheapo fags with you.'

Good point. I swapped the packet of Silk Cut in my pocket for some Embassies and set off. I couldn't afford at this late stage in the war to have my reserve of good smokes wiped out by Roger's insatiable appetite for other people's cigarettes. Rog, as every smoker in the half-squadron convoy knew, would scrounge a fag off a corpse if he got the opportunity.

As soon as I lifted the edge of his cam-net, the RSM told me the reason for the summons: I was to lead a recce that night into a place RHQ had earmarked 'the triangle of death'.

'Why?' I asked. 'What's going down?'

'I don't know,' Roger replied.

'Does RHQ?'

'Maybe, maybe not.'

'What the fuck does that mean?'

'They said they wanted us to check it out for the hell of it. But I got the impression there was a definite reason for the mission in there. Be careful tonight, all right?'

It took a lot to bring out Roger's more sensitive side. Somewhat shaken by his concern for us, I promised I would.

We looked at the map.

The 'triangle' wasn't big; its total area was probably no more than thirty square kilometres. It was bordered on three sides by roads, hence the first part of its monicker. The death bit was harder to get a handle on, but bending over the map, you could tell that it wasn't your average house of fun.

Getting in wasn't the real problem. Half the reason for our survival to date was the fact we had the entire desert at our disposal. The triangle was different. If we got a contact, the enemy could move troops along the roads and seal the place. Then, it would simply be a case of trawling it till they fished us out, dead or alive.

'What do you think's so special about this place?' I asked.

'Search me,' Roger said, slapping his pockets as he went through the first of what I knew would be many a bogus fag search ritual. I cut this one short and offered him an Embie. He gave the packet a sneer, but took one anyway.

'I s'pose in the end you don't put three roads around a patch of bloody desert for nothing,' he said.

'Right.' The logic was sound, but I still couldn't figure out why they didn't just send an aircraft.

Roger must have detected the note of scepticism in my voice. He looked up and said: 'Your job is to recce a bloody route into that place, nothing more. You're to take one other vehicle. You'll leave at last light and be back by first light the following day. Got it?'

'Sure, Rog. No problem.'

Then, he bent over the map. 'Report back your route before you go, but if you ask me that looks like the place you want to head for.' He gave me a conspiratorial wink, which was meant to convey a sort of have-that-one-for-nothing, on the house kind of comradeship.

I looked down and blinked. Roger was pointing at the bottom right-hand apex of the triangle. From the way the roads converged it looked like a major intersection, undoubtedly topped off by a fucking great bridge. I searched his expression for signs of a wind-up, but as usual with the RSM, you couldn't read a whole lot behind those eyes. I simply about-turned and left.

On the way back, I rounded up Taff. The Welshman was not just a sound reccier, he also had the right vehicle for the job. It wasn't so much the Milan I was interested in – our brief, after all, was to avoid enemy contact at all costs – as its MIRA night-sight. The MIRA, which cues on heat, is able to pick out a camouflaged tank on a pitch-black night at around twenty klicks. This gives it a great recce capability, one that, on this patrol, I figured I might just need.

With Tom looking over our shoulders, Taff and I spread the map on the bonnet of my 110. I told them about Roger's bridge suggestion and asked them what they thought.

'Nah,' Taff said, 'he's taking the mickey.' Tom nodded in agreement.

That settled, we went about searching for a proper way in. What we needed – and what was evidently lacking on a first trawl across the map – was a safe way of crossing the autobahn that ran along the southern edge of the triangle.

Eventually, we found it, but only after some detective work that would have got each of us an A grade with distinction if we'd been sitting a bloody geography exam. By following the contour lines in the immediate area, it was apparent that a lot of water needed to cross this road during the rainy season. Having traversed the autobahn on our mission to Victor Two, we knew it was a serious piece of engineering. That meant the Iraqis would have left nothing to chance.

'If you ask me,' I said, summing up and pointing to the map, 'there are culverts, here, here and here. That's our bloody way in. We don't go across the motorway. We go under it.'

Cue a flurry of further scrutiny by the other two, followed by nods of assent. We had us a plan.

I wandered back to Roger's vehicle with the map. The only thing that niggled was the memory of what D Squadron had done to their vehicles back at the Forward Mounting Base. They'd removed their rollbars to lower their profile and to allow them freer access to tunnels like these. We'd dismissed it at the time. Now, I found myself wondering if we mightn't end up getting beaten by a few measly inches of headroom.

I started to go over our handiwork to Roger, but suddenly he cut me short. 'I thought I'd made myself clear. Now do as you're told and go over it again. The bridge, Cammy. Use the foockin' bridge.'

It takes a lot to get me riled, but I left his wagon seething. You want the fucking bridge, I thought, I'll give you the fucking bridge.

I dropped by Tony's wagon and ran it past him, just in case I was the one who was losing it. But the mobility man's verdict was clear: using the bridge was madness. 'If I were a betting man, I'd put a month's wages on there being swarms of ragheads on it,' he said. 'You poor, sorry-arsed fucker, Cammy. Looks like it's suicide time all over again.'

Great, I thought.

Taff and I adjusted our nice, safe route to the culverts with a run that would take us as close to the bridge as we dared. As far as we were all concerned, we now had two objectives tonight: find a way into the triangle; and bring back proof that the bridge was occupied to prevent Roger killing the entire bloody convoy.

We set off after dark with the rest of the wagons, peeling off when they reached their observation point overlooking the MSR. For the next two hours, we moved slowly, our vehicle leading. Tom, who was driving, scoured the ground ahead for signs of trouble. He was wearing a pair of the massive PNGs that most drivers consider mandatory for traversing hostile territory by night. The rest of us scanned like crazy with our hand-held night optics. These are good for general observation of the terrain, but have nothing like the power of the PNGs. It came as little surprise, therefore, when Tom pulled up abruptly while we were still about eight klicks from the bridge and just sat there staring into the black emptiness ahead.

'What is it?' I whispered. At the same moment, I started to scan, but saw nothing.

'Dunno,' he shot back. 'Something's out there . . .'

'What do you mean? Where?'

He leaned forwards. 'Dead ahead. Something dark and very big. About thirty metres away.'

Now I see it. A big black expanse in front of the vehicle. In my mind's eye, I read it as an enormous boulder obstructing our path. I got out of the wagon and started walking. As I moved, the outline changed. Suddenly, it had shape-shifted into something quite different. Not solid at all, but empty. Like a trench . . .

A trench. No question.

And then, I was hit by a second realization, more heart-thumping than the first. What if it was manned?

Jesus, Cammy, a month in this place and you fall for that one hook, line and sinker, you stupid bastard.

I dropped down onto my haunches, trying to slow

the tempo of my breathing. I needed to scan, but I also needed to listen.

I approached it slowly, my M16 with 203 grenade-launcher attachment in one hand, my optic scope in the other. I peered over the lip and into the base of the trench, half-expecting to see bodies huddled in sleep or, worse, staring up at me through the darkness.

Empty, thank Christ.

We still weren't out of it. If we'd found one slit trench, chances were there would be others.

Nick and I moved forward a hundred metres, then fanned out a further 300 to the sides. Taff and one of his blokes did the same to the rear. Forty minutes later, we reported back. There were other trenches, but they were all unoccupied. The big question was, would they stay that way when we came back the following night?

We decided to push on, even though there was just a chance that what we'd stumbled upon was a forward position of some formidable defence system stretching in front of us. To minimize the risk, Nick and I decided we'd walk a hundred or so metres ahead to provide that little bit of advance warning, just in case this did turn out to be some kind of enemy shindig in depth.

We passed a couple more trenches during the next hour, but progress was painfully slow. Conscious of the need to press on, and deeming the risk to be low, we saddled up again. Nick took over the driving, giving Tom's poor old eyes a well-earned break. PNGs can be murder on the vision. So much so, that Nick elected to drive without them.

The ground started to become more rugged. The wagon was bucking like a wild steer. We kept going, counting down the klicks to the bridge. We were only about five kilometres away, when suddenly there was a tremendous lurch and the next thing I knew I was catapulted forward onto the dash, my head only just missing the butt of the GPMG.

There was a hideous shriek of brakes, then a wild crunching noise as the tyres bit into the crumbling sandstone. A black void filled my vision. I prepared myself for the moment when the vehicle went over. Funny, I remember thinking, but the night my number came up, it wasn't a stake that got me, but several tons of Land Rover. And then a momentary flash, like a pulse of electricity through my brain: What if it's down there, pointing upwards, in the blackness, just waiting for me . . .

Unlike me, Nick, to my right, was free of any such thought. He yanked on the hand-brake and jumped. He must have presumed he was going to hit solid ground, but he dropped off the side of the vehicle and fell like a stone. He didn't scream. He didn't utter a sound. All I heard was the noise of his body bumping on the rocks below and the scrape and rattle of stones, earth and boulders tumbling in his wake.

My stupor left me and I was up and out of my seat, scrabbling across the back of the vehicle. Tom had already gone. I found him by the side of the precipice calling down into the abyss. I joined him, calling and listening by turns.

'Jesus Christ,' I said. 'He's gone.'

'How deep's this thing?' Tom panted.

'Fuck knows.' I called down into the darkness some more.

Nothing.

Then Taff and Dean showed up. The four of us yelled for Nick to respond. Still, nothing.

'Get a pocket-scope,' I blurted. 'Let's see if we can pick him up on that.'

Taff jogged back to his vehicle and returned a moment later with the requisite optics.

I pointed it into the void and started scanning. It took me a while to adjust to the darkness. The wadi was deep. There was much less ambient light than the surrounding terrain. I swept past something I thought was a large cluster of rocks. Then, they moved.

'Nick,' I yelled.

This time, I got a very faint response. Thank Christ. He was alive.

Five minutes later, the BFG had recovered sufficiently to check himself over. He'd fallen sixty feet and knocked himself out for a moment. As it turned out, though, it looked like he had escaped with cuts and bruises and perhaps a bit of concussion. Behind his bravado, however, I could tell he was in a lot of pain.

He tried to climb up the side of the wadi, but gave up after five minutes. It was just too steep. He was in no fit state to do any mountaineering.

It was Taff who suggested we lower some tow chains down. Nick tied himself to the hook and we started to pull him out.

Slowly, slowly, we caught our monkey. In a couple of minutes, he was back at the top. He was bleeding quite badly from multiple abrasions, but waved aside offers of help. I guess he knew we needed all hands on deck to shift the Land Rover from its precarious perch on the lip of the ravine.

Fair enough, I said. We'd patch him up later. For the moment, I told him to sit tight and take it easy.

We put sentries out and got to work. The times when we need to tow a vehicle are the moments when we are most vulnerable. With the chains attached, Tom got behind the wheel of our vehicle, while Taff did the pulling. Those of us who weren't on stag or in the vehicles could only stand around and watch. Both drivers were trying desperately to keep the noise of their engines to a minimum. As a result, our Land Rover looked as if it wasn't going anywhere.

In the end, I could stand it no longer. I ran over to Taff and yelled: 'Forget the fucking noise. Just do it and let's get the hell out of here.'

Taff nodded and hit the accelerator. In the vastness and the silence, the noise of those screaming engines felt like they'd be heard by every living thing for miles.

Then, suddenly, there was a whirl of motion and our 110 staggered back from the edge.

Everybody's nerves were frayed. We rebelled against our urge to drive like the clappers and forced ourselves to sit there and cool it for a few minutes. We broke open our flasks and waited in the darkness, smoking and sipping our brews until our battle-senses returned. I couldn't help but curse Roger for sending us on this bloody stupid route. Around me, I heard the odd mutter about the patrol being jinxed.

Half an hour later, we got eyes-on the motorway. A moment or two after that, the bridge swung into view. It was every bit as big a piece of engineering as we'd thought it would be; like any large flyover you'll see crossing the M25. The bridge itself was devoid of any lighting, though on either side of it the autobahn was bathed in the same orangey strip-lit glow we'd come to recognize from our forays to and from Victor Two.

We broke out the MIRA and took a long look. To my immense surprise, I saw nothing; not so much as a blip of heat. Thinking we might be a tad too far even for the MIRA's super-cooled, super-sensitive optics, I took us forward to within a thousand metres of the flyover. We scanned again and still saw nothing.

'Fuck me,' I said, thinking of Roger's smug bloody grin when I told him, 'he can't be right; he just can't be.'

Tom and I went forward on foot, stopping when we got to within 200 metres of the bridge's massive concrete stilts. I'd left my M16 and 203 behind to carry the MIRA. I swept the shadows under the flyover for a good fifteen minutes, but still the night-sight registered zip. Now, I decided to do a 360-degree scan of the surrounding desert, just in case we'd missed anything.

Tom kept his back to mine so he could watch my six o'clock as I scanned. We'd pirouetted a fair way round, when suddenly I dropped down onto my haunches.

'What is it?' Tom whispered over his shoulder.

'Something . . . I saw something.' In the reflex-action that felled me I'd lost it. But something was out there, all right. On the MIRA it had burned a white-hot hole onto the screen. That meant it was big – and close.

I panned across the horizon in front of me. Then, my heart stopped.

Tom must have heard my sharp intake of breath. 'What the fuck is it?'

'Vehicles,' I said, trying to keep my voice even. 'Two of 'em. Less than a klick away. Shit, and they're crawling with fucking troops.'

Tom didn't speak. I expected him to say something. But it was like he had been struck dumb.

'Tom?'

'Yeah.' He paused. 'Crawling, you say?'

'Well, there's more than three registering on the scope.'

'How about four blokes, all told?'

I half-turned. 'You can see 'em?'

He dug me hard in the ribs. 'I don't need to. They're ours, you plonker. Those are our fucking one-one-ohs you're looking at.'

I was hit by a moment of disbelief. Then, I hung my head and smiled ruefully. I'd been so fixed on scanning, I'd forgotten about the Land Rovers. A wave of relief washed over me. I was surprised Tom didn't kill me on the spot.

We moved forward a little closer to the flyover for one last check. This time, Tom took the MIRA and I watched our tail.

Suddenly, I was overcome with an acute need for a dump. I crap regular as clockwork soon after breakfast whether I'm on ops or not, so the urge to drop one here, now, came as something of a surprise. I told Tom, endured a few insults in response, and edged backwards till I found a boulder, my very own throne under the stars.

I dropped my combat fatigues, pulled down my NBC trousers and hung my arse out over the rock.

The package was mid-way when Tom, no more than six feet away, suddenly turned and rasped: 'Cammy! Enemy!'

For the second time in half an hour, my ticker almost died on me. 'Where?' I shot back. My attention was seized by the flyover. I couldn't see a thing on it, but that didn't mean there wasn't anybody there. Tom had gone into a low crouch. He'd lowered his head to reduce his profile, something he'd only do if the enemy was close. Like within spitting distance.

That did it.

I pulled up my trousers and unholstered my sidearm in a fluid movement that ended with the gun in my hand and a truck-load of squashed shit in my pants. My sixteen was on the vehicle. I'd left it there to carry the MIRA. Fucking typical.

I crawled towards Tom, a gargoyle-like figure silhouetted against the distant lights of the autobahn.

I touched him lightly on the shoulder. 'Where?' I whispered, so low I could barely hear myself.

Tom's body had gone rigid. I could feel it convulsing slightly, like it had gone into spasm or shock.

He turned, biting his lip. There was a wild look on his face.

'Cammy?'

'What, for Christ's sake?'

'It's a wind-up, mate.'

And then he collapsed laughing.

I don't know why I didn't shoot him. I sat there for a moment, letting the realization sink in. We weren't going to die. I was so relieved, I didn't have room for anger. For a second or two, it was the best bloody feeling in the world.

Then a whiff hit me and I remembered the package in my noddy-suit.

We set off back to the vehicles at a steady lope. I was feeling uncomfortable, but I kept my little secret to myself. I figured that if an NBC suit could keep mustard gas out, it could definitely stop a heavy seepage of shit escaping from the inside out.

After briefing Taff and the others, we drove onto the slip road and up onto the bridge itself. When we were half-way across, we stopped and looked out over the edge. That was when we saw the bomb-damage. Either side of the flyover, craters dotted the ground. A line of electricity pylons lay where they'd fallen. The attacking aircraft had missed their target, but done a thorough job of ploughing up the local country-side. It was only when you got above it that you saw it. It also explained why there was nobody here. They'd legged it and not come back.

We drove on about 200 metres past the bridge and then left the road. Getting into the triangle would not present a problem. We could forget about culverts. As long as we put in a big dog-leg south of the autobahn to clear the trench positions, we'd be all right. I just didn't know how I was going to break the news to Roger: against all the odds, and by a fluke of botched flying, his kooky scheme for entering the Triangle of Death had paid off.

For good measure, we drove back to the RV via our newly plotted dog-leg. Tom drove. I sat next to him. Along the way, I decided to forget my self-respect and go for a little payback. I tugged at the elastic of my NBC trousers and wafted a curtain of grim odours in his direction. The atmosphere was as unpleasant as anything you'll find at Porton Down, the chemical and biological warfare establishment in Wiltshire.

He pulled a face. Seeing I was on-target, I kept fanning. Just the thing, I figured, to help the concentration over the rough terrain we'd started to encounter.

Tom endured this for thirty minutes, then snarled, 'All right, all right. It was just a bloody joke, OK?'

'*Now* you know why they call us crap-hats,' I said. I looked at my watch and smiled. By my reckoning there was another hour to go before we hit the RV.

The day passed normally except for two things. The more worrying of the two concerned Nick, who wasn't in a good way. He was putting on a brave face, but you could tell he was hiding the full extent of his injuries. A more thorough examination of his body had led him to the conclusion he had a couple of cracked ribs. He was also pissing blood.

There was little chance of a CASEVAC out. And in any case, the BFG was insistent on staying. I didn't like it, but in the end we had no choice.

The second problem concerned my NBC trousers, which were about to become a serious bio-health hazard. How to wash those suckers when water was in such short supply? I tried to persuade Tom it was his responsibility, but, for some reason, he wouldn't wear it. Tom's a great bloke, but he'd make an awful wife.

In the end I decided the trousers were beyond redemption and buried the bastards.

With commendable self-restraint, Roger never made a big deal over his sixth-sense instinct regarding the bridge. He briefed us on our mission in the afternoon. The plan was simple: check into the triangle, check it for activity and check out again pronto.

We set off as soon as it was dark and reached the bridge without a hitch. Tony and I moved our vehicles onto the flyover where we both kept watch. We sent a couple of bikes back to guide the others over. They came across two at a time. The process was done and dusted inside forty minutes, no fuss, no trouble.

We started patrolling at about one in the morning. We'd got no more than a few kilometres when we realized we had a big problem. The terrain had become a never-ending series of undulating hills. You could be a few hundred metres from the enemy at any time and not even know it – a situation that's potentially fatal for us.

The head-sheds quickly came to a decision. We stopped driving and closed the vehicles down. We put guards out and hunkered down for the night, sleeping where we sat, in our vehicles. We'd patrol again in daylight, when at least we could see slightly further than our own noses. It was a big step, but one that had to be taken. We'd never seen country like this before. Coupled with the fact we were hemmed in by three major roads, it called for extreme measures.

We began patrolling again at eight. It was a weird feeling moving by day – like the time when we'd first crossed the border, we scanned for trouble every which-way, our eyes bulging like rats.

After a couple of hours with no sign of the enemy, we started to relax. Then, just before lunch, the convoy pulled up abruptly. Tony's lead vehicle had stopped just short of a mound. The mobility man got out, scrabbled up its rocky slope and settled into a prone position on the ridgeline.

He remained there, immobile for five minutes that soon drifted into ten. If Tony deemed it sensible to hang around watching whatever it was that had seized his attention for the rest of the day, that was good enough for me. But Roger, several vehicles behind us, lost the plot completely.

Suddenly, his 110 hared past us full tilt. I jumped out of my seat and ran after it, wondering what the hell had got into him.

Roger floored the accelerator and tore up the side of the mound, stopping just short of the brow in a cloud of dust. The watchers on top turned, their faces a uniform picture of the Planet Gobsmack.

When I got to them, Buzz and Roger were having a full-blown argument. I found out later that, as the watchers had stared back at him slack-jawed, Roger, aka General George Patton, had stood up in his seat and yelled: 'What the foock are you lot waiting for?'

To which Buzz retorted: 'A shit-load of incoming, unless you wind your fucking neck in and get that wagon off this mound.'

That was when it degenerated into a dangerous slanging match, the two of them squaring up to each other like a pair of pugnacious bulldogs.

Shit, I thought, as I pounded up the mound. So, this is what happens when you overstay your welcome. A month ago, this would never have happened. We were all pretty much one big happy family. Maybe we were starting to lose it. Maybe it was time to go home.

Blokes waded in and pulled Roger and Buzz apart. It had been so bad that for one moment I thought Buzz had been about to hit him.

When I peered over the crest of the mound I saw why.

Stretching away in front of us was an enormous antenna farm. Dozens of tall, thin masts sprouted from the desert over an area the size of a couple of football pitches. We'd hit some kind of listening post in the desert, a very sophisticated one.

This, I guessed, must have been the real reason we'd been sent into the Triangle. RHQ would have been aware of the signals coming from this place, which was almost certainly another comms node – a major one – in Saddam's Scud launch network. Looking at it now, though, I saw that it would have been damned difficult to detect from the air. Because the masts were thin and spread out, an overflying pilot would probably have missed them. Yet, listening stations in Saudi would have calculated the position of this thing to an area within the Triangle. We couldn't recce something that hadn't been found. So, they dispatched us into the Triangle to see what we could see and report back.

Gazing out over the antenna farm, I realized something else, too. Despite what we'd done at Victor 2, the Scuds were still operational. The Coalition hadn't erased them at all. This simple weapon could still hold the allies to ransom and win the war for Saddam. No way could we head home yet. General Schwarzkopf still needed us here.

Roger got the gist and backed up the Land Rover. He had no time to dwell on his mistake. We held a quick meeting of the head-sheds and decided to get the place fixed and lased as quick as we could. That way, we'd be able to provide the mission planners back in Riyadh with a precise set of coordinates for the flyboys when they came visiting in their F-15Es and F-16s.

Suddenly, a cloud of dust sprang up from the desert to our right. All eyes locked onto the source of it; a vehicle moving fast down the flank. Somebody got the binoculars out and said the dreaded words, ZSU-23/4.

The ZSU-23/4 is a Russian-built tracked vehicle fitted with a formidable radar-guided quad-23 mm gun system. It was designed to shoot down aircraft and helicopters, but it's also pretty damn good at blowing the shit out of soft-skinned land vehicles.

We edged back off the ridge and watched.

The vehicle kept going and didn't stop. We had no idea if it had seen us or not. And then somebody hit on the notion that it was part of some posse that had been sent out to encircle us. We got back in the vehicles and drove for five kilometres, just to get away from the antenna farm, scanning all the while in the direction we'd last seen the mystery Iraqi vehicle. But it had disappeared.

We carried on patrolling the triangle, but the combination of this incident and the fact we were now driving around in the full glare of the sun had spooked us. We were glad when the job was done and we could get the hell out of there, back to the wide open desert where entrapment wasn't so much of a threat.

We got back to the motorway that night. Except for one thing, the approach went relatively smoothly. We stopped about a kilometre short of the bridge. I got out the MIRA, expecting to do a quick scan and see nothing, but instead I got a small, but positive heat signature. It had all the properties of a guard on stag.

'Foockin' 'eck,' Roger said, 'I never did like the look of that bloody bridge anyway.'

After the fuss over the culverts, I couldn't quite believe I'd heard this. I opened my mouth to say something, but thought better of it. I worked off my anger by tabbing over towards the bridge with Taff for a closer inspection.

Five hundred metres from the road we did another MIRA check and, bingo, there it was again – a single blip on the screen. We settled down and watched. If there was one bloke, there would be others. Forty minutes later, our lone heat source hadn't moved. Not a muscle. I figured that our guard was either a Zen Buddhist or had fallen asleep.

A last possibility, of course, was that it wasn't a guard at all, but something inanimate. Taff and I ran back and held a quick meeting with Tony.

'What the hell,' Tony said, 'if it is a guard, we'll Milan the poor bastard. He won't know what's hit him.'

Fortunately, the 'guard' turned out to be a concrete post. It must have absorbed the heat of the sun and cooled more slowly than the surrounding flyover. The MIRA's super-cooled optics are that sensitive. It was a surreal ending to a place we were glad to see the back of. The Triangle had had us all spooked.

We crossed the motorway without incident and headed south. The general feeling was that our days of going north were over. Given the comms node we'd found, though, I couldn't help wondering whether we might, after all, soon be on our way back.

THIRTEEN

The next morning, Sunday, we awoke to the news we'd been expecting for days. At 4 a.m., allied forces began pouring through selected points along a 500 km stretch of the Iraqis' defences around Kuwait. The attack had opened with an artillery barrage the like of which had not been seen in this neck of the woods since El Alamein. Except for the weather, which had turned to rat-shit, things appeared to be going to plan, but it was difficult to read the picture accurately from the garbled reports we were picking up on the BBC.

At eight, Roger convened the head-sheds. RHQ had been on the horn. We were to work our way towards the Saudi border and await further instructions. Because no one had the least idea how the land offensive would go, they wanted us to remain inside Iraqi lines, just in case we needed to head full-tilt for Baghdad and rub out the Moustachioed One.

One other directive was of significance. From now on, we would do all our moves by daylight. This stemmed from two changes in the big picture: one, the Iraqi Army was deemed to be more preoccupied with what was happening in Kuwait than with a handful of Brits wandering around their backyard; and two, we'd stand a much better chance of identifying our own forces – and them, us – in daylight than at night and in weather that was truly appalling. In the excitement of a conventional war, soldiers had a nasty habit of shooting first and asking questions later. All told, we reckoned we'd come too far to get taken out by our own side.

As we drove, we started to do what I thought they only did in second-rate movies about the Second World War: we dreamt about what we'd do when it was finally over.

Tom was looking forward to a long holiday with Helen. Nick, who was looking a little better today, wanted to start one or two building projects around the home. He figured with all the money he'd saved during our time on ops he'd be able to do that extension he'd been promising himself for a year or two now. Nick's idea of recreation is to lay down the foundations of a house in the morning and build the son of a bitch that afternoon. When we caught up with Jeff, he noted with satisfaction that Schwarzkopf had timed his coup de grace to coincide neatly with the culmination of the rugby season. A couple of afternoons at Twickenham would sort him out, then it was on to the next war.

'And you,' Tom asked, 'what are your plans, mate?'

I was about to open my mouth, when he stopped me. Maybe something in my eyes had given me away.

'No, no, no. Don't tell me. Instead of passing some quality time with that gorgeous woman and delightful family of yours, you're going to spend the first three bloody days in camp sorting your fucking kit out, aren't you?'

I shrugged. 'You know it makes sense.'

I have an admin-head and a happy-head, but I can't don the happy-head till I've sorted out any admin that's hanging over me. It's just the way I am and Tom knew that.

'You are one fucked-up crap-hat,' he said.

What could I do, but nod? I had a distinct feeling he was right.

Come mid-morning, and a break in the weather, we stopped for a brew and some scoff. The move was beginning to take on the quality of a Sunday afternoon drive in the country, when suddenly somebody spotted a glint of silver in a patch of clear sky above the horizon.

Tony didn't hang around. He grabbed a TACBE and wandered a little way away from the vehicles. The TACBE is a black box about six inches square that can operate in two modes. By leaving a pin in the top, it's a straightforward transmit and receive set, with a limited line of sight range. Pull the pin out and it becomes a tactical beacon – hence its name – capable of sending an automatic distress signal to anyone who happens to be in the vicinity.

The rest of us watched Tony anxiously, occasionally casting a glance back towards the aircraft, which we could now hear quite distinctly. With the binos, it was plainly identifiable as an F-16. There was no doubt it had seen us. Like a vulture, it had pulled into a circling pattern about eight klicks in front – easily within the stand-off range of its Maverick air-to-surface missiles.

Tony's voice drifted towards us.

'Unidentified aircraft, unidentified aircraft. Be advised we are friendly forces ten kilometres due north of your position. Unidentified aircraft, are you receiving, over?'

A light static hiss reached us on the wind.

Again, Tony tried to raise the aircraft. I was just thinking what a pisser it would be to get blown up by a couple of missiles when suddenly Roger appeared.

'What's going on?' he asked blithely.

'We're about to have the shit blown out of us by that aircraft over there,' I said, pointing at the diminutive dot above the horizon. 'Tony's trying to do something about it.'

Roger squinted in an attempt to find the plane, then gave up and strode over to Tony. The mobility man was still trying to contact the pilot.

'What the bloody 'ell do you think you're doing?' Roger asked him.

Tony attempted to explain. 'There's an aircraft up there. I think he's seen us, Boss.'

Roger stood there with his hands on his hips. 'So?'

'Unidentified aircraft, unidentified aircraft, we are friendly forces 10 klicks north of your position . . .' Tony began again, then stopped when he realized what Roger had said.

'So, I'm trying to stop a repeat performance of what happened to D Squadron.'

Roger threw up his hands. 'Ah, bollocks,' he said, 'the bloody thing's miles away. Stop pissing about and let's get the foockin' show on the road again. I don't know about you, but I'm about ready to go home.' And with that, he walked off back to his wagon.

Tony and I looked at each other. Just then, there was a crackle from the TACBE and a rich American accent came through loud and clear: 'Acknowledged, friendly forces. Over and out.' That was it.

To me, it was apparent from the guy's business-like tone that we had been a hair's breadth from getting locked up and launched at by a Maverick.

Roger, sadly, was too far away to have caught the acknowledgement. But even if he had, I doubt it would have made a whole lot of difference.

The dot on the horizon peeled away to the south and we headed after it. We drove hard all day, eventually reaching a suitable LUP approximately twenty kilo-metres north of the border. We dismounted, set up shop and waited for our next set of orders, keeping our eyes and ears peeled all the while for anything resembling an aircraft.

Monday came and went in a weird way. From what we could glean off our radios and the snatches of information we were getting from RHQ, the fighting for Kuwait was going on some way to the south-east of us. There was no longer any call to camouflage our vehicles – in fact, if the near-run thing with the aircraft we'd encountered and the planes we'd seen since were anything to go by, our only chance of not getting vaporized by our own side was to be as open as possible about what and where we were.

After a month of totally covert ops, it felt peculiar in the extreme to be camped out on the table-top desert of Iraq with nothing more substantial for pro-tection than a couple of blokes on stag and a bloody great Union Jack in our midst.

We passed the time stagging-on, sleeping and sitting around listening to the World Service. We also fell into cliques. Each person gravitated towards the group with which he had formed a particularly close bond during the campaign. There was Chris and Keith over by the Unimog, drinking brews and shooting the shit about nothing in particular. Alec and Roger stood around Roger's vehicle talking about football, dog racing, snooker, tiddlywinks and any other sport that Roger wanted to talk about and maybe take a punt on. As for us, we tended to flow between Taff's vehicle, Tony's and my own.

The contrast with our early days across the border could not have been more pronounced. Then, organization and tidiness had been the order of the day – you finished with your sleeping-bag, you put it in your Bergen immediately and packed the lot away in the vehicle just in case you needed to make a hasty departure. Here, there were no cam-nets and it was not uncommon to see maggots and items of clothing all over the place, so they could get a bit of an airing. In time, the weather picked up and the atmosphere became quite pleasant. The scenery was much as it had been throughout the campaign: flat, rocky and dusty, with a scattered hint of vegetation. We had sentries out, of course, but if the enemy had come for us, we'd have clocked them around ten klicks out.

Nick, Tom, Jeff and I spent a lot of time with Tony, Frank, Buzz, Taff, Dean and George. We took it in turns to play poker with Dean's single deck of cards and we told each other stories of mad times both before and during Desert Storm. We also listened to the BBC a lot for news of the war. Most of us were keen Margaret Thatcher supporters and made quite a few references about the unfortunate timing of her demise from politics in the run-up to the conflict. We all felt pretty sure that if Maggie, and not John Major, had still been around, we'd have been in Baghdad, combing the streets – and the bunkers that lay beneath them – for Saddam and his cronies.

After the constant rush of living life on the edge, our appetite for horseplay and tomfoolery had pretty much run its course. Just about the only gag we still had the time or energy for were news wind-ups. And it was always Taff's crew, none of whom had a radio, that ended up on the receiving end.

A typical news wind-up would go something like this. Buzz would suddenly run over to where most of us were sitting around, drinking brews or playing cards, and say: 'Shit! You'll never guess what's just come over the news.'

To which we'd reply (most of us knowing the score): 'What? Spill the beans.'

'John Major's just been caught nobbing some high-class whore. The government looks like it's about to fall. The Coalition's crumbling and all because John couldn't keep his wick dry.'

At which point, Taff would look up and go: 'No! I don't believe it.'

Buzz would nod vigorously: 'Straight up, mate. It's absolutely true.'

He looked so earnest that even I, despite being in on this pathetic jape, almost found myself believing it.

Those not in on the gag would then divide between those who thought the PM had been a complete tool for letting the side down at such a critical juncture in world history and those who thought he wasn't such a bad type after all.

'Well bugger me,' Taff ended up saying. 'Good old John. I never knew he had it in him.' It was amazing how many variations of this gag we could pull on Taff and still have him believe us.

After thirty-six hours and still no sign of a recall, we were starting to go mad. The yearning to do something, or simply to get home, was killing us. Surprisingly, the one person we thought would go ballistic from all the inactivity didn't. Roger did the rounds between the vehicles, chatting amiably about the way things had worked out and telling a never-ending stream of amusing stories. When he wasn't charged with the intricacies of a knife-edge special forces campaign against a wily and sophisticated enemy, he was great company; a good bloke to have around.

By early Wednesday, and with the land war going spectacularly, we received an update from the FOB. We were to stay in place until the hostilities were concluded formally, with something like a proper declaration of surrender. Without it, there was no knowing what tricks Saddam might try. RHQ wanted at least one squadron in place across the border ready for contingencies. That squadron was us. So, until it was done and dusted, all we could do was to continue to sit around and wait. What made it all worse was the knowledge that both D Squadron half-convoys had made the crossing already.

Even though we were loath to admit it, most of us understood the reasons for RHQ keeping us on. Saddam still had a few Scuds left. And he had a chemical arsenal he had not used. With the Iraqi army in full retreat, his regime was like a badly wounded animal. It could have tried anything. The bastard had promised the world the Mother of All Battles and it hadn't happened. We, meantime, had seen enough in the past few days – the dead goats and the antenna farm comms complex, to boot – to know that his Scud capability was still a threat. A couple of chemically tipped missiles lobbed into Tel Aviv and it could all still change. Then, we'd have to shake ourselves down and get stuck in again.

That afternoon, I'd just got back to the wagon from Tony's when Tom told me Alec had been round looking for me. He'd sent me over to Tony's vehicle, but somehow we'd missed each other on the way.

'Fuck,' I said, 'I was just going back there again. Maybe, I'll hang around and wait till he's buggered off.'

'This is eating at you, isn't it?' Tom said.

I turned to him and nodded. 'It's been a fantastic bloody experience, the whole jaunt,' I replied. 'There's not a damned thing I regret. There are some valuable lessons we can all learn from this, of course, and I hope we will. But the biggest bloody disappointment of all – for me, at least – has been Alec. I'll never go to war with that man again.'

Tom offered me a smoke. 'Fuck me, you are wound up.'

I took his roll-up and lit it. 'Yeah, well. You should have heard the way he tried to screw Tony to elevate himself in Roger's eyes.'

'Listen,' Tom said, 'why don't you go over there and have it out with him. You can't let this thing fester.'

I pulled on the straw-thin smoke and gazed out towards the horizon. 'Yeah,' I said at length, 'maybe you're right.'

In the event, we ran into each other half-way. Maybe Alec had been wanting to have it out as badly as I did. Maybe, it was just a fluke. We strolled a little way into the desert, far enough away to be out of earshot from the rest of the group, and sat down.

'I'm going to give you a heads-up on this,' I began. 'I'm never going to work with you again. And what's more, as soon as we get back to camp, I'm going to put down a warning order with the squadron OC.'

Alec never asked me why. I guess he already knew how it had come to this. But behind his eyes I could see his brain working overtime on how he could sort out this mess to his advantage. This would be a big gig back at Stirling Lines. Alec and I were senior NCOs in the same troop – he, in fact, was senior to me. In my seven years with the SAS, I'd never heard of two head-sheds being openly at loggerheads with each other. But here was I telling him that I'd be requesting an OC's interview to explain why I'd never work with the man again. And just so he was in no doubt, I told Alec now. I kept my voice even – we both did – but beneath the veneer, I was seething.

'You were deceitful towards Tony and you played Roger's game for your own personal career ends, even when you knew that his wasn't the way we should necessarily have been doing things. Fuck, Alec, you sold out, mate. And for that, I'm giving you due warning of my impending action.'

And with that, I got up and walked back to Tony's. It was the last word I addressed to him outside of a head-sheds' meeting for the rest of the campaign.

On Thursday morning at 5 a.m., somebody woke us with the news: President Bush had gone on air to announce his suspension of all offensive action, with effect from 8 a.m. our time. The latter stages of the Iraqi withdrawal from Kuwait had, by most accounts, turned into a duck-shoot. The highway from Kuwait City to Basra had jammed with the vehicles of Iraqis trying to flee to the banks of the Euphrates. Because much of the traffic had comprised tanks and other military vehicles, allied helicopters and aircraft had pressed home attack after attack, turning the Basra road into a bloodbath. By late afternoon – early Wednesday evening, Washington time – the US president had had enough. Two hours later, Schwarzkopf ordered a stop to the killing.

Thursday drifted into Friday. The radio thundered the extraordinary success of the land offensive. In the war as a whole, fewer than 150 allied soldiers and airmen had lost their lives against an estimated 100,000 Iraqis. It was, even we were forced to admit, a stunning victory.

But for all that, there was still no word of our recall. The team of allied officers that had been trying to negotiate the official cease-fire was still parleying with Iraq's generals in the desert. Particularly at stake, according to radio reports, was the return of tens of thousands of Kuwaitis believed to have been abducted by the Iraqis since the invasion in August.

And then, suddenly, at our early morning 'sched' on Saturday, Roger told us the news: we were to start making our way back. No fanfare, no fuss. Just come on in, all's forgiven.

Because next to no one knew we'd gone into Iraq in the first place, returning was not as simple as it sounded. We were given a specific aim-point on the border, a set of coordinates next to an old fort. One of our liaison officers would turn out to meet us there so as to smooth things over with the Saudis.

It was just as well. Glancing from face to face, I realized only now how bad we all looked. Our clothes were faded and worn. Some of us were dressed as Arabs, some of us stank like pigs. We had hair past our ears and beards that would have won prizes in Alabama's Craziest Backwoodsman of the Year Contest. The Land Rovers, which had served us so magnificently, looked like they'd been through some kind of apocalyptic demolition derby. Without someone to tell the Saudis we were on their side, they might think we were a band of die-hard Iraqis on a suicide mission or upwardly mobile djinn, evil spirits of the desert that had taken to driving Land Rovers. Either way, I half-expected them to call down an artillery barrage on us.

At the allotted time, we drove out and made for the border. We headed for a spot several kilometres west of our designated crossing point, then drove east, keeping five kilometres from the border-line as we gained on the fort. That way, at least, we figured the Saudis could get a good look at us and our Union Jacks, a flurry of which were flying from masts on our vehicles.

Then, in the distance, we caught our first glimpse of the fort. It was pointless trying to raise the Saudis on the radio as we knew they wouldn't be listening. We drove up the slight incline that led to the gates still not entirely convinced that the troops inside weren't preparing some kind of hostile reception for us. When we got there, however, the gates were open, so we drove on in. A small delegation of bewildered Saudi border guards came over and checked us out. From the look on their faces we might as well have winged in from Mars. But at least they tagged us as friendly.

We hung around for ten minutes, securing the vehicles and generally shutting things down. The next thing we knew, the fort commander came over accompanied by a bunch of his subordinates clutching cans of cold drinks. I'd rather have a brew any day, but the gesture was much appreciated.

While we sat around sipping Cokes, Fantas and Seven-Ups, the Saudi officer told us we'd been expected for a while. The LO had been there a day earlier to prepare the way. I got the impression, though, that nothing could have readied him for the band of renegades that now occupied his fort.

We got on the horn and asked RHQ for instructions.

By three in the afternoon, we were on the move again, this time to a place called Arar. The plan was to stop and load up with fuel at a US Army depot there, before proceeding on to our forward mounting base.

For the next three hours, it was like nothing had changed. The sky was the same and the scenery identical to that which we had left in Iraq. Outside the vehicles it looked like business as usual. You had to pinch yourself every five minutes or so as a reminder that the war was over, that we weren't about to find ourselves locked in battle with the Republican Guard or homing in on some vital intelligence target.

For the rest of the afternoon, we bumped our way across the dunes until we reached the road that borders the Saudi tap oil line. We turned left and floored it for Arar. With the sun setting behind us, I turned to check on the boys. Tom gave me a smirk from behind the wheel and Nick forced a grin between the pot-holes that made his ribs feel as if the devil himself was putting the boot in.

It was a moment in which something unspoken passed between us. We'd weathered the ultimate test and come out the other side. All of us on the convoy had been changed by our five weeks of unrelenting ops. For some it would mean a better appreciation of the little things in life; for others, a life-long search to recapture the rush of a forty-day pass in the Iraqi theme-park. I realized then that I belonged in the former category – and that I was happy with it. Experience said that the blokes who fell into the other bracket only rediscovered that rush in the split-second before their brains were excised by a burst of 7.62.

For now, I didn't dwell on any of that. Exhaustion hit me like a spade flat in the face. I sat back and listened to the tyres singing on the tarmac and the flap of the Union Jack above our heads. A light drizzle had started to fall from clouds heavy with oil-smoke from the burning wells of Kuwait. I scarcely even noticed.

Ahead, lay a dead straight road with next to no traffic on it; behind, a convoy that, unbeknownst to the few vehicles that passed us, had 'done some things' across the border.

As work-outs went, I thought this one had gone pretty good.

FOURTEEN

We reached the FOB at five the following morning following a quick pit-stop at Arar. We were greeted by Phil, the RQMS, but most of us were too knackered even to speak. We parked the vehicles behind a mess-hall used by the Americans and crashed out on the spot. What the Yanks must have thought of these down-and-outs camped on their door-step I don't know. Luckily, we were beyond caring about anything very much.

After barely three hours' gonk we were up again and readying for our debrief. We filed into a large tent and made our way to the front, where somebody had had the decency to set out a table with several flasks of piping hot tea and coffee – and real milk, too. The atmosphere was quite informal as we ranged ourselves around a couple of tables with maps spread across them. None of us sat. What with the hanging around near the border and the seventeen-hour drive to the base, we'd all parked our arses enough.

Presently, a number of people trooped in. The CO was amongst them and several other badged officers, but the main contingent was made up of Green Slime – Int Corps. You could feel the temperature drop a notch or two.

The guy who stepped forward was a good friend of the squadron, a bloke we'd worked with on a number of CT exercises called Sparks. I didn't envy him his job much today. He sat down and went straight into a brief on what British special forces had achieved in Iraq. It was quickly apparent that what we had been involved in hadn't been some kind of side-show, but an integral part of the way the war had been run. Between the four half-squadron convoys that had gone across the border, the Regiment had achieved its objective. We'd reduced the Scud launches on Israel sufficiently to keep the Israeli Defence Force out of the war. Had it been any other way, Sparks told us, Schwarzkopf's carefully stage-managed campaign would have stalled almost as soon as it started.

'When it became clear to Saddam that you guys pretty much had the run of his desert in the west, he moved a lot of his Scuds up to the north-west and fired them against the Israelis from there,' Sparks said, matter of fact. 'But they didn't have the range or the accuracy to do a whole lot of damage – certainly not enough for the Israelis go to war over. And, in any case, the Yanks soon sent their SF guys up-country to do a little Scud-bashing of their own. Based on your experiences, we were able to give them a pretty full briefing on what to expect.'

Another day, another place, we might have crowed a bit about that. As it was, nobody spoke. For a few awkward seconds, the only sounds were the flapping of canvas and the crackle of charts as a breeze got up and riffled through the tent.

Sparks coughed and continued his discourse about the war, how it had gone in a more general sense. By now, none of us were listening too carefully. The atmosphere was charging up by the second. It wasn't just us. You could see it in the faces of the officers ranged along the other side of the table.

It was Scouse who broke the tension. Sparks was in mid-flow, when a Liverpudlian accent cut him dead.

'What happened at Victor Two, mate?'

Sparks looked up. There was a weariness on his face that I had not seen earlier. I guess he'd been expecting this question for a while. Now that it had come, he seemed almost relieved.

'It was an important target.' He paused, looking at several of us in turn. His tone, when he spoke again, was definitely defensive. 'You guys were there. You saw what kind of a place it was. It had to be taken out.'

'I wasn't talking about its tactical value,' Scouse said. 'Tell us about the bloody enemy.'

'What do you mean?'

'Tell us how many Iraqis you thought were at Victor Two,' Buzz said, picking up the baton.

'You received a signal on that before the attack . . .'

'To the effect that there were thirty men,' Taff said.

'Try ten times that number,' Frank added.

Sparks frowned and shook his head. Behind him, the other Int Corps officers exchanged a series of puzzled glances.

Then, Tony stepped in, unflappable as ever. 'Look, you told us there'd be thirty blokes on-target. What the guys are saying is right. It was more like three hundred.'

'Thirty?' he queried. 'No way. We knew all along that Victor Two would be well-defended. As I recall, and I don't have the figures in front of me, we thought there were about 300 men there. Maybe, there was an encoding error on your part.'

'Encoding error? That's bollocks!' Frank said. 'And what's more, you know it.'

Before everybody joined the fray, the CO took a step forward and held his hands up. Within seconds, the volume subsided. He told us there would be a full debrief when we got back to Hereford.

'We're not going to have a rerun of what happened after the Falklands,' he added. 'The Regiment will benefit from the lessons of this campaign. Nothing is going to be brushed under the carpet, all right?'

He swept us with his gaze. It was enough to exorcize the madness. I think if we hadn't been so tired the subject would not have reared its head – not now, at least, and not in this way.

Sane heads know that intelligence mistakes get made in war. If we could cut down on the possibility of something like this happening in the next one, though, then we'd done our bit. The post-Falklands wash-up, according to those who'd been there, had been a travesty. Now, the CO was telling us that everything would be reviewed and, where necessary, remedies implemented. I don't think any of us could have asked for more.

Just as we were about to leave, the CO called for our attention. We looked up. Most of us knew what was coming. The CO was the guy who had braced us 'to expect the worst' before we left Hereford. Now he was going to tell us how that prediction had panned out.

'I guess some of you already know what happened to Bravo Two Zero,' he said. 'You may not know that three of the guys didn't make it.'

He read out their names. We knew them all, but none better than Vince Phillips, who had originally been one of us, an A Squadron sergeant. It was rotten bloody news.

It was then, too, that we were told about Shug, cut down in a firefight following an attack by his half-squadron on a convoy in the final days of the war. He would be sorely missed. They all would.

'Better news,' the CO said, after a few moments'

silence. He looked at his watch. 'As we speak, more or less, the surviving members of Bravo Two Zero are being handed over to the Red Cross. Andy McNab and the rest of his team are OK. From the little we know, it's a hell of a story, and this isn't the time or the place. Suffice to say, they've been to hell and back, but they're alive.'

He wasn't done. There was one other name still unaccounted for.

'The last good bit of news is that the sarn't major is alive,' the CO said.

I'd been preparing myself for the worst. As it was, I could scarcely believe it. I suddenly realized I was cheering and that I wasn't alone. We all were.

The CO waited for it to subside. Then, he continued. As we'd heard previously, Robert had been wounded – terribly so – when his Land Rover had been shot to pieces as it had traversed an Iraqi trenched position. The Iraqis had picked him up and carried him back to Baghdad where the surgeons operated on him and pulled him back from the brink. He was still in a bad way, but off the critical list and due for imminent hand-over to the Red Cross.

A few moments later, we all filed out. Our heads were still spinning from the news. There was so much to take in, I didn't know how I felt. Joy and sadness competed for the upper hand, leaving all of us disoriented. I dealt with it the way we all did – by losing myself in work.

After all, there were vehicles to degunge and not a bottle of bloody Domestos for miles.

Officially, we were still on readiness to go back to Iraq. The peace was fragile and everybody sensed it. In reality, though, we knew in our bones that we were going home. The question was, when.

We were in a garrison town – a military city. There are no cinemas, no shops to speak of, no nothing; where we were, there wasn't even so much as a TV, and nobody had any books. So, having cleaned out the wagons and topped them up with oil and water, ready to go back if they had to, we did what we'd done for the previous week: nothing; except listen to the World Service. We couldn't even call our wives or girlfriends to let them know we were all right. We trusted, though, that others had done that for us.

We were into our third day of this interminable routine, when suddenly word came down the line that Schwarzkopf himself was flying in. He was breaking his frantic schedule specially to see us. This was very flattering, but it was also a bit of a pain. Suddenly, everything had to be spit and polish and pronto. We'd cut our hair and trimmed our beards a few days earlier, but now we'd have to go the full nine yards. Tom was even thinking of a manicure.

A couple of hours later, we lined up the vehicles on the airfield and waited. Within minutes, the Bear's plane was circling the field and coming in to land.

Finally, the blue and white Gulfstream taxied over to our little line-up and shut down its engines.

What happened next had most of us pissing ourselves, but, because of the importance of our visitor, we tried desperately not to let it show.

We thought maybe Norm or one of his aides would be first down the steps, but we hadn't reckoned for his bodyguards.

The first BG stuck his nose out the door, all crewcut, shades and earpiece. Then, he was down the stairs and going through the routine: pointing the Uzi, assuming the Starsky and Hutch position, scanning the horizon for signs of trouble, then going through the whole rigmarole again.

Within moments, he was joined by two or three of his mates, all of them doing the same thing. The only thing they didn't do was run around the place going *hut-hut-hut*.

I'm not quite sure what they were expecting. The SAS Forward Operating Base, being a garrison, is about as secure as you can get in the Middle East. Maybe, given the shit state of our appearance, there was some intel going about that Iraqi death squads had taken to infiltrating Saudi bases dressed as the SAS. Or maybe this was *Norm – The Movie*, and we missed the cameras.

When it was finally safe for the Bear to emerge, he swept down the steps and shook hands with our brass, then moved down the line, talking to each of us and pressing the flesh. He was every bit as impressive as the TV had shown him to be; all in all, a remarkable guy who deserves his place in the history books.

When it came to my turn, he looked me in the eye, shook my hand firmly and said: 'Thanks.'

It was a simple, yet meaningful gesture and I felt moved to respond in kind.

Somehow, though, it got a bit scrambled between my brain and my lips. 'Cheers, mate,' I replied.

He smiled and moved on down the line.

A few minutes later, it was over and Norm was heading off again. We swept back into our hangar and wondered, what next.

The short answer was bog-all.

It was almost another week before the RAF's hard-pressed C-130 special forces flight arrived to take us back to Victor, our forward mounting base in the United Arab Emirates. The squadron left in two sorties, our wagon, of course, being on the second flight out.

Shortly before midday, good old Tarakiwa, Maori god of war, was rolled up onto the ramp of the aircraft and secured. Moments later, we lifted off and swung south-east for the warmer shores of the Gulf, our flight-plan neatly avoiding the charred hell-hole of newly liberated Kuwait.

At Victor, the Regiment greeted us in the form of Paul, a half-colonel and badged member of some twenty-five years who was managing the camp. He gave us the rundown on the place, although, in truth, nothing much had changed since we'd last been there. Paul immediately dispensed two bits of solid wisdom. First, if we wanted to let our hair down, there was a bus leaving for Dubai that evening – it'd be first come, first served. Second, if we had any scores to settle after six weeks of unrelenting ops, then now was the time to do it, not later, when we were pissed to the eyeballs in the flesh-pots of Dubai.

After five weeks behind enemy lines, there were plenty of simmering tensions between various members of the group, but – other than Alec and me – nothing that couldn't be solved over a brew and some fags and with Paul standing by as adjudicator. I know several people did avail themselves of the facility. As I wandered over to our hangar, I knew Paul was right. If any guys did need to get things off their chests, much better to do it here and now – gloves off, if need be – than in a place where civvies were around. It's all right for two soldiers trained in lethal forms of warfare to kill each other, if that's what they're hell-bent on doing, but not so good if they take innocent bystanders with them.

Luckily, Alec knew better than to come with us.

I strolled into the hangar and took a look around. Again, nothing much had changed since our departure. Even our kit was where we had left it, on the end of our camp-beds.

It was like being in a time-warp. Little things became enormously meaningful. At mealtimes, my plate filled with funny little green balls, sliced-up orange bits and large, round white things; vegetables, I think they were called. In Iraq, when we had taken time out to have what we euphemistically called a 'stew', all the vegetables were mashed in with the meat to produce a revolting-looking green-brown paste. It hadn't exactly been culinary, but it had seen us through.

In comparison with the FOB, Victor was luxury. We had beds, showers, a TV, videos, books – and access to civilization. I scooped up my mail from the big table in the middle of the hangar and sprinted out the door to the bus. On the trip to Dubai, I read letters from friends and family, all wishing me well on the eve of Desert Storm. In the hold-up at the censors, none of the other post had got through. There was no letter from Jade, but then, because of our agreement, I hadn't been expecting one.

Dubai was unreal. I didn't need to chuck beers down my throat to unwind. I found myself walking down its brightly lit streets like I was in a dream. Around me, people went about their everyday lives. Shops were still trading and punters were still buying as if nothing had happened. I had to tell myself a couple of times that only a week earlier I'd been on the endless flat plain of the Iraqi desert, wondering which part of the horizon the Republican Guard would appear from.

As reality checks went, it was a weird one.

The next morning, life went on. At squadron prayers, standing amidst the green faces and bloodshot eyes of my fellow men, I was reminded again of the way Desert Storm had receded as surely as if it had never happened. The groups we'd formed to go into Iraq had been disbanded. We were no longer in convoy running-order, but back in our respective troops – boat, air, mobility and mountain.

We'd even lost Roger. He was back with the brass in a different hangar from us, doing his RSM thing again. No doubt, he was giving them a 'foocking doosting'.

Our new OC designate, a boat-troop captain who was slated to replace poor old Graham, told us we could be at Victor for anything up to two weeks. This was a major bloody downer, but necessary because of what was now happening in Iraq. Having lost to the big boys, Saddam, brave lad that he is, was picking on people he knew he could beat the shit out of: the Kurds in the north of the country and the Marsh Arabs in the south. It wasn't inconceivable that we'd be called back to take the bastard out. Frankly, it would have been a pleasure.

Thankfully, there was plenty of work to take our mind off things. All the vehicles – not just ours, but D Squadron's as well – needed to be de-kitted; that is, everything of any worth on them had to be taken off and packed away. Weapons, thermal-imagers, PNGs, all the hardware that had seen us through the past six weeks, was crated up and put into storage. The idea was to leave it all, along with the Land Rovers, in-theatre, just in case things blew up again and we'd have to come back and do it all over again.

It was during this time that we became aware of all the ammo we had lying around. Some of it was still boxed-up, the seals unbroken. But a hell of a lot of it wasn't. Technical officers were running around like crazy trying to find stuff that was salvageable, but you could tell from the looks on their faces that most of it was useless, as far as the Army was con-cerned. Too volatile for shipment, it would all have to be rounded up and dumped in the sea. What a bloody waste. Walking through the ordnance storage area you could see how much was destined for the fishes. There were 66 mm anti-tank rockets, mortar bombs, bullets, grenades – even Stinger and Milan missiles – all lined up for disposal.

Imagine our delight, then, when, at a head-sheds' meeting one afternoon, the new OC told us the plan. We were all headed to the ranges for some target practice.

We set off at 5 a.m. the next day. The drive down took us a good six hours. The ammo had gone on ahead in four four-ton trucks. All of us were looking forward to the next few days. We'd been promised an abundance of pyrotechnical mayhem. Ahead of us, at the ranges, nigh on five tons of ordnance was being pre-positioned for our personal use. There were fifty of us, give or take a few blokes, which meant one hell of a lot of kit per man to dispose of. Officially, it was marked down as a training exercise – and it *was* good training. But above all, we knew it was just going to be fun. Our idea of a good way to unwind after a bit of a work-out.

We split up by troops and headed off into different corners of the range, each of us clutching as much ammo as we could carry. First things first: we belted off all our .50 ammunition, firing so much I thought the bloody gun would melt.

'Take that, you temperamental son of a bitch,' Scouse yelled, shouting at the .50 like he really meant it, as he poured another volley of shots into a ruined shack a few hundred metres away. This was the Liverpudlian's revenge for the stoppage that had given the entire Fire Support Group a heart-attack at Victor Two.

We did the same thing with a Mk19, loosing off round after round into the dunes, until, in the quadrant we'd been aiming at, there weren't any dunes anymore, just flat, empty desert, diffused with a light curtain of cordite mist.

Next up, grenades. We'd long since disposed of anything remotely resembling a target, so we started to lay out objects that would give us the semblance of an aim-point: an old bucket, a hubcap, a spent ammo box; sticks, even.

Of course, we weren't bound by the same safety rules that were so rigorously observed at UK ranges. There, you've got proper concrete walls to duck behind when you've lobbed your grenade. There are blokes in towers with binoculars, too, who'll tell you when there's a problem, like something you've just chucked hasn't gone bang. That's not to say we weren't being safe here; we were – kind of. We always yelled when something was in the air and anyone too stupid not to duck behind the mound of sand we used as our base-camp soon got the message. Tom, who laboured under the curious impression he was some kind of lady's man, complained for days afterwards that he was brushing bits of shrapnel out of his hair.

Three hours later, I was suffering from the nearest thing I'd ever had to tennis elbow. It came as something of a relief, therefore, when somebody looked in the grenade bucket and pronounced it empty. In a year, a green army grunt is lucky if he gets to throw three grenades. I'd just thrown seventy.

The next day, it was the turn of the mortars. Because none of the convoys had had a single mortar engagement during the entire war, they all had to go – 81 mm, 51 mm, the lot. The desert rang to the plop-boom of mortar-fire and detonations long into the afternoon. We ended up dispensing with the quantity of rounds a brigade normally uses for training in a year inside of a few hours.

On the third day, the experience ramped up a notch

from being fun to something approaching nirvana. Today was the day we started to get rid of the Milans and the Stingers. Again, an average infantry battalion will fire five Milan anti-tank missile rounds a year. We had to dispose of forty.

Given the cost of these things, we figured it would be an awful waste just to fire them off indiscriminately. We'd blown up everything there was to blow up in a desert now, which wasn't saying a lot to begin with. It was time, therefore, to start getting a little imaginative. We looked around, umming and ah-ing, until we spotted the solution: mortar lume rounds. Eighty-one millimetre and 51 mm illuminating rounds will burn for 75–80 seconds. You plop one down the tube, then wait till it goes pop high above your head some way down range. The white-phos pot descends on a little parachute till it either burns out or hits the ground.

The perfect challenge.

We all had a go. Some people had several. Our Milans were mounted on the roll-bars of the Land Rovers, a fit that was non-standard, but worked well. When it came to my turn, I waited for the lume round to burst high in the middle distance, then begin its lazy float towards the earth. Next, it was a case of zeroing the MIRA sight's cross-hairs on the phos-pot and pulling the trigger.

Being next to a missile when it goes off is an experience even we don't get that often and there's a moment when the flash of the launch throws you. Within a couple of seconds, though, you readjust and make sure that you're still lined up on the target. The Milan is a semi-automatic command to line of sight, or SACLOS, missile system, which means to pull off a kill, you have to keep the sight on the target throughout the missile's time of flight. Computers within the MIRA and the missile do the rest. The Milan is an anti-tank weapon, but we scored just about every time. Several people even managed to sever the strings between the parachute and the phos-pot – all from a couple of kilometres. It's that accurate.

When we got bored of firing the Milan on its own, we decided to race it against the Stinger. Because the Milan is subsonic and the Stinger supersonic, we'd launch a Milan first, wait five seconds, then fire a Stinger. It was fifty-fifty which of the two would make it to the lume round first, but nine times out of ten, one of them hit the thing smack-on. If the entire British Army were allowed to train in this way, no one would ever dare go to war with us. Trouble is, the nation would be bankrupt before anyone ever got the chance. Around forty Stingers were disposed of in this and other juvenile ways. It was great sport.

We saved the best till last, however. The *pièce de résistance* was a mound of explosives – around 400 lb – that was considered too unstable for travel. Because of the lack of targets, we started by seeing how far we could shoot boulders the size of cars with a quantity of judiciously placed plastic. When somebody reminded us that the session was meant to have some vague educational value, we set about teaching the non-dems specialists how to set up different kinds of ambushes. Some relied purely on the killing power of the explosive itself; others on the fragmentation effect of things that you attach to it. Out here, of course, we weren't short of things that increased the blast effect of the plastic. In fact, we were swimming in it. We ended up by building the most complex, but effective ambushes I'd ever done, an intricate web of destruction comprising 66 and 94 mm anti-tank rounds, mortar bombs, white phos and regular grenades, all primed to go off from different locations, but all directed towards a single spot. The effect was awesome. In case Saddam or some other such nutter is planning another event similar to Kuwait, and is reading this: be warned, mate; it's not worth it. Next time, we're going to be back with some new tricks up our sleeves.

And so the days passed, broken only by sleep, eating and inter-troop football matches – a sport in which I have two left feet – until there was nothing left to blow up and the time came for us to board our wagons and coaches for the return trip to Victor.

From now until the time we left, which could be anything up to ten days, we were told it was freebie time. There was nothing left for us to do except put on the Union Jack shorts and sit around soaking up the rays prior to our return to rain-lashed England. At

Victor, wherever you looked, the blokes were getting some serious tanning in. It was particularly bad in the area between the hangar and the mess-hall. Being a heat-trap, it was wall-to-wall posers and lizards.

One day, Tom and I were walking past to get some scoff when we saw Taff, complete with aluminium foil reflector around the face.

''Ere, Taff, you coming to get some grub, mate?' Tom yelled.

'Nah,' the Wee Welshman replied, 'I've still got the front of me to do yet.' He waved us off, rolled over and proceeded to rub another handful of expensive-looking suntan lotion over his hairy torso.

Two hours later, he was still there. 'Jesus,' Tom said, 'he must be cooked by now.'

Apparently not.

We looked at each other and the germ of a plan lodged in our brains. While Tom raced off to get the principal ingredient, I strolled over and engaged Taff in conversation. The rate at which he was knocking the Cokes back said it wouldn't be long before we got a chance to put the strategy into effect. In fact, by the time Tom reappeared, Taff was already lifting himself off his makeshift beach-bed to go and take a leak. That was when we went into action.

While I kept watch, Tom emptied three-quarters of Taff's Ambre Solaire down the drain. He then topped it up to where it had been before with gun-oil.

Presently, the Welsh One took his place in the sun

again. There was an anxious moment when he picked up the bottle and poured another lakeful into his hand. Because it was mixed up with some of the original stuff, however, it still managed to retain enough of its original exotic coconut smell and Taff never suspected a thing. He just went right ahead and smeared it all over his body.

If I'd tried to speak, my face would have cracked in a thousand places. But Tom was brilliant. He egged Taff on with little comments like, 'you've missed a bit there, mate,' or 'blimey, this must be crap sun-oil, you're still white as a sheet' – all the while keeping a straight face. Taff fell for it hook, line and sinker. He slapped the oil on like there was no tomorrow.

Now, Tom employed a new strategy. ''Ere, careful, mate. You're gonna burn something rotten if you do too much of that.'

'Bollocks,' Taff said, by now glistening like a small, hairy, but very well-oiled porn-star, 'I was fucking born on a sun-bed, wasn't I?'

Well, we did warn him.

At 9 p.m., Taff limped into the mess-hall looking like a parboiled, but very live and angry, crustacean. There was a chorus of titters from the boys. Taff did his best to rise above it, pretending it was situation normal. He didn't help things, however, by blushing to his roots, which made him look like he was about to explode.

Far from being contrite, Tom just kept right on at

him. 'Christ, mate,' he said, 'you got well ripped off with that sun-oil. You look a right bloody mess.'

Poor Taff. I think he went back to the place where he'd bought his Ambre Solaire in the souk and accused the stall-owner of having pissed in it. It could have caused a minor diplomatic incident. He never did find out the secret of his tan. So, that's something off my conscience, at least.

Thirty-six hours later, we were on a C-130 back to Lyneham in Wiltshire. We arrived as we'd left; quietly, no fuss, after dark. Just the way we like it. The only people who sussed us were Her Majesty's Customs. In my first inkling of the extraordinary gratitude that people held for us, they checked our bags and waved us through, no matter how many cartons of fags or how much booze we had on us. To be held in some kind of respect by these people is sobering indeed.

True to form, it was pissing down when we emerged out the other side. Several unmarked buses were waiting to take us back to Hereford. We climbed aboard and settled down for the journey home.

There were no songs, no jokes on the road north. In the darkness, I felt the presence of the men we had left behind. And from the silence that surrounded me, I knew the others did, too.

EPILOGUE

Desert Storm is well and truly consigned to the history books now. The comprehensive defeat of an overwhelming force by an opponent sustaining so few casualties ensured that. This and other factors – not least, the role the media played in conveying it live to our living rooms – made it a weird war, but its phenomenal success has already set the agenda for the next conflict. Smart weapons, stealth, information warfare, lightning-fast manoeuvres and psy-ops will be at the heart of it. So, too, will the SAS.

How do I know? Because just as the political map has changed since the Cold War, so, too, has the Regiment. Our enemy isn't the Soviet Union anymore, but a plethora of foes. The West's intelligence agencies have declared open war on rogue political regimes, international terrorists, narcotics traffickers, the mafia and other organized crime lords. The weapon of choice for eradicating this threat, which collectively is just as wily and sophisticated as the old Soviet war machine, is the same crack special forces that headed for Saddam's kitchen in 1991. Only, like the enemy, special forces are evolving, too. They have to. Certain aspects of twenty-first century SF warfare will read one day like *Mission: Impossible*. I only hope that the people in charge don't let all the high-tech stuff go to their heads.

Fifty years separated our activities in Iraq from those of the Long Range Desert Group, our distinguished forebears, in North Africa during the Second World War. Apart from odd items of equipment, our foray across the border showed that little had changed. The allied Coalition had all the weaponry at its enormous disposal to erase the threat posed by Victor Two and Saddam's Scuds, right down to stealth bombers and nuclear weapons. But, in the end, their fate was sealed by a handful of blokes with rifles and a bit of savvy. As long as that aspect of the Regiment never changes, no bad guy will ever rest easy in his bed at night. And that's how it should be.

I left the SAS in 1996. I'd had about as good a time as anybody could hope for in the army. My twenty-two years were up and it was time to return to civvy street. I miss aspects of the life, obviously, but like the Regiment I knew I had to move on. I'm settled in a good, kosher job that employs some of the skills I learned at Hereford. Life goes on in the outside world and I'm happy with it. Multiple nights under the stars with the Republican Guard breathing down our necks had given me plenty of time to focus on the things in this world that matter most. Three of them are right here under my roof.

Many of those with whom I fought in that desert winter of 1991 are serving today. Most, I know, look back on it as the ultimate adventure.

Graham returned to his parent unit and, as far as I know, remains there to this day, his career-path seemingly unaltered by his experiences in Iraq. Some people sail through the armed forces wearing a bomb-proof suit of armour, gaining promotion, despite themselves, all the way to the top. Graham, I guess, is one of those blokes. Good luck to him.

Roger is still serving. For all his quirkiness on the field of battle, he is, as RSM, the Regiment's backbone and a highly popular individual at Stirling Lines. Of course, he is still the scourge of ditherers and mealy-mouths everywhere. Occasionally, at dead of night, I can still hear the boom of his voice. If there is another big conflict in the near future, Roger will be there, snorting like a bull, ready to give 'em a dusting.

Gazza, like Graham, also emerged from Desert Storm unscathed, much to everyone's surprise. He came back two years afterwards as our squadron commander. It was not a good time for the unit and many key blokes left. He is still in the Regiment and one day will probably command it. I can't explain the

Teflon-like way people like him manage to avoid shit. I guess it's just the way the world turns.

Jeff left the Regiment and went back to the green army and trained to fly helicopters. Now he's a fully fledged pilot in the Army Air Corps; Tom and Nick are still serving. The BFG was none the worse after his fall; that is, if you don't count the jokes he had to endure when the boys found out how he'd stepped off the vehicle, with all the aplomb of Buster Keaton, into the inky void below. They are great guys. Despite the different paths our careers have taken, we meet regularly to shoot the shit. Tom still has appalling taste in clothes and Nick manages to avoid sugar in his tea, in spite of our best efforts in Iraq.

Tony and Alec remain in the SAS. After Desert Storm, I made a point of breaking all contact with Alec outside of work. Even then, the OC did his best to keep us apart. In a unit as tight as ours there are bound to be disagreements, but to have two head-sheds at each other's throats is rare. Tony, I'm sure, will go on to great things. As the bloke who probably did more than anyone else to hold us together in Iraq, he certainly deserves to.

Frank, Buzz and George all left the army and are pursuing careers I know not where. I only hope, for the sake of world harmony, that they haven't decided to team up and go into the demolition business. In the deregulated world of satellite television, there is probably room for a minority show with Frank and

Buzz as its stars. When it happens and becomes cult viewing, never forget that you read it here first. Then, I'll claim my ten per cent.

Taff and Dean are also still with the SAS – another good reason for the world's criminals and terrorists to chuck in the towel now. The photograph of Dean's prize package – courtesy of the Odd Couple – was sent to the Guinness Book of Records, but fortunately there is no category in that distinguished tome for this truly grotesque sight and it was impolitely returned.

As for Harry Taylor, the guy who kept me sane while I was stranded in the Himalayas following the invasion of Kuwait, he went on to climb Everest without oxygen, a remarkable achievement in anyone's book. Maybe, one day, I'll get to follow in his footsteps.

Regarding what happened at Victor Two, we never did get to the bottom of the number of enemy garrisoned at the facility and who knew this and when. We who were there reject the possibility of an encoding error, since all signals were checked and double-checked by many different members of the convoy. Without the original transmission, it will always remain a mystery. So long as people learn from the whole incident, it's probably better left that way.

The principal villain of the piece, the Scud, is still very much alive and kicking, though not in Iraq, where, according to the United Nations, Saddam's missile arsenal has pretty much been eradicated, at least for the time-being.

Since the war, rogue nations that didn't already possess the missile have gone out of their way to acquire it. They are also working on the chemical, biological and nuclear warheads that promise to turn it into a truly devastating piece of technology. A half century after Nazi V2 rockets first struck London, the Scud and its long-range successors are still out there. Some of them are well capable of hitting the capital all over again, this time from launch-points across the Middle East. As long as they are stored deep underground, all the fancy bits of weaponry the West possesses can't destroy them. It's a worrying thought.

Fortunately, as General Schwarzkopf found in 1991, there is an antidote.

GLOSSARY

AFV	Armoured Fighting Vehicle
B-52	Heavy US Air Force bomber
Cannon	Motor bike
CFSG	Close Fire Support Group
Chinook	US-made heavy transport helicopter
Crap-hat	Para nickname for infantryman
C-130	Veteran RAF four-engined transport aircraft, built in USA
Endex	End of exercise or mission
Exfil	Exfiltration or extraction of personnel or equipment, usually covertly
FOB	Forward Operating Base
Four Tonner	British Army Bedford truck
FSG	Fire Support Group
F-16	US multi-role fighter aircraft
GAZ	Russian-made jeep
GIAT	French-made heavy-calibre gun

Gonk	Sleep, rest
GPS	Global Positioning System; satellite-based navigation aid
Green army	Regular army
IR	Infra-red
LSRV	Landing Site Rendez-Vous, usually for helicopters
LTD	Laser Target Designator; device used to direct air-launched laser-guided weapons onto target
Maggot	Sleeping bag
MATS	Remote-controlled aircraft used as target for ground-to-air weapons training
MILAN	European-made anti-tank missile
MIRA	Milan Infra-Red Attachment; special night-sight for the MILAN missile
Mk19	Grenade-launcher
M16	Semi-automatic rifle
M202	Incendiary round
NAPS	Pill administered to Coalition troops to counter effects of chemical and biological warfare
NBC	Nuclear Biological & Chemical (warfare)
NCO	Non-commissioned officer
OC	Officer Commanding
PNG	Passive Night-vision Goggles

Rodney	Like a Rupert, only more so
RQMS	Regimental Quarter Master Sergeant
RSM	Regimental Sergeant Major
Rupert	Lower ranks' nickname for officer; somewhat derogatory
Sat-nav	Satellite navigation system
SIS	Secret Intelligence Service; otherwise known as MI6
Stinger	US-made shoulder-launched anti-aircraft missile
Two i/c	Second in command
T-72	Russian-made Iraqi main battle tank
Unimog	4 by 4 Mercedes Benz, used as support vehicle
Victor	Codename for Regiment's Forward Mounting Base in Saudi Arabia
Victor 2	Iraqi communications relay post for control of Scud missiles
White Phos	Smoke grenades
.50	Heavy calibre machine-gun
110	Long wheelbase Land-Rover
203	M16 rifle with 40 mm grenade-launcher attachment

He just wanted a decent book to read ...

Not too much to ask, is it? It was in 1935 when Allen Lane, Managing Director of Bodley Head Publishers, stood on a platform at Exeter railway station looking for something good to read on his journey back to London. His choice was limited to popular magazines and poor-quality paperbacks – the same choice faced every day by the vast majority of readers, few of whom could afford hardbacks. Lane's disappointment and subsequent anger at the range of books generally available led him to found a company – and change the world.

'We believed in the existence in this country of a vast reading public for intelligent books at a low price, and staked everything on it'
Sir Allen Lane, 1902–1970, founder of Penguin Books

The quality paperback had arrived – and not just in bookshops. Lane was adamant that his Penguins should appear in chain stores and tobacconists, and should cost no more than a packet of cigarettes.

Reading habits (and cigarette prices) have changed since 1935, but Penguin still believes in publishing the best books for everybody to enjoy. We still believe that good design costs no more than bad design, and we still believe that quality books published passionately and responsibly make the world a better place.

So wherever you see the little bird – whether it's on a piece of prize-winning literary fiction or a celebrity autobiography, political tour de force or historical masterpiece, a serial-killer thriller, reference book, world classic or a piece of pure escapism – you can bet that it represents the very best that the genre has to offer.

Whatever you like to read – trust Penguin.